SALVATION MEANS CREATION HEALED

Salvation Means Creation Healed

The Ecology of Sin and Grace:

Overcoming the Divorce between Earth and Heaven

HOWARD A. SNYDER
WITH JOEL SCANDRETT

CASCADE *Books* · Eugene, Oregon

SALVATION MEANS CREATION HEALED
The Ecology of Sin and Grace: Overcoming the Divorce between Earth and Heaven

All biblical quotations are from the New Revised Standard Version (NRSV) unless otherwise indicated.

Cascade Books
An Imprint of Wipf and Stock Publishers
199 W. 8th Ave., Suite 3
Eugene, OR 97401

www.wipfandstock.com

ISBN 13: 978-1-60899-888-3

Cataloging-in-Publication data:

Snyder, Howard A.

   Salvation means creation healed : the ecology of sin and grace: overcoming the divorce between earth and heaven / Howard A. Snyder and Joel Scandrett.

   xviii + 260 p. ; 25 cm. Includes bibliographical references and indexes.

   ISBN 13: 978-1-60899-888-3

   1. Creation. 2. Salvation—Christianity—Biblical teaching. 3. Eschatology. 4. Mission of the church. I. Scandrett, Joel. II. Title.

BS651 S59 2011

Manufactured in the U.S.A.

For Janice—a true healer

Contents

Preface

"Heaven is a wonderful place."

Oh, really?

Even as a young Christian, I felt vaguely dissatisfied with the promised afterlife we celebrated in church. Salvation was all about going to heaven. Heaven was the truly ultimate thing. Yet descriptions of "heaven" seemed static, bland, and colorless compared to the beautiful world around me.

It seemed that not much happened in heaven except unending worship, and I didn't find that particularly attractive. As a child and teenager I liked worship services well enough, but was certainly glad they weren't eternal. At times they seemed that way, and that wasn't good. It may be that according to the standard Christian view, as medievalist Jeffrey Burton Russell (my old prof) puts it, "Heaven is the opposite of boredom, because the joys always increase."[1] But that's not the way I felt.

Of course, I understood that this vision of heaven was *supposed* to delight me. It's what was really important, so I should long for it. If I didn't, the problem must be with me. I wasn't spiritual enough. And much of the preaching about heaven and spirituality, even when good and sometimes entertaining, seemed designed precisely to convince me that I wasn't spiritual enough.

Our church insisted on Jesus' actual resurrection in space and time. "Up from the grave he arose." We held firmly to the resurrection—we just didn't quite know what to make of it. I see now that we did precisely what N. T. Wright warns of in *Surprised by Hope*. We thought that "belief in Jesus's bodily resurrection is all about God's supernatural action in the world, legitimating an upstairs-downstairs view of reality—a dualism, in other words—in which the supernatural is the real world and the natural, the this-worldly, is secondary and largely irrelevant."[2]

Looking back over a lifetime in church, I have gained new insight into the journey I traveled. It has *not* been a journey from "matter" to "spirit"—from materiality to spirituality—as I initially imagined. No, it has been a pilgrimage toward the union

---

1. Russell, *Paradise Mislaid*, 11.
2. Wright, *Surprised by Hope*, 220.

of matter and spirit, the marriage of heaven and earth—toward an understanding of salvation that *includes* creation.

I now see how for my whole life (at least the last sixty years), I have been pursuing a mostly unconscious longing to wed earth with heaven. This has been a journey toward seeing salvation as creation whole and healed—which, it turns out (surprise, surprise!), is precisely the biblical vision. That biblical vision, and the church's long struggle to embrace it, is the burden of this book. My own pilgrimage mirrors a much bigger story.

Faced with a view of reality that says matter and spirit are literally two different worlds, we have several options. One option is to accept that understanding as the Christian worldview and try to live our lives accordingly, doing our best to avoid schizophrenia, but living with unresolved tension. Alternatively, we can opt for matter over spirit, abandoning spirituality as irrelevant or unattainable, even if possibly real. (As a teenager, my oldest brother dropped Christianity because "non-Christian kids were having a lot more fun.") Or we can opt for spirit over matter, trying our best to be "spiritual" and denying, despising, or ignoring the material world as best we can. That's long been the dominant impulse in the Christian tradition. Finally, we can become thoroughgoing dualists, holding a split-level worldview, operating as though "spirit" and "matter" were two unconnected worlds with incompatible software and different sets of rules. This fourth option seems to be the most popular in American Christianity as I've experienced it.

Not one of these options is satisfactory. None is biblical. *The starting assumption is wrong.* The Bible offers a better insight: Spirit and matter are not two different worlds. They are interlaced dimensions of the one world God created in its entirety and intends to redeem, save, liberate, and heal in its entirety.

This book may look like a radical shift from my earlier writings. Not so. The seeds are all in my previous books. However, this book does explore the fruit of a major shift in my thinking that's been long in the making. And its source is twofold.

First, when I was in seminary, I learned a concept that continues to be a radical one: inductive Bible study. We study the Bible not to confirm what we already believe but to find out what it actually teaches, whether that cements or shatters our assumptions. I have continued to pursue inductive Bible study over the years, and it has been an ongoing voyage of discovery marked by key moments when new insights crystallized beautifully. My primary source has been and continues to be Scripture.

Second, I am nonetheless influenced by the times we inhabit. Some may see a red flag here, but in biblical interpretation "it was always thus." The Holy Spirit has always worked through the cultural context of the church in order to bring the truth of Scripture to light. The early church developed the doctrine of the Trinity in response to the philosophical and cultural currents of Hellenistic society. The Reformation was triggered in part by the cultural context of medieval Europe. The church eventually came to clarity on the evils of slavery as the moral offense of the colonial slave trade (and the exploitive economic system it sustained) weighed more and more on people's consciences.

Likewise environmental concerns today are prompting a fresh look at biblical teaching about creation, stewardship, and the healing of creation.

This is exciting! Salvation means creation healed, and that is shocking and stupendous news. The good news of Jesus is even better than we thought.

Introduction

A Healthy Church on a Sick Planet?

Can there be a healthy church on a sick planet? If salvation means the healing of creation, then the ultimate answer is "no." If the world is sick, the church is also infected. The body of Christ is not immune or antiseptic. The church does not live in a germ-free, pristine bubble, untouched by the world's ills.

But, though infected, the church can still be a sign and agent of healing—if God's healing grace enlivens and flows through it. Our hope in writing this book is to nurture the growth of healthy churches on a sick planet, churches that by God's Spirit become agents of both present and future healing.

WHAT IS SALVATION?

Our primary concern here is salvation itself. This book focuses on the root questions: God, the nature of the world God "so loved," incarnation, atonement, resurrection, and Jesus' promised return to earth "with power and great glory" (Matt 24:30; Luke 21:27). We focus especially on the key biblical portrayal of salvation as *healing* and attempt to show what this means for church, mission, and society today. We aim to overcome impoverished views of salvation that focus mainly on inner spiritual experience, eternity in heaven, or even narrowly on church health and growth.

This is not a book about environmental ethics. Ethics, environmental and otherwise, come up in due course, but as a *consequence*, not a cause. Much Christian environmental thinking today is lifeless because it does not begin with foundational questions regarding God's salvation of creation. Similarly, most books on creation care start at the wrong place and don't plow deeply enough. This book does engage environmental stewardship and related matters, but that is not its central focus.

SALVATION MEANS CREATION HEALED

The great concern of the church is *salvation* and, biblically speaking, salvation ultimately means *creation healed*. God promises to hear humanity's cries "and heal them" (Isa 19:22). God pronounces "Peace, peace, to the far and near" and pledges, "I will heal them" (Isa 57:19). "Return, O faithless children, I will heal your faithlessness" (Jer 3:22). When God's people truly turn to him, he promises to "heal their land" (2 Chr 7:14). In fact, the Bible promises a healed, restored "new heavens and a new earth" (Isa 65:17; 66:22; 2 Pet 3:13). We recall that the Old Testament word for peace, *shalom,* means comprehensive well-being—healthy people in a flourishing land.

Healing the world: now this is *good news!* Jesus applied Isa 6:9–10 to himself, proclaiming that if people would turn to him, he "would heal them" (Matt 13:15). Jesus was the Great Healer. His healing miracles powerfully signaled the presence of God's kingdom, the restoration of creation. He sent his disciples out "to proclaim the kingdom of God and to heal" (Luke 9:2). When he preached the kingdom of God he was preaching healing, *shalom,* the kind of peace and healing only he could truly promise and truly bring.

Of course, the gospel is also about justification by faith, atonement, forgiveness, and new birth. But the larger truth that encompasses all of these is healing—complete healing, creation restored, true *shalom.* The tree of life in the book of Revelation bears leaves "for the healing of the nations" (Rev 22:2). The prophet Isaiah says of the Messiah, "Surely he has borne our infirmities and carried our diseases . . . he was wounded for our transgressions, crushed for our iniquities; upon him was the punishment that made us whole, and by his bruises we are healed" (Isa 53:4–5). "He himself bore our sins in his body on the cross, so that, free from sins, we might live for righteousness; by his wounds you have been healed" (1 Pet 2:24). As Joel Green makes clear, *healing* is

> a remarkably rich metaphor for working out the nature of salvation in the biblical materials . . . From Scripture itself, we receive an all-encompassing perspective on human health in the cosmos and in relation to God, as well as well-developed ways of identifying the sickness that spreads like a cancer throughout the human family, even eating away at the world that humans call home. . . . In this view, healing does not allow the categorization of the person or his or her salvation into "parts," as though inner and outer life could be separated. What is more, in a significant sense, healing does not allow us to think of the restoration of individuals, as it were, one at a time, but pushes our categories always to embrace the human community and, indeed, the cosmos. People are not saved in isolation from the world around them. For healing, attention falls above all on the power and initiative of Yahweh as healer, and on Jesus, Yahweh's co-regent, through whom the renewing beneficence of God is made available. Finally, the metaphor of healing serves as an invitation to the people of God, not only to be recipients of God's good gifts of salvation, but also to be agents of healing, to be a community of compassion and restoration.[1]

How and when does this healing take place? These are the issues we must explore.

1. Green, *Salvation,* 52–53.

DIAGNOSIS FIRST

What does it take to establish healthy churches on a sick planet—churches that are more a part of the cure than a part of the disease?

What is needed first, of course, is *diagnosis*. What ails us? What ails the world? What ails the church? Christians believe that the Bible provides a true diagnosis, and that we find the cure in Jesus.

Typically we say that the problem is sin. But what is sin? While we often think of sin as the violation of God's law, the Bible often pictures sin as a more fundamental moral disease that has infected every part of human existence, even the land itself. The prophet Hosea pictures this graphically:

> There is no faithfulness or loyalty, and no knowledge of God in the land.
> Swearing, lying, and murder, and stealing and adultery break out;
>   bloodshed follows bloodshed.
> Therefore the land mourns, and all who live in it languish;
>   together with the wild animals and the birds of the air,
>   even the fish of the sea are perishing.
> (Hos 4:1–3)

People have died from misdiagnosis. We have all heard such stories; maybe it has happened in your family. The doctor was wrong, or the disease was undetected, or medical knowledge had not advanced enough to discern what was happening. Or perhaps the patient ignored the symptoms and didn't seek help.

The church has a misdiagnosis problem. On the one hand, we have insisted that sin is comprehensive ("*total* depravity"), but on the other hand we have not adequately explored the meaning of sin as moral and spiritual infection ("total *depravity*"). Instead, especially in Western Christianity, we have tended to reduce sin to matters of *law* that are disconnected from *life*. Consequently, we have failed to see that God's cure is as comprehensive as the disease. We have ignored or bypassed key biblical insights regarding both the nature of the problem and the nature of the solution because we have overlooked the biblical theme of sin as disease.

Consequently, the world faces a profound two-pronged problem: the moral disease called sin, and the symptoms of conflict, alienation, discord, violence, injustice, and oppression that result from that disease. We can address these symptoms to some extent, but the solution is to deal with the disease itself, to find a comprehensive cure.

Here the biblical revelation is absolutely essential. The Bible is remarkably comprehensive and realistic about the nature of our moral disease. This disease is, in fact, a major theme of Scripture. From Genesis to Revelation, the Bible is filled with passages that attest to the moral corruption that affects all human beings and the world in which we live.

Take, for example, the horrific story in Judges 19. A Levite mistreated his concubine and allowed her to be raped and abused by others. When she died, "he cut her into twelve pieces, limb by limb, and sent her throughout all the territory of Israel," calling for revenge on the abusers (Judg 19:29).

Judges does not moralize about this story, and yet the moral is clear. Something has gone horribly wrong on earth, and it affects—infects, really—everything. Scripture is very clear that this problem is at once spiritual, moral, theological, social, economic, political—and yes, physical. We can't simply isolate one strand of the problem and separate it from the rest of the diseased reality that is our fallen world.

The human and earthly problem is, in other words, *ecological*—our entire human existence in all its dimensions is diseased. The spiritual, the physical, the social, and political are all intertwined. This means that piecemeal solutions won't work. They won't do more than treat one part of the problem, and in the process can actually leave other aspects of our situation even worse than they were before.

We intentionally use the concept of *ecology* here because ecology is the most comprehensive conceptual frame we have for visualizing the complex interrelationships of factors that make up human life and the life of our planet. In an ecological understanding, everything is related to everything else. The study of ecosystems helps us grasp the nature of these interrelationships and learn how to work for stable and flourishing systems, overcoming the maladies that harm or even destroy an ecosystem over time. As we will show later, this ecological conception is biblical at heart and can be an important tool in helping us understand the comprehensive healing message of the gospel.[2]

OVERVIEW

Salvation means creation healed. But in order to understand this we must first heal some theological maladies and close some gaps in Christian teaching.

One of the worst of these is the gap, the divorce, between heaven and earth that has developed in Christian theology over the course of history. This divorce of earth from heaven and the resulting over-spiritualization of salvation are addressed in *Part One* of the book. Here, as throughout the book, we strive to hold things together that tend to fly apart—avoiding, for instance, any "under-spiritualization" of salvation, as well.

Part Two is diagnostic: the disease and the cure. Humanity suffers a vicious and deadly moral disease that affects everything. This section deals with the nature of sin and describes the gospel as a complete cure. It shows how the good news of Jesus Christ is the healing medicine for the disease of sin, and thus for healing all creation. It discusses the cycles of death that mark the human condition and the cycles of life that God brings by his Spirit.

---

2. The case for an ecological understanding of salvation is argued in Snyder, *Liberating the Church*, chapters 2 and 3; *Models of the Kingdom*, chapter 11; "Coherence in Christ" and *Decoding the Church*, chapters 4 and 7, as well as by other authors, as will be noted later.

Part Three considers the healing mission of God. The mission of God (*missio Dei*) is the healing of creation, beginning with men and women in their relationship with God. This mission envisions and promises complete fulfillment of the biblical promises of "a new heaven and a new earth." In considering mission as healing, this section also reexamines the meaning of the kingdom of God.

Part Four describes the Healing Community—the church, the body of Christ. What does it look like for the church to be God's healing community on earth, embodying and extending healing in all the interrelated dimensions of heaven and earth?

We conclude with a meditation on living New Creation now.

This book is unique in several ways. First, it mines the biblical material on sin as disease and salvation as healing—much neglected but essential *biblical* emphases. Second, it takes a comprehensive ecological approach, seeking intentionally and consistently to overcome gaps, bridge polarities, and heal blind spots that often constrain the telling of the Christian narrative. Third, it takes history seriously, tracing trajectories that must be understood if the church is to be comprehensively faithful and healthful today. Fourth, it takes *the earth* seriously. Biblically speaking, the gospel is about God's people and God's land, but often land simply disappears or disintegrates in Christian theology and is largely ignored in our discipleship.

Finally, the book provides new images, and deepens traditional images, of the church. Books on the church continue to pour forth, but few view the church comprehensively as God's healing community on earth and harbinger of the New Creation which already presses upon us.

PART ONE

The Divorce of Heaven and Earth

1

The Great Divorce in Christian Theology

The arm of the Lord is not too short to save, nor his ear too dull to hear.
But your iniquities have separated you from your God;
your sins have hidden his face from you, so that he will not hear.

(Isa 59:1–2 TNIV)

SALVATION MEANS CREATION HEALED. But why does creation need healing? The
short answer is that all creation is diseased because of sin. First comes the mystery
of Satan's fall, followed by humanity's fall into sin, pictured so graphically in Genesis
3. With sin came moral disease, a fourfold alienation of man and woman from God,
from themselves, from each other, and from the earth. All of this, and especially the
disease of sin, is explained in a new way in chapters 5 and 6 of this book.

The disease of sin brought alienation, a divorce, between people and their maker
and between people and their world, their habitat, which is planet earth. *Divorce* is an
apt metaphor for the whole problem of the relationships between God, humans, and
the earth. Sin, in effect, triggered a divorce between heaven and earth. And salvation
is about overcoming this divorce both now and in the future. Ultimately salvation
means the final marriage of heaven of earth in the New Creation. Thus, the book of
Revelation speaks of "the marriage supper of the Lamb" (Rev 19:9).

But there is a fore-story here that must first be told. There is another divorce, a
secondary divorce that also cries out for healing. This is the great divorce *in Christian
theology* between heaven and earth. This theological divorce has to be faced. In fact,
healing this theological divorce is key to grasping the larger healing that salvation

implies and promises. So we begin this book with the intriguing but mostly untold story of a great divorce in Christian theology. We will show how the divorce happened, so that healing and reconciliation can begin.

First, we need a basic theological diagnosis. Think of it this way: A married couple is heading for divorce. Their problems are deep and seemingly insoluble. They seek out a trusted counselor, perhaps a pastor, and share their pain. Can reconciliation happen? Yes, but there's a preliminary problem: the counselor discovers that the couple misunderstands marriage itself. They think it has to do only with emotional and sexual "compatibility," not understanding the many other moral and spiritual dimensions of Christian marriage. The counselor has to diagnose the problem before he or she can introduce a reconciliation process. The couple first needs to come to a fuller understanding of marriage before they can live it out.

So also with the church. Just as a counselor has to hear the couple's story in order to have a healing influence, so we have to understand the story, the history that led to the theological divorce of earth from heaven. In the following three brief chapters, we show how the theological divorce between heaven and earth came about, then we point a way forward.

But does this great divorce really exist? Yes. We testify to it whenever we:

- think salvation is about the soul only, not the body;
- see no spiritual significance in material things;
- view life on earth as something unreal or of little importance;
- view physical death as the end of our earthly life;
- think that beauty in this life (nature, people, art, music) is ultimately unimportant, except as it points to spiritual beauty;
- see this present world as evil or totally under Satan's control;
- overlook the biblical mandate for creation stewardship;
- see spirit and matter as two opposite and irreconcilable categories.

Wherever such symptoms abound, we have evidence of the great theological divorce between heaven and earth that exists in the Christian tradition. Perhaps the most glaring evidence of this divorce is the church's longstanding carelessness (with a few exceptions) about tending the garden, the earth that God has given us. Devastated, polluted, and barren spots in the garden are signs of the divorce. They shout to us that we have missed something basic. A quick review of church history shows why.

THE RISE OF CHRISTIANITY, 30–330 AD

After Peter's message on the Day of Pentecost, "those who welcomed his message were baptized, and . . . about three thousand persons were added. They devoted themselves to the apostles' teaching and fellowship, to the breaking of bread and the prayers" (Acts 2:41–42).

This is a new story, but of course it is also the continuation of the Old Testament story. Now, Old Testament promises of a Messiah, the outpouring of the Holy Spirit, and the renewal of God's covenant are being fulfilled.

The Jerusalem church was not really the "New Testament church," however. The Acts 2 church is not the full biblical model, as some suppose. It is the embryo, the initial episode, the beginning of the story. After the scattering in Acts 8, and especially with the birth of the church in Antioch, we begin to see what the New Testament church really is—its visibility, its dynamic, its vision and mission. In the rise of Christianity as a global movement, Acts 11–13 more fully paints the birth of the church than does Acts 2. But it's all part of one story, of course.[1]

By the close of the New Testament, the church has spread to many key cities of the Roman Empire. The Book of Acts ends in Rome with Paul's ministry there. The letters to the seven churches in Revelation 2–3 give us a glimpse of the church in Asia Minor (present-day Turkey) about 90 AD. The church has grown remarkably, but we should remember that it is still a tiny, "illegal," mostly underground sect within the Roman Empire. However by this time the faith has erupted also beyond the Roman Empire, spreading to Syria, India, North Africa, and Armenia, which would become the first Christian nation.

Within the Roman Empire the church was still running mostly "below the radar screen" of public notice. It was essentially a network of home-based fellowships, with no church buildings until about the mid-200s.

Then comes a key tipping point. By about 300 AD Christians were so numerous throughout the empire that they could not be ignored. The conversion of the Emperor Constantine (c. 272–337) in 312 brought a rapid and historically critical shift. Christianity moved quickly from a despised minority to the favored religion of the Empire. This period of the rise of Christianity reached its climax in the early fourth century with the official toleration of Christianity (Edict of Milan, 313) and the Council of Nicea (325). The Christian church, it seemed, had won—it had conquered the Roman Empire.

The rise of Christianity from about 30 to 330 AD is an amazing story. We can summarize these three hundred years by tracing three key themes: *God's narrative, God's redemptive plan*, and the *visible church*.[2]

The Narrative, the Plan, the Visible Church

The years from the end of the book of Acts to about 330 AD give us a sense of the church's continuity, of an unfolding story. Early Christians knew God was at work among them, despite trials and persecutions. The church was multiplying—in numbers, geographic spread, influence, organization, and theological sophistication.

1. Ray Anderson in *An Emergent Theology for Emerging Churches* draws sharp contrasts between the Jerusalem and Antioch churches, showing why we should pay more attention to Antioch.

2. These themes partly reflect the emphases of the 2006 "Call to an Evangelical Future" formulated by the late Robert E. Webber in collaboration with a large network of people. For a summary and exposition, including the text of the Call itself, see Webber's *Ancient-Future Worship* and *Who Gets to Narrate the World?*, both published posthumously.

Heresies arose and were countered; cultural barriers were crossed; essential consensus was reached on the canon of Scripture. Yet the church was more and more diverse, with varying forms of organization and leadership, differing doctrinal emphases in different places, and a range of conflicts and controversies.

The Council of Nicea in 325 (widely viewed as the First Ecumenical Council) and subsequent councils gave us the Nicene Creed—a key marker of early consensus on essential doctrinal points, particularly with regard to the identity of Jesus Christ.[3]

The Nicene Creed affirmed that God created "all things visible and invisible"; that God provides salvation through the incarnation, life, death, and resurrection of Jesus Christ; and that Jesus will return again and establish God's everlasting kingdom, with "the resurrection of the dead" and ongoing life under God's reign.

The early church clearly understood that God's redemptive plan centers in the story of Jesus Christ and the victory of the Creator-Redeemer God in Jesus. This included the expectation of Jesus' return within history, the physical resurrection of the dead, and God's everlasting reign. Thus the narrative of Jesus builds upon and extends the Old Testament narrative, which is essentially the story of God, God's people, and God's land.

Drawing on Eph 1:10 and other passages, some early Christian writers developed a theology of the "plan" or "economy" (*oikonomia*) of God—a potent theological idea that is being reexamined today.[4] Probably the greatest contribution to the church's understanding of God's redemptive plan during this period was the great "recapitulation" theology of Irenaeus of Lyons, who died in 202 AD. Irenaeus saw the divine redemptive plan as *creation–incarnation–re-creation*. Robert Webber notes, "These three words capture the basic framework of biblical and ancient thinking" and contrast with the creation–sin–redemption paradigm which later became dominant in the Western church.[5] This creation–incarnation–re-creation framework is also consistent with the God–People–Land structure of the biblical narrative, as we will see.

The "economy of God" concept can be especially useful in helping us explore the significance of *ecology,* a related concept,[6] and in healing the divorce of earth and heaven, so we will return to this in later chapters. It is helpful also in understanding the nature and visibility of the church.

The Nicene Creed actually says very little about the church. The original creed of 325 did not mention the church at all. Fifty-six years later, the first Council of Constantinople formulated the revised Niceno–Constantinopolitan Creed (381 AD), which describes the church in just four words—"one, holy, catholic, apostolic." These

---

3. See Davis, *First Seven Ecumenical Councils.*

4. E.g., Reumann, *Stewardship and the Economy of God.*

5. Webber, *Ancient-Future Worship,* 169. For a brief summary of Irenaeus' thought, see ibid., 94–98, 169–77.

6. The word "ecology," based on the Greek word for "household" (*oikos*), "was coined by the German zoologist Ernest Haeckel in 1866" and has proved increasingly useful as humanity has progressively come to understand the complexity and interconnectedness of all of life and its intricate relationship to the earth. Carl Safina, *View from Lazy Point,* 28.

four key descriptors soon came to be viewed as the "marks" or "notes" of the church.[7] Significantly, the creed makes no distinction between a "visible" and an "invisible" church. The church is at once visible and invisible.

Visibility is always important in the church's witness. How was the body of Christ in fact visible during the first three centuries?

Even by 300 AD the Christian church was still mainly a network of house church- es. Clearly "church" referred to Christian community—local Christian fellowships scattered throughout and well beyond the Roman Empire. In a more general sense, "church" signified the entire Christian community on earth. Since believers who had died were also considered part of the church, the church was more than the sum of its visible parts. Wherever there is genuine Christian community, there the church is both visible and invisible.

So the early church was mainly a network of visible local communities of people worshiping Jesus Christ and seeking to visibly live the life of Jesus within their societ- ies and neighborhoods. Although visible Christian leaders had emerged—apostles, bishops, elders, deacons, and others—the church was visible primarily as *koinonia,* as Christian community gathered around and marked by Jesus Christ. The visibility of the church was not yet a matter of church buildings or institutions or public offices.

As a result, during this early period church and mission were united. Early Christians believed not that the church "had a mission" but that the church *was* God's mission in the world—the living body of Christ, the actual visible embodiment of the good news. Church and mission were not two different things. This was key in God's plan, God's economy.

Four Troubling Tendencies

The church was thus dynamic, growing, and visibly countercultural during its earliest centuries. This was due in part to the fact that the church was viewed with suspicion and often oppressed by established Greco-Roman society during its early centuries. But as time went on the church began to enjoy greater cultural acceptance, and four tendencies developed that would prove troublesome in later centuries—tendencies that helped open the door to a theological earth-heaven divorce.

First, in terms of doctrine and self-understanding, *the church was shifting away from a comprehensive narrative toward abbreviated doctrinal formulations.* The theo- logical focus began to shift from story to creed. This was an inevitable apologetic and theological move as church leaders and apologists engaged the (primarily) Greek phi- losophies of the day. Under pressure to defend and consolidate orthodox doctrine, early Christian theologians labored to articulate core Christian beliefs in dense, yet memorable statements of faith. This process led to remarkable doctrinal achievements, particularly concerning Christology and the Trinity.

---

7. The creed often cited today as the "Nicene Creed" (325) in most cases is actually the Niceno- Constantinopolitan Creed of 381.

So arose the church's great ecumenical creeds. On the one hand, these served (and continue to serve) as extremely important anchors of the Great Tradition of Christian belief. On the other hand, such a focus on the creeds began to eclipse the church's larger story of redemption and mission and tended to shift the church toward an over-reliance on formal doctrine itself.

This is not to argue against creeds. The church's great creeds are signposts of key confessional truths; crucial points of consensus. They are stakes that anchor central doctrines; facts of history that are essential to the story. Indeed, creeds themselves encapsulate story. Most creeds are pared-down and very selective summaries of the Christian story, emphasizing the particular doctrinal points currently at issue. This selectivity means that other crucial dimensions of the larger redemptive narrative are neglected— and with time easily forgotten, which then distorts the central narrative itself.

The problem grows when the church substitutes creed for story—or when it reduces the church's story to the abbreviated story told by the creeds. When the larger narrative is eclipsed by creed, mission easily becomes the defense of doctrine rather than proclaiming and living the good news of Jesus in the world. Creeds—which can serve as useful resources in mission and discipleship—become the central focus and thus may supplant mission.

The great creeds are, of course, a part of the Christian story; they are embedded in the church's narrative. But when they supplant the story, both Scripture and mission are diminished. At its best, the church has held creed and story together. At its worst, it has focused on creeds and the defense of doctrine to the detriment of the Christian story and mission contained in Scripture.

In the doctrinal debates that gave rise to the early creeds, the story itself was altered. The church began shifting away from seeing itself as a community of "aliens and exiles" (1 Pet 2:11), "strangers and foreigners on the earth" (Heb 11:13), a pilgrim people on a journey. Increasingly the church saw itself as a *settled* community, bound together by doctrine and liturgy.

We must not push the distinction between narrative and creed too far, however. The early "rules of faith"—proto-creeds apparently developed as declarations of faith uttered by converts at baptism—existed by the end of the first century. Such memorable distillations of faith were extremely helpful for the illiterate majority and weren't at odds with the larger biblical narrative. They were *distillations* of the Christian narrative. Early formulaic statements can in fact be found in the New Testament itself (e.g., Philippians 2).

A second and related trend was *the growing influence of Neo-Platonic dualism*. Despite the achievements of Irenaeus and others, Neo-Platonic conceptions of spirituality and doctrine began to drive a wedge between Christian understandings of spirit and matter, undermining the integrated wholism of the biblical worldview, and favoring the spiritual over the physical.[8] The impact of such views on biblical interpretation

8. Neo-Platonism (or Neoplatonism), a revival of the philosophy and worldview of the Greek philosopher Plato (c. 428–347 BC), makes a radical and unbiblical distinction between spirit and matter, strongly valuing the spirit world over the physical. Although Neo-Platonism sought to overcome

was significant: Neo-Platonism began to distort the way in which the spirit/flesh distinction in Jesus' teachings and in Paul's writings (for example in John 3:6, 6:63; Rom 8:3–13) was understood.

On this point, many scholars have noted the abiding influence of the early Greek father, Origen (c. 185–254). Alister McGrath calls Origen "a highly creative theologian with a strongly Platonist bent, who held that the resurrected body was purely spiritual." Though a radical spirit/matter dualism was "commonplace within the Hellenistic culture of the New Testament period," it was "vigorously opposed by most early Christian theologians,"[9] McGrath notes. Nevertheless, Neo-Platonic dualism seriously infected Christian theology, with effects that continue today. Origen put matters starkly: "The invisible and incorporeal things in heaven are true, but the visible and corporeal things on earth are copies of true things, not true in themselves." Thomas F. Torrance comments, "The implications of that dualist way of thinking were very far-reaching."[10]

A third development which distorted the biblical story came with the end of the age of the martyrs and the rise of asceticism—both of which resulted from Constantinian toleration. As saintliness came more and more to be understood ascetically—that is, as literally fleeing the world of human society and denying or repressing the physical passions—the Christian story became more and more otherworldly. The good impulse of wholehearted devotion to God was compromised by the unbiblical Platonic spirit-matter dualism prominent at the time.

With these three shifts the Christian narrative became less about the journey from Jerusalem and Antioch to the "ends of the earth" (Acts 1:8) and the visible kingdom of God, and more about the journey from earth to heaven. The direction of discipleship was now mainly *upward* rather than *forward*. Salvation ultimately became a movement from matter to spirit. We find the roots of this tendency already here in this early period. Its full flowering came later, as we will see.

A fourth key shift during these early centuries was *from community (koinonia) toward hierarchy (ierarchia)*—from the sense of being the charismatic "one-another" body of Christ to being a hierarchically structured institution. By 300 AD the tripartite hierarchy of bishop, presbyter, and deacon was firmly in place in much of the church. The divide between "clergy" and "laity" was pretty well sealed.[11]

---

some of the dualism in Plato's philosophy, it remained dualistic with regard to spirit and matter. (The term Neo-Platonism itself derives from the nineteenth century.) A very similar dualism was found in Gnosticism, an early Christian heresy that New Testament writers like John and Paul were already having to combat.

9. McGrath, *Brief History of Heaven*, 33–34.

10. Torrance, *Trinitarian Faith*, 34–35. Torrance here quotes Origen from *In Canticum canticorum* 2.

11. Debates over this drift toward a more hierarchical structure produced some of the church's earliest divisions, which in turn actually reinforced the institutionalizing tendency. Snyder's *Signs of the Spirit* shows how reactions to the church's "first charismatic movement," the New Prophecy ("Montanism") in the second and third centuries, brought greater emphasis on structure, authority, and hierarchy in the church—all this a familiar pattern in the sociology of religion.

These four significant tendencies were clear departures from the biblical picture of God's plan. They testify to the influence of Greco-Roman society, especially Greek philosophy and Roman social and political organization.

To summarize: The rise of Christianity in the first three centuries saw the rapid multiplication of local Christian communities throughout and well beyond the Roman Empire. These communities of disciples were firmly committed to Jesus and his mission, and strong in the hope of resurrection and ongoing life in God's everlasting reign. Jesus' followers held fast to the hope of full salvation, creation healed, when Christ returned. In the meantime, they were busy living the life of God's kingdom, being God's healing community on earth.[12]

Yet at the same time the church was moving away from biblical narrative toward a focus on doctrinal propositions, and from participatory "charismatic" community toward settled hierarchical organization. This and other factors would eventually reshape the church's understanding of salvation. Theologically speaking, the church was heading toward the divorce between heaven and earth.

Then—amazingly—the Roman Emperor converted to Christianity, and the world changed. Constantine's conversion would dramatically impact the church and world history. The emperor's conversion eased the lives of most Christians. But over time, the fallout from this event would make it ever harder for the church to understand salvation as creation healed.

12. See Stark, *Rise of Christianity*.

2

Church History

Sealing the Divorce

So, for the sake of your tradition, you make void the word of God.

(Matt 15:6)

E VERY FIVE HUNDRED YEARS or so "the church feels compelled to hold a giant rummage sale," says Phyllis Tickle in her book, *The Great Emergence*. Institutional Christianity gets shaken up every now and then, and new movements and patterns emerge—in the process also enlivening the old.

Tickle believes that the church is once again at "the hinge of a five-hundred-year period," a major change time. We can "gauge our pain against the patterns and gains of each of the previous hinge times through which we have already passed." The Great Reformation of the 1500s, the Great Schism of 1054 and its surrounding events, and the rise of Pope Gregory the Great about 590 just as the Roman Empire was disintegrating, she argues, were key rummage-sale times that God used to breathe new life into the church.[1]

Whatever we may think of Tickle's theory, it does raise the important question of the dynamics of church renewal. Yet it sidesteps the key question of how salvation itself was understood, and so misses the crucial theological divorce between heaven and earth. That key dynamic can better be understood by seeing the story differently. The big story is not the Great Emergence but the Great Earth-Heaven Divorce.

1. Tickle, *Great Emergence*, 16–31. Tickle credits Episcopal Bishop Mark Dyer with the 500-year "rummage sale" idea.

The complex tapestry of church history is a work of great beauty. Yet we must not overlook the troubling tears, the rough edges, and the burrs caught in the fabric. Over the centuries, the power of the gospel was both expressed faithfully and abused shamefully.

Christians today know of the abuses of the Crusades, the outbreaks of Anti-Semitism, the merchandising of salvation through indulgences that later touched off the Reformation. But behind and even more basic to all these, and a key contributing cause to them, was the divorce of heaven from earth. Church history from about 330 to 1500 is the story of sealing that divorce, short-circuiting the gospel hope of creation healed.

This chapter traces the steps leading to the divorce, and some of the results. The news is not all bad, of course; God's Spirit was always working. It is wrong to view the church's story, or history in general, either as a downward slide or a steady ascent (two common mistakes). The reality is more complex and more interesting. A narrative is unfolding.

The twelve hundred years following Constantine's conversion divide naturally into two periods, 330–800 and 800–1500. In both periods we must note the storyline or *narrative*, the way God's *redemptive plan* was viewed, and how the church was actually *visible*.

CULTURAL ENGAGEMENTS AND COMPROMISES, 330–800 AD

The five centuries from 330 to 800 were momentous ones for the church. By 800 most Asian and African churches had fallen under Muslim control. The "eternal city" of Rome was overrun by "barbarians" in 410. The Roman Empire crumbled and was carved into pieces. Yet the church survived among pagan tribes to the north—especially in Ireland, through the ministry of St. Patrick (c. 389–461) and the Celtic missionary movement that sprang from his influence. The Christian faith also spread to China during this period with the Nestorian mission led by Alopen in the 600s.

For our purposes, though, the main storyline runs through Europe. The key events of this phase came at the beginning: The conversion of Constantine, the recognition of Christianity as the official state religion in 380, the fall of the Roman Empire, and the corresponding rise in influence of Constantinople (present day Istanbul), founded by Constantine in 330.[2]

Throughout these five centuries the union of church and state was almost universally assumed—except, of course, in Muslim areas. It is hard to overestimate how much the marriage of church and state in Europe altered the church's self-understanding, and how much it contributed to the divorce of heaven and earth. The Age of Christendom, which would last for 1700 years, had begun.[3]

---

2. The fullest flowering of Byzantine (Constantinopolitan) Christianity came under the Emperor Justinian (reigned 527–565) and Empress Theodora (c. 500–548).

3. The fact that most historians put the transition from the early church to medieval Christendom in the 500s rather than the 300s shows how much the established-church mindset took over within Western Christianity, and how little understood is the revolutionary transition of the 300s, even today.

How was salvation understood during this period, and how did people literally *see* the church?

The Narrative, the Plan, the Visible Church

If recognition of the church by the Roman Empire and the fall of Rome just thirty years later changed the Christian story dramatically, it was Augustine of Hippo (354–430) who reshaped the storyline. In *City of God*, the North African saint's influential masterpiece, Augustine reinvented the story of salvation, seeing it as the ongoing struggle between the "City of God" and the "City of Man"—to end ultimately with the victory of God's City. According to Augustine, Christians should focus their attention on the City of God. This city was essentially the mystical New Jerusalem, the Heavenly City, more a spiritual than an earthly or political reality, though still partly embodied in the institutional church. The business of the church was above all the mystical City of God.

An unbiblical "spirit is perfect, matter is imperfect" view permeates much of Augustine's writings, for his worldview was strongly shaped by Neo-Platonic thought. Augustine so emphasized original sin that the original goodness of creation was eclipsed.[4] The biblical affirmation of the image of God in humankind and the manifestation of God's glory in nature was largely forgotten. Though Augustine did see creation as displaying God's glory, he did not seem to value the very materiality of creation as God's good gift, nor to fully understand the place of the earth in God's plan.

Meanwhile the church went on developing its doctrine, liturgy, and structures. Two great innovations were the Christian Year, a liturgical way of celebrating the great acts in the drama of salvation, and the Liturgy of the Hours, which was widely practiced in monastic communities and useful for structuring our days in the service of God. Though the storyline had changed, many common Christians continued to lead devout and holy lives.

By 800 all the great Seven Ecumenical Councils had been held. Through these councils the church, East and West, reached historic creedal consensus on key doctrinal points. Given the complex political, cultural, personal, and church-institutional plots and machinations involved, only the Holy Spirit could have brokered this remarkable consensus![5]

Major monastic movements arose during this period, most notably the Benedictine Order. St. Benedict of Nursia, (c. 480–547) founded the first Benedictine community at Monte Cassino near Rome in the early 500s; his twin sister Scholastica is said to have started a community of women nearby. Monasticism had begun earlier in Africa, but the amazing growth and expansion of the Benedictines throughout Europe set the dominant pattern for dozens of later orders (of both men and women) and thousands

---

4. Meyendorff, *Byzantine Theology*, 143–45; Pelikan, *Emergence of the Catholic Tradition*, 292–301, 313–18.

5. This is not to overlook the growing rift between East and West as Western theology was increasingly shaped by cultural differences and by Augustine's thought. In the East, Augustine's views on sin and depravity had almost no influence, though neo-Platonism was strong.

of monasteries. Meanwhile the Celtic orders (mentioned earlier) were key during this period in evangelizing Scotland, England, and northern Europe.

The monastic orders were a renewing force, a source of vitality to the church throughout this period, though they often assumed or promoted a body-soul dualism. The legacy thus is mixed and, in fact, testifies to a critical shift in the Christian narrative, in two ways.

First, Augustine's type of theology—which stressed human sin and depravity and neglected the Bible's emphasis on humanity created in the full image of God and the goodness of the created order—became the dominant worldview. In 529 the Council of Orange endorsed Augustine's doctrine of sin and grace, tilting the Western church toward an overemphasis on depravity and sinful carnality and an underemphasis on holistic discipleship as the norm of Christian experience.

Second, Jesus' teachings on costly discipleship were demoted to mere "counsels of perfection" for the select few—mainly monks, nuns, and ascetics—rather than being the pattern for all Christians. A split-level view of Christian experience was the result. This was perfectly understandable, given the marriage of church and state that essentially viewed Christian clergy as something like civil servants. A great many Christians were nominal believers; essentially baptized pagans.[6] Fortunately, vital Christianity and serious intellectual study were kept alive in many of the monastic communities. But no one, other than some fringe or "heretical" groups, questioned the view that devout discipleship was for the spiritual elite, not for the many.

Reviewing this period centuries later, the Anglican John Wesley saw the church-state alliance that began with Constantine ("Constantinianism") as the greatest disaster in church history. Wesley said,

> [The greatest wound true Christianity] ever received . . . was struck in the fourth century by Constantine the Great, when he called himself a Christian, and poured in a flood of riches, honours, and power upon the Christians; more especially upon the Clergy . . . [Thus,] when the fear of persecution was removed, and wealth and honour attended the Christian profession, the Christians "did not gradually sink, but rushed headlong into all manner of vices." . . . Then, not the golden but the iron age of the Church commenced.[7]

But the medieval worldview taught that true saints could flee this sad reality and live a higher life. By about 800, ideal Christian spirituality had come to mean an ascent to the realm of the spirit, a journey to the spirit world; enjoying a timeless "beatific

---

6. A measure of vital Christian faith and discipleship was kept alive among many persons and families through the "third orders" (tertiaries) which drew their inspiration and guidance from local monastic communities.

7. Wesley, Sermon 61, "Mystery of Iniquity," Par. 27 (Wesley, *Works*, 2:462–63). Wesley adds: "And this is the event which most Christian expositors mention with such triumph! Yea, which some of them suppose to be typified in the Revelation, by 'the New Jerusalem coming down from heaven!' Rather say, it was the coming of Satan and all his legions from the bottomless pit: Seeing from that very time he hath set up his throne over the face of the whole earth, and reigned over the Christian as well as the Pagan world with hardly any control" (Par. 28; ibid., 464).

vision" that was seen as the essence of eternal life. Saints could already inhabit heaven while still living on earth.

How was the church visible during this period? Where could you see it? Primarily in its structures, institutions, hierarchy, and sacraments. The church's most obvious visible emblems were church buildings and the multiplying monastic settlements. It was also visible in its clergy, especially the hierarchy, which by this time made extensive use of vestments that combined Old Testament priestly imagery with elements from the royal court.

By 800, then, the church was visible in a very different way from the way it had been visible in the first three centuries. It was visible, not in local Christian communities, families, house churches, and common folks of the earlier period, but in sacred buildings, vested clergy, and separated monastic settlements. The church had developed a rich liturgy, but for the majority of people it was a liturgy more to be watched than to be "done" as the ongoing everyday "work of the people" in serving God (the true meaning of *liturgy*).

Here then is a stark and dramatic contrast between two modes of being church; two expressions of the Christian faith.

THE DIVORCE OF HEAVEN AND EARTH, 800–1500 AD

Now comes the third act in the drama, the great 700-year period from about 800 to 1500, climaxing in the "High Middle Ages."

The Eastern church and parts of the African church survived, often under Islamic repression or limited tolerance. About 1000 AD the Russian Orthodox Church was born, and a significant missionary movement followed. Stephen Neill notes, "The world owes a great debt of gratitude to those missionaries who from AD 1000 onwards spread Christian culture throughout Russia." With the fall of Constantinople to Islam in 1453, the Russian Orthodox Church came to see Moscow as the "third Rome" and true heir to Orthodox Christianity. "The first Rome has fallen into heresy . . . The second Rome, Constantinople, has fallen under the dominion of [Islam]. Moscow alone is left, called into existence by God to be the centre of the world in these later times."[8]

Meanwhile Europe suffered cultural, ecclesiastical, and political tensions between southern Europe, centered in Rome, and northern Europe, where Christianity was emerging in more distinctly Frankish (later French), Germanic, Celtic, Anglo-Saxon, Scandinavian, and Slavic forms. In various ways the pagan tribes of Europe were Christianized, or at least partly so. Medieval Christian culture formed and took root. This was a dynamic period as medieval Christianity struggled through the ongoing clash of cultures, tribes, worldviews, ideas, kingdoms, and personalities.

From the year 800 on, medieval Christianity was held together politically and ecclesiastically through something called the Holy Roman Empire. This, as has often been remarked, was neither "holy," "Roman," nor even a real "empire," but it was still a

---

8. Neill, *History of Christian Missions*, 77, 180.

synthesizing force. Its key figures were Charles the Great, or Charlemagne (747–814), King of the Franks, Pope Leo III, and their respective successors. As Stephen Neill puts it, "When, on Christmas day 800, Pope Leo III crowned [King Charlemagne] in Rome as emperor, that strange archeological fiction the Holy Roman Empire came into being, and was destined to last for just over a thousand years." Charlemagne—a man of faith, learning, political skill, and sometimes ruthlessness— "set in motion that Carolingian Renaissance which is one of the brightest spots" of the medieval period.[9] This resurgence was a precursor of the Renaissance to come later, in the 1400s.

Throughout this period, the reigning assumption was that church and state were one. A kingdom or nation could have but one faith. (On this, at least, Christians and Muslims agreed.) So emerged the medieval Christian synthesis: Western medieval Christianity.

Six key elements of this synthesis should be noted:

1. *Scholastic theology*, epitomized in the *Summa Theologica* of Thomas Aquinas (1225–74). Aquinas brilliantly combined Augustine's theology with Aristotle's philosophy, which had been recovered through Islamic and Jewish sources. This established the "scholastic" model by which Roman Catholic and, later, Protestant theology were practiced until the mid-twentieth century (though Protestant scholasticism obviously differed in content).

2. The multiplying *medieval Gothic cathedrals* were a theological declaration, expressing worldview as much as architectural genius. "Church" and "church building" were now almost synonymous. We'll say more about this shortly.

3. The *increasing centrality of the Mass*, which was understood through the doctrine of transubstantiation as the repeated actual, physical sacrifice of Jesus Christ for our salvation.

4. The *system of seven sacraments*, in which the Mass was central but ordination was key. Ordination conferred an "indelible mark" that empowered priests, exclusively, to administer the other six sacraments, especially the Mass. So clergy held the key to salvation. This system amounted to a functional "sacramental technology" in which the right religious techniques produced guaranteed results.

5. The church on earth as a *holy hierarchical institution*—the indispensable earthly, visible reflection and agent of the celestial hierarchy and sole dispenser of grace, all of which was centered in the papacy.

6. *Latin as the church's sacred language*, which inevitably fostered theological ignorance, superstition, and magical conceptions of Christian faith and practice. The Latin for "this is my body" (*hoc est corpus meum*) was the basis for the phrase "hocus-pocus."

We can understand the significance of these six elements more fully by seeing them through the lenses of narrative, plan, and visibility.

9. Ibid., 67–68.

The Narrative, the Plan, the Visible Church

By 1500 the divorce between heaven and earth was nearly fixed and final. *The marriage of church and state brought the divorce of heaven and earth.* Now Christianity is seen as the journey from this world to the next; from the world of fallen matter to the world of perfect spirit. God has dictated the way to heaven, and it is through the church and its sacraments and institutions. Only a few special people can be expected to practice the "counsels of perfection" on earth and live a devout and holy life. In one sense the metanarrative is now cyclical—the cycle of earthly and liturgical seasons. Yet it is also linear. Out of the narrative extends a vertical line—up to heaven, as emphasized by the great cathedral spires—rather than a horizontal line that moves forward with the narrative into time, history, and God's reign on earth. The central biblical story of God's people serving faithfully in God's land is now long forgotten.

Thus God's plan was to save souls through the church's sacraments so that they could escape from the physical sufferings of this life to an ethereal state of unending bliss. Hell, however, was pictured as a very physical place, with literal fire and ingenious torments. Many visions of hell were painted or penned in this period, leading eventually to Dante's *Inferno* and Milton's *Paradise Lost*.

Heaven was also viewed as a place, though of a very different kind. In the concentric Ptolemaic worldview of the time, heaven was out beyond the farthest stars, presumably the realm of pure spirit. It was as far away from earth as you could get. Medievalist Jeffrey Burton Russell notes,

> In the sixteenth century, people generally still believed that heaven was a place and that it had a specific direction—up in the sky.... Dante's description in 1321 of moving *up* from the round Earth through the spheres of the moon, planets, and stars to the empyrean [realm] fit the geography and astronomy both of his time and that of two hundred years later. As late as 1600, only a very few people were aware of the heliocentric Copernican model that removed Earth from the center of the solar system.[10]

The church was still wedded to the older worldview. So both church and culture became unsettled as the discoveries of Galileo (1564–1642) began to undermine the traditional heliocentric worldview. So "by 1700 not many educated people believed in the ancient geocentric cosmology any more."[11]

In the 1500s, however, the ancient worldview still held sway. And in this model the church's sacramental system and hierarchy, structures, and traditions, its monasteries and cathedrals, all fit together as one neat divine plan, God's "economy" of salvation. The view of history was that God had orchestrated the development of the church and its traditions. The sharp contrast between the early church and its state now was not evidence of unfaithfulness; rather it showed the glory and providential wisdom of God through history. In the twelfth century Bishop Otto of Freising wrote,

---

10. Russell, *Paradise Mislaid*, 17 (emphasis in the original).

11. Ibid., 17. Copernicus (1473–1543) showed that the earth was not the center of the universe, but revolved around the sun; Galileo showed that neither earth nor the sun was the center of the universe.

"Speaking frankly, I do not really know whether the current prosperous condition of the church is more pleasing to God than its earlier humility. That earlier condition was perhaps better, but the present one is more agreeable!"[12] Otto identified the kingdom of God with the church and saw God's kingdom coming to fruition in the political and ecclesiastical order of his day.

Now the Christian church was very visible—increasingly so as the "cathedral crusade" got underway in the 1100s.[13] The great cathedrals, monasteries, and parish church buildings all across Continental Europe and the British Isles, and similarly throughout much of Russia, were the new visible face of the church. The church was visible also in its statues and icons and vestments, and in its sacraments. By 1500 the church was also becoming visible in the rise of the cathedral schools at Paris, Oxford, and Cambridge. The monastic orders—which had long been centers of learning—gave birth to institutions that would become Europe's great universities, while drawing on Muslim sources and precedents.[14]

The amazing rise of scores of Gothic cathedrals in the 1200s fits precisely into the theological architecture of the Middle Ages. The great cathedrals combined technical innovations, creative fundraising, and religious zeal. The key architectural breakthroughs were the pointed (rather than rounded) arch, flying buttresses which could support ever higher walls and wider arches, and ribbed vaulting.[15]

Some churchmen denounced the cathedral mania as an evil epidemic. "It is a sin to build the kind of churches which are being built nowadays," one Parisian wrote in 1180. "Monastic churches and cathedrals are being built by usury and avarice, by cunning and lies, and by the deception of preachers." But this ran counter to popular opinion and the passion of the growing medieval bourgeoisie to outdo one another in the splendor of their edifices. "Nothing was too splendid or too big," historian Jean Gimpel notes. "The house of God was being built in the image of the Heavenly City, and this house of God was an admirable thing: it was the place of worship and the home of the people."[16]

Gimpel adds, "We can no longer appreciate this duality of the Christian world which was symbolized" by the austerity of St. Bernard of Clairvaux, on the one hand, and the luxury and ostentation of cathedral builders like Abbot Suger (1081–1151, "father of the Gothic style"), on the other.[17] But behind this is the dualism of the medieval Christian worldview, a spirit-matter dualism with long roots, as we have seen. The cathedral with its soaring spires and holy high altar was the precious, sacred

---

12. Chenu, *Nature, Man and Society*, 240.

13. Gimpel, *Cathedral Builders*, 27–41.

14. The "oldest active university in the world" is Al-Ashar al-Sharif in Cairo, Egypt, the main Sunni Islamic university. Zahniser, *Mission and Death of Jesus*, 1.

15. The pointed arch would become the most recognizable emblem of the Gothic style, as it still is today. See for example Loth and Sadler, *Only Proper Style*.

16. Gimpel, *Cathedral Builders*, 32, 38.

17. Ibid., 18.

channel between heaven and earth. So (as with the Old Testament temple) nothing was too good or too expensive.

The symbolism of medieval cathedral construction was a theological statement. The towering spires and exalted naves pointed worshipers upward, away from earth, toward the dwelling place of God. Cathedrals said, in effect: Look up! There is your true destiny; there you will spend eternity, escaping this fallen world. This is holy space; the divinely-approved essential portal to eternal spiritual reality.

Heaven and Earth, Church and State

We said above that the marriage of church and state brought the divorce of heaven and earth. This happened in three ways: It introduced a distinction between the sacred and the secular; it reinforced the slit between clergy and laity; and it paved the way for the Crusades. To elaborate:

The union of church and state introduced the sacred/secular distinction. The Old Testament, of course, underscores the difference between holy and common, but this is not the same as the sacred/secular divide. "You are to distinguish between the holy and the common, and between the unclean and the clean; and you are to teach the people of Israel all the statutes that the Lord has spoken to them through Moses" (Lev 10:10–11). But the Old Testament nowhere suggests the category of "secular" in the modern senses of "amoral," "irreligious," "unspiritual"—in other words, outside moral, ethical, or spiritual consideration. Quite the opposite: God is sovereign over all, and even the "common" and "unclean" fall within the sphere of God's concern, judgment, and potential redemption.

Both the Old Testament covenants and the new covenant are about the hallowing of all of life. Nothing is beyond the scope of the kingdom of God; nothing is outside the sphere of the work of the Holy Spirit. There are not two sets of ethical rules; nothing is "secular." In the new covenant in Jesus the ritual hallowing of the Old Testament becomes a matter of the heart and of actively claiming God's rule over "all things" as a part of faithful discipleship. Jesus "declared all foods clean" (Mark 7:19). The word *secular* (Latin, *saeculum*) means, literally, "the present age." So "secular" has come to mean "connected with the world and its affairs; of things not religious or sacred; worldly."[18] But the New Testament makes clear that the gospel is about both this age and the future. The risen Christ now has authority over all other powers, "not only in this age but also in the age to come" (Eph 1:21).

Since Constantine, things spiritual have increasingly been seen as sacred and otherworldly, while the material world and its affairs are secular and "worldly"—not really expected to operate by the ethics of Jesus. The church struggled mightily with this conundrum—theologically, politically, economically, and even militarily. For the most part, the church has embraced the sacred/secular split. The major underlying question through one thousand years of medieval history was where to draw the line

---

18. *World Book Dictionary*, 2:1881.

between sacred and secular—how to blend them or keep them apart. (Martin Luther later would try to solve the problem with his doctrine of "two kingdoms.")

This is the main way the marriage of church and state hastened the divorce between heaven and earth. But second, this marriage also *reinforced the clergy/laity split*. The division started earlier, as we have seen, but the church-state union reinforced it. In fact, since clergy were now government-supported, the eventual result was a three-tiered society: church (that is, clergy, the First Estate), government (that is, the nobility), and everyone else (peasants). So society was divided roughly between "those who prayed," "those who fought," and "those who labored" and produced the food. (This applied only to men; the "feminine estates" were virgin, wife, and widow.)[19]

The clergy/laity split, along with the sacred/secular distinction, got so woven into the medieval Christian worldview that it became conceptually invisible; just part of the fabric of reality.

Third, *the marriage of church and state paved the way for the Crusades*. The logic is pretty self-evident. When church and state are one, the church has access to armies and swords. The new politico-religious empire of Islam had captured Jerusalem in the year 638. After the fall of the Roman Empire, Europe was in disarray and the church too weak in worldly terms to do anything about it. By the year 1000, however, feudal princes had gathered armies around them, and much of Europe was loosely networked through the Holy Roman Empire. Now the idea arose of a Holy Crusade to liberate the Holy Land from the unholy "infidel." The two-hundred-year period of the Crusades was underway. The church had found its new, exciting, and militarily possible mission.

All this is unimaginable without the marriage of church and state.

Some of the church's most capable and most pious saints, like the great monastic leader and reformer Bernard of Clairvaux (1090–1153), supported the Crusade movement. The First Crusade began in 1095 and four years later French Crusaders liberated Jerusalem. Historian Norman Cantor describes this as "the breakthrough moment." The First Crusade "inaugurates the era of the High Middle Ages of the twelfth, thirteenth, and early fourteenth centuries. This was the time when Western Europe exhibited unprecedented creativity in literature and the visual arts and remarkable advances in theology, philosophy, popular piety, government, and law, as well as a population boom and commercial and urban expansion."[20] These developments also triggered the rise of capitalism. Money was in short supply. Historian Niall Ferguson in *The Ascent of Money: A Financial History of the World* writes, "The Crusades, like the conquests that followed, were as much about overcoming Europe's monetary shortage" as they were about spiritual conquests.[21]

Much of the dynamism of the High Middle Ages, including the "cathedral crusade," was thus facilitated by these military Crusades. But this dynamism and creativity were put into the service of a faulty worldview.

19. See online: http://cla.calpoly.edu/~dschwart/engl430/estates.html.
20. Cantor, *Inventing the Middle Ages*, 26, 27.
21. Ferguson, *Ascent of Money*, 25.

Medieval Biblical Interpretation

Bible study flourished during the High Middle Ages. Compiling texts and manuscripts and rigorous, persistent study in monastic communities and cathedral schools laid the groundwork for two vital developments. First was the emergence of the great European universities that grew out of the cathedral schools. Second, later, came the distribution of Bibles, commentaries, and theological texts flowing from the newly-invented printing press.

Ironically however, this flowering of Bible study did not lead to a recovery of the biblical vision of creation healed, as might have been expected. The reasons are instructive for us today. Three trends in medieval biblical exegesis actually widened the gap between heaven and earth: a preference for Paul's writings and the Psalms over the Gospels, preference for symbolic and mystical interpretations of biblical texts, and a new interest in the Hebrew language and the Old Testament.

1. The *preference for Paul* traced back to earlier centuries. As Beryl Smalley writes, "The pre-eminence of the Pauline Epistles and of the Psalter [over the Gospels] in the teaching of Scripture is common to East and West alike."[22] The limiting tendency to interpret all Scripture through the lens of Paul, rather than the other way around (still with us) traces back well before the Protestant Reformation. (In contrast, some fringe groups, "heretical" sects, and reformers like Francis of Assisi pointed to the Gospels and the actual earthly example of Jesus as the pattern for Christian faith and discipleship. Later the Anabaptists and their heirs would make this following of Christ a major focus.)

2. Added to this preference for Paul was the persistent tendency, also dating back centuries, to *interpret much of Scripture symbolically or mystically*—to find its "spiritual sense" beyond its "literal sense." When controlled by Scripture itself, this is legitimate. But the preference for symbolic and mystical interpretation easily opens the door to Neo-Platonism and to spirit-matter dualism.

Robert Grant notes, "In the late patristic period and in the Middle Ages" exegetes developed "a system of allegorization" which found four, and sometimes up to seven, meanings in biblical texts. Most commonly the four meanings sought were the literal, the allegorical, the moral, and the anagogical or mystical. By far the "most important and characteristic method of biblical interpretation . . . was not literal but allegorical."[23] Smalley explains further, "The Latin Fathers, followed by the assistants of Charlemagne, made Bible study serve their present needs. They retained both the literal sense and textual criticism, but only as a basis for the spiritual interpretation." Bible study was put in the service of mystical spirituality, on the one hand, and of defending the church's doctrines and place in the social-political order, on the other. In general, Bible study "subordinated scholarship . . . to mysticism and to propaganda."[24]

3. An *increasing preference for Hebrew over Greek* was another factor that tended to split earth from heaven. This is highly ironic! One might suppose that focusing on Hebrew and the Old Testament would counteract Greek Neo-Platonism. Quite the

22. Smalley, *Study of Bible,* 361.

23. Grant and Tracy, *Short History,* 85.

24. Smalley, *Study of the Bible,* 358.

opposite happened, partly due to the two tendencies just noted, and partly for socio-cultural and even geographic reasons.

With time, Western scholars were increasingly cut off from their early Eastern roots. Yet they were influenced by the early Greek Fathers, especially Origen, "the boldest allegorizer of the ancient church" who applied "the metaphorical method of the Greek mysteries" to the Jewish Scriptures.[25] Hebrew was "mysticized," one might say, rather than being taken simply as human language. It came to be viewed as the "language of heaven," having "a magical pre-eminence over others," writes Smalley. "Greek must have seemed to have little sanctity compared with the alpha and omega of speech."[26]

Smalley notes that a Western scholar wanting to master Greek "would have to make the journey to Byzantium [Constantinople] or to southern Italy or Sicily, while he could [simply] learn Hebrew from the Jew next door."[27] The local Jewish rabbi or scholar was "a kind of telephone to the Old Testament." Contemporary Jewish biblical interpretation was highly mystical, however. Smalley suggests that the Christian biblical scholar "in his dealings with the Synagogue . . . abstracted his disapproval of its present-day representatives from his veneration for its past. The Jew, however despised and persecuted, could put him in touch with the patriarchs, the prophets, and the psalmist." "No such obvious source for the study of the New Testament presented itself." As a result, "the medieval Latin scholar [tended] to concentrate his forces on the study of Hebrew and of the Old Testament, leaving the New high and dry."[28]

Smalley shows how "veneration for the mystical properties of Hebrew persuaded the medieval Hebraist that his studies were taking him to the crux of the matter. He was penetrating the innermost spring of meaning of his text."[29] In other words, exegetes were attracted to the Hebrew biblical texts, but their interpretation of these texts was heavily shaped by the then-current *mystical* Jewish interpretation of Scripture. The study of the Old Testament thus did not lead to a holistic biblical worldview, but rather to an increasingly mystical, otherworldly one.

The fundamental mistake here was to see the Old Testament as allegory rather than real salvation history—an error still found in popular Christianity today. The Hebrew Scriptures became the *mystical typological background* of the gospel, not the *necessary historical context* within which the gospel can only properly be understood.

Allegorizing the Bible is, above all, a way to get around the embarrassing materiality, physicality, passions, and historicity of the Old Testament. The great scandal of the Old Testament—today as in the Middle Ages—is that it is so earthly, so earthy. Job says "in my flesh," not spirit, "I shall see God" (Job 19:26). The earthiness of the Old Testament is an embarrassment to Neo-Platonic thought. The solution is to turn most of it (and even some of the New Testament) into allegory; to search out the Bible's "real," higher, "spiritual" meaning. In such exegesis, then as now, the symbols

25. Grant, *Letter and Spirit*, 101.

26. Smalley, *Study of the Bible*, 362.

27. Ibid.. 361–62.

28. Ibid., 362–63.

29. Ibid., 362.

are biblical, but the worldview is Platonic, not Hebraic. The result: further sealing of the earth-heaven divorce.

Such Old Testament interpretation largely explains the popularity of Paul over the Gospels, even today. Medieval exegetes preferred a spiritualized Jesus over the historical Jesus who was and remains fully human while fully God. This was not Paul's fault. Though Paul sometimes used allegory to explain the divine economy, his allegory was always controlled by the actual history. In most later biblical interpretation, however, the history was controlled (and reinterpreted) by the allegory.

This is not to say the medieval biblical allegories were all wrong. The point is that the allegorical interpretation uprooted and supplanted the more literal, plain-sense, historical interpretation, giving biblical history a different, more "spiritual," theological meaning. The interpretation and the worldview were more Platonic than Hebraic—thus further distancing earth from heaven.

The Rediscovery of Nature

The 1200s brought a new focus on nature and the natural world. Would this mean a recovery of the biblical emphasis on land and the earth in God's plan? It could have, but it didn't. Due to the theological gap already opened between earth and heaven and the dominance of mysticism, the new stress on nature led not to its proper, biblical theological appropriation but rather to its secularization!

Smalley notes, "All creatures, whether works of nature or art, [now became] worth examining." A growing "interest in the working of natural processes in man and the universe [led even] to inquiries into the physics of Bible narratives," with "a driving desire to understand exactly how things happened." But because of the spirit/matter worldview split, such Bible study did not translate into a sense of salvation as creation healed or the marriage of heaven and earth. It led rather to a further sealing of the divorce. Notes Smalley, "we are watching a stage in the secularization of medieval thought."[30]

Here then was a widening gap: secularization on the one hand, mysticism on the other. This gap climaxed in the mystical-historical-eschatological writings of Joachim of Fiore (c. 1135–1202), an Italian abbot who wanted to reform the church and particularly the Cistercian Order. In his *Harmony of the Old and New Testament* and other writings, Joachim worked out a theory of three ages of history that became immensely popular.

Up until Joachim, the mystical-spiritual interpretation of Scripture "had worked within recognized limits" and without extensive eschatological speculation.[31] Joachim however mixed together the doctrine of the Trinity, the book of Revelation, and the mystical-symbolic interpretation of Scripture, concocting a theory of three ages—a dispensational theory that in some ways parallels the premillennial dispensationalism of John Nelson Darby six centuries later.[32]

30. Ibid., 371–72.

31. Ibid., 286.

32. See chapter 4. For a summary of Joachim and his influence, see Snyder, *Models*, 30–33.

Joachim's dispensational model was novel in its creativity and basic simplicity. Biblical exegesis had already established the principle that what was prefigured in the Old Testament was fulfilled in the New, making heavy use of allegory and typology. "Why [then] should not Old and New Testaments prefigure some third period?"[33]

Joachim identified the Old Testament with the Father, the New Testament and the church age with the Son, and a new, dawning age of renewal with the Spirit. This new Age of the Spirit was about to begin. It would bring the full flowering of the gospel promise, a dispensation of love in which people enjoyed intimate fellowship with God. The church's monastic orders, filled by the Spirit, would play a leading role, largely replacing the church's hierarchy. At this very time the new Franciscan Order was flourishing and expanding. Many people saw the Franciscans as the leading edge of the coming Spirit Age.

Joachim was creative in his ideas and his mathematics, like John Darby much later. Based on passages such as Rev 11:3 ("I will grant my two witnesses authority to prophesy for one thousand two hundred sixty days") and 12:6 ("the woman fled into the wilderness, where she has a place prepared by God, so that there she can be nourished for one thousand two hundred sixty days"), Joachim concluded that the new Age of the Spirit would begin in the year 1260. The logic seemed self-evident, once Joachim pointed it out.

Only in the Age of the Spirit would people fully understand the Bible's deepest spiritual secrets. The husk of the literal sense of Scripture would be cast aside.

Thomas Aquinas (c. 1225–74) refuted Joachim's ideas in his landmark *Summa Theologica*. Joachim's fellow Italian, Dante Alighieri (c. 1265–1321) in his *Divine Comedy* pictured him in paradise, however. This is understandable, since Dante viewed the highest, ultimate reality as pure nonmaterial light; "for him the ultimate truth is that the soul is dazzled by the light."[34]

In Joachim we see the recurring lure of apocalyptic speculation. His novel theory seemed to explain much about the world and the church. And it inspired hope: God was about to do a new thing. That "new thing" was not though the marriage of heaven and earth; rather it was an intensified spiritualization of all things material. In this sense Joachim's views can be seen as "the culmination of the patristic tradition which had indentified the letter with the flesh, and regarded the spiritual interpretation, the special prerogative of religious, as its antithesis," as Beryl Smalley suggests.[35]

Countercurrents of Renewal

And yet, significantly, fresh renewal currents really were stirring. In part this was a reaction, even revulsion, to the Crusades with their excesses and the ostentation they brought to people in power in church and state. Many people longed for a return to the simplicity of early Christianity.

33. Smalley, *Study of the Bible*, 287.
34. Edwards, *Christianity*, 259.
35. Smalley, *Study of the Bible*, 289.

This yearning eventually became a self-conscious impulse toward reform, leading to what some have called "the evangelical awakening of the twelfth century."[36] This impulse reached its spiritual high point in Francis (c. 1182–1226) and Clare (1194–1253) of Assisi and their thousands of youthful followers. The multiplying communities of Franciscans and Poor Clares made the church visible in new ways.

God told Francis, "Go, rebuild my church, which is in ruins." Francis's first response is telling, for it shows what "church" meant in his day. He naturally assumed God wanted him to repair church *buildings*. (Today in the elaborate Church of St. Francis high on the edge of the old city of Assisi one can see a fresco of Francis symbolically propping up a tilting church building.)

Taking "rebuild my church" in a physical sense, Francis and his friends started repairing the old chapel of San Damiano, down the hill from Assisi. Gradually, though, Francis came to understand what God really meant. The church was the people of God, not buildings. Today, one of the most inspiring sights at San Damiano is a small bas-relief sculpture of Francis receiving his divine commission: "Go, rebuild my church."

Within just thirty years or so, thousands of Franciscans, Clares, and others were making the church visible through lives of simplicity and service. It was one of the greatest of all movements in Christian history. Once again the church was visible in ways that reminded people of the early church. An observer said that the Franciscans "have in a short time so multiplied in number that there is hardly a province in Christendom where they do not have some friars." Another noted how this "completely new form of life" of the Franciscans attracted youth, especially.[37]

The Franciscans, Clares, and to a lesser degree the Dominicans renewed the life of the church throughout much of Europe. The supposedly heretical Waldensians (Peter Waldo, 1179–1218) were also a renewing force in this same period.

Even so, the church continued to be visible mostly through its physical structures and its hierarchy, allied with the state. Though many common people were discovering God through the Franciscans and others, still everyone knew that the church bore the cross in one hand but (through the state) could bear the sword in the other. After all, this was not only the age of the Franciscans but also of the Crusades, from which we still suffer.

CONCLUSION: THE DIVORCE CONFIRMED

We speak of "the divorce of heaven and earth" because that phrase captures the key long-term development over twelve hundred years of church history. Jesus' incarnation and resurrection united heaven and earth. In Jesus Christ the kingdom of God appeared visibly. When the Roman Empire became Christian, and especially when the

---

36. Chenu points out that the aspiration to restore the church to its primitive state not only provoked a drive toward moral reform but also nourished a deep inquiry into the Christian faith that brought significant advances in theology. The two directions of that renewing thrust are symbolized in the names of Francis and Clare, on the one hand, and Thomas Aquinas on the other.

37. Esser, *Origins of the Franciscan Order*, 37–38.

great Byzantine Christian empire was established, it seemed indeed that the kingdom of God had come on earth.

But with the decline of Rome, the conquests of Islam, the increasing politicization of the church, and the absence of daily discipleship among the Christian masses, heaven grew more and more distant—far, far above. The earth was not "full of God's glory" except as one might glimpse it through the sacraments or otherworldly mysticism. "The end of the age" came to mean the time when "Christ will appear in his glory and will come to look for his own to take them away with him" to heaven, wrote Henri de Lubac, rather than the reconciliation of heaven and earth—the healing of creation.[38]

Randy Maddox neatly captures the basic trend:

> While Scripture speaks of God's ultimate salvific goal as "the new heavens and earth" (i.e., transformation of everything in the universe), . . . Christians through the first millennium [came] to assume increasingly that our final state is "heaven above" . . . seen as a realm where human spirits dwelling in ethereal bodies join eternally with all other spiritual beings—a category that did not include animals!—in continuous worship of the Ultimate Spiritual Being. By contrast, they assumed that the physical universe, which we abandon at death, would eventually be annihilated.[39]

By 1500 this earth-heaven divorce was nearly complete. It was challenged only by some millenarian, spiritualist, or proto-Anabaptist groups like the Waldensians—which were considered heretical by the official church—and to some degree by the Franciscans, Clares, and others who embraced the ideal of "apostolic poverty." We say "to some degree" because, for all his love of nature, Francis (in understandable reaction to the official church) manifested an overly ascetic, world-denying life that glorified suffering and extreme poverty. Theologically he did not really bridge the earth-heaven divide in a fully biblical way. In some ways, he reinforced it.

By 1500 the Christian church, both East and West, fully accepted the divorce of heaven and earth. Indeed, the church more than accepted it: it unconsciously assumed it as part of the Christian worldview. The chasm between earth and heaven could be bridged only through the sacraments and mystical experience. At death, the soul escaped earth and entered the timeless bliss of a spiritual heaven. Much medieval art dramatically depicts this worldview. It is well captured for example in Dieric Bouts the Elder's "Ascension from Restored Paradise" (1450). And yet, unknowingly, the church stood at the brink of major reform and renewal!

---

38. De Lubac, *Four Senses*, 179.

39. Maddox, "John Wesley's," 47. Maddox notes that John Wesley "imbibed this understanding of our final state in his upbringing, and through much of his ministry it was presented as obvious and unproblematic." In his last decade, however, "Wesley reclaimed the biblical imagery of God's cosmic renewal, shifting his focus from 'heaven above' to the future new creation" (ibid., 47).

The Flemish painter Dieric Bouts the Elder imagined redeemed people rising from earth to heaven in *Ascension from Restored Paradise* (1450).

3

Streams of Renewal

Hope for Reconciliation

There is hope for a tree, if it is cut down,
that it will sprout again,
and that its shoots will not cease.
Though its root grows old in the earth,
and its stump dies in the ground,
yet at the scent of water it will bud
and put forth branches like a young plant.

(Job 14:7–9)

FRESH STREAMS OF RENEWAL began stirring the church around the year 1500. Renewing currents have ebbed and flowed, but continue right up to the present.

Succeeding waves of renewal revived the church and extended its witness over centuries. These renewal movements did not begin with the Protestant Reformation. Renewal has always been a part of church history. But a significant new era began in the 1500s.

This chapter traces these renewal currents in two phases: 1500 to 1800, and 1800 to the present. The second phase we call the "age of gospel globalization." The key question: did these fresh winds of renewal finally birth a vision for the reconciliation of heaven and earth? What happened to the earth-heaven divorce, the split that undercuts the full power of the good news as the message of creation healed?

JOURNEYS OF RENEWAL, 1500–1800

Renewal movements stirred Western Christianity repeatedly, and quite broadly, over the three hundred years from 1500 up to the early 1800s.[1]

The Catholic Reformation (or "Counter-Reformation") in southern Europe, and the remarkable rise of global missions through the Society of Jesus (Jesuits), breathed new life into Roman Catholicism. Granted, these movements were not as "evangelical" as Protestants might wish. They still involved the political ambiguity of the church-state alliance. Yet God's Spirit seemed to be remarkably at work in people like Teresa of Avila, John of the Cross, Ignatius Loyola, and Francis Xavier. As the Protestant Reformation arose in northern Europe, Roman Catholics were already sending devout missionaries to India, China, and the Americas, accompanying or following in the steps of Spanish and Portuguese world-ranging explorers. Today in the Church of St. Ignatius Loyola in Rome (opened in 1650, built on the site of the ancient Temple of Isis), visitors gaze transfixed at dramatic ceiling frescoes of early Jesuit missions in Asia, Africa, and the Americas.

Yet the Protestant Reformation was the major source of the renewals that shaped this three-hundred-year period. The reforms of Luther, Calvin, Zwingli, Menno Simons, and the early Anabaptists set the stage for great awakenings in Continental Europe, the British Isles, and (later) North America. Through these movements, the church in various ways and places was stirred, renewed, chastened, and then inspired to global mission as never before.

To a large degree these renewals accompanied the rise of European colonialism. So their story is a mixed one. Despite this ambiguity, the Holy Spirit was at work both in renewing the church and in expanding its global missionary vision.

Here we encounter a crucial point. During the Reformation period only the Anabaptists and a few earlier "heretical" groups, such as the Waldensians, challenged the church-state marriage. Protestants, like Catholics (and Muslims in their own way), simply assumed that church and state must be one. That was their worldview. The religion of the people must be that of the king. Those who disagreed were not mere dissenters; they were political subversives, heretics deserving death or banishment. That was the logic of the divine right of kings and the church-state marriage.

The Anabaptist or Radical Protestant movement is often misunderstood at this point. These earnest Christians were labeled "Anabaptists"—that is, "rebaptizers"—because of their insistence on adult believers' baptism, and were widely rejected by Catholics and Protestants alike. The issue wasn't so much baptism, however, as it was their challenging of the church-state alliance. From the traditional perspective, if church and state are one, then baptism and citizenship are one. To be a Christian is to be a citizen, and vice-versa. Against this view, the Radical Protestants insisted on adult believers' baptism in order to draw a clear line between church and state.

---

1. To a degree this was true also in Eastern Christianity and even within Judaism and Islam, but we focus especially on Western Christendom.

Christian faith required a conscious decision to follow Jesus, not just a passive acceptance of the state religion.

Adult believers' baptism was a protest against the marriage of church and state. This was the great Anabaptist heresy! The irony is that the much-maligned Anabaptists pioneered at great cost the view of the church that today most Christians take for granted.[2]

After the Protestant Reformation it took two hundred years for the marriage of church and state to be seriously questioned by anyone *within* established Christianity. Gradually, with the growth of various dissenting groups—including some Baptists in England and then, notably, the Quakers—"Dissenters" won the right to live and to worship as conscience dictated. The free religious economy we now take for granted arose not from enlightened policy or theological breakthroughs, but because independents and dissenters grew so numerous that they *had* to be tolerated.[3] In North America, the United States from the beginning was so religiously mixed that no group could become an established state church, except briefly in a few of the colonies. The United States was born guaranteeing freedom of religion—an amazing innovation, much celebrated by Thomas Jefferson.

The Narrative, the Plan, the Visible Church

The Narrative and the Plan. These renewal currents shifted the Christian storyline a bit. Hope grew that God was doing a new thing. In Continental Europe, the Thirty Years War (1618–48) and weariness with Protestant doctrinal battles over precisely correct belief (sometimes called "Protestant Scholasticism") awakened a longing for renewal. Pietists and the renewed Moravian Brethren on the Continent, together with Puritans in England, sought to recover the potential unleashed by the Reformation a century and a half earlier.

The revival and renewal movements of the mid-1600s through the 1700s changed the mindset, and thus the direction, of the Christian narrative. Philip Jakob Spener, a Lutheran pastor key in the rise of Continental Pietism, spoke of "hope for better times" and the possibility of "new birth" or "rebirth," not only of persons but of the church itself. People stopped looking back to Luther and started looked ahead to new things the Spirit would do. A similar mentality marked the early Methodists and the larger Evangelical Revival in England. This was true also of the Great Awakening in North America.[4] Today historians still debate the role of the Great Awakening in shaping America's national destiny.

---

2. A particularly good overview is Durnbaugh, *Believers' Church*.

3. Here was an ironic parallel with the fourth century when the (pagan) Roman Empire eventually had to tolerate Christians because they had become so numerous and were having such a leavening influence, as shown for example by Stark, *Rise of Christianity*.

4. Among the many sources, see especially Snyder, *Signs of the Spirit*; Ward, *Protestant Evangelical Awakening*; Noll, *Rise of Evangelicalism*.

Despite these great renewals, the central Christian narrative didn't change much. The global expansion of Europe, the encounter with other peoples and religions, and the Industrial Revolution all contributed to a dynamic, expansionary sense of a world full of potential and opportunity. But church and state, and thus Christianity and empire, were still tightly linked—not only within Roman Catholicism but also in most branches of Protestantism. This produced decidedly mixed messages during the great period of Protestant missions, which was about to dawn.

And the divorce of heaven and earth was not healed. Land—the created order— played little or no role in God's plan except as something to be conquered, dominated, and made to produce economic gain and extend empire. It was not to be nurtured, protected, or redeemed.

In Europe, covenant or federal theology (from the Latin word for "covenant," *foedus*) in the 1600s seemed to offer hope for a more biblically-based view of salvation. Stressing the biblical covenants, federal theology made room for human agency and historical processes in the divine economy. Here was a way around the rigid orthodoxy of Reformed scholasticism. Unfortunately however, key covenant theologians such as Johannes Cocceius largely ignored God's covenant with the earth itself (Gen 9:8–17; Jer 33:20, 25). Earth, as earth, was still virtually invisible; the focus was solely on the covenant between God and humans.[5] If American Puritans sometimes made connections between the biblical promise of land and America as a new promised land, that blessing was a corollary of God's covenant of grace with his chosen people, not a distinct covenant with the land or earth itself.

Renewal and revival movements did nurture a broader sense of personal responsibility and holy living. But for the most part, those Christians affected by the renewals—whether Methodists, Baptists, Congregationalists, Lutherans, or the new restoration movements in North American—understood God's redemptive plan to mean eventual translation from a material earth to a spiritual heaven. Of course, this was the worldview they had inherited. Christians had little expectation of the restoration of heaven and earth; little real, lively hope for God's will being "done on earth as in heaven" as a realistic present-time possibility.[6]

The still-popular hymns and gospel songs from the mid-1800s and the 1900s make this abundantly clear. They are full of lines like these:

> In the cross, in the cross, be my glory ever
> Till my raptured soul[7] shall find rest beyond the river
> ("In the Cross")

5. Johannes Cocceius (1603–69), despite his concern to be biblical, focused almost exclusively on the relationship between God and humanity, with little or no reference to the earth and God's relationship with the earth—understandable, given the nature of the debates at the time. See McCoy, "Covenant Theology of Johannes Cocceius."

6. The many utopian communities in the U.S. and elsewhere in the 1800s (and earlier) are best understood in this context, by way of contrast. See for example Holloway, *Heavens on Earth*.

7. Fanny Crosby wrote this before the rise of premillennial dispensationalism, so "raptured soul" here has no reference to "The Rapture" but rather carries the more traditional sense of spiritual delight or ecstasy.

> Then he'll call me some day to my home far away
> Where his glory forever I'll share
> ("The Old Rugged Cross")

> I have a future in heaven for sure, there in those mansions sublime
> ("Heaven Came Down," 1961)

"When the Roll is Called Up Yonder" (by James M. Black, 1856–1938) celebrates "that bright and cloudless morning when the dead in Christ shall rise, and the glory of His resurrection share," but the destination is "their home beyond the skies," not the renewed heaven and earth. The problem here is not the vision of "rest" and an eternal "home," but rather the idea that the final Christian future consists of "ransomed souls" in a "home far away" from any kind of material world—rather than the reconciliation of heaven and earth. This is clearly unbiblical.

These ideas did not begin in the 1800s, of course. They were already well embedded in evangelical theology and experience in the revivals of the 1600s and 1700s. Isaac Watts (1674–1748) wrote,

> When I can read my title clear
> To mansions in the skies.

The hymns of Charles Wesley (1707–88) make an interesting case study because of their seeming ambivalence about the Christian hope. Taken together, Wesley's hymns give a mixed message. Some speak positively about resurrection, new creation, transformation, and God's coming kingdom. But many picture earth as "a dream" (a rather bad one), something to escape from, and death as a liberating friend. So we find lines like these:

> The voyage of life's at an end;
> The mortal affliction is past:
> The age that in heaven they spend,
> Forever and ever shall last.
> ("Weep Not for a Brother Deceased")

Or these:

> Nothing is worth a thought beneath,
> But how I may escape the death
> That never, never dies!
> How make mine own election sure;
> And when I fail on earth, secure
> A mansion in the skies.
> ("And Am I Only Born to Die?")[8]

Meanwhile John Newton (1725–1807) wrote,

---

8. One of Charles Wesley's worst (from a biblical standpoint) and most escapist hymns is "Leader of Faithful Souls," which speaks of "travel to the sky," meeting "our Saviour in the skies," "Our everlasting home above," and "This earth" as "not our place."

As the winged arrow flies
Speedily the mark to find;
As the lightning from the skies
Darts, and leaves no trace behind,—
Swiftly thus our fleeting days
Bear us down life's rapid stream;
Upward, Lord, our spirits raise;
All below is but a dream.
("While, With Ceaseless Course, the Sun")

Christians rightly celebrate the gospel promise of eternal life. That promise, though, is not ultimately about escape from earth but about the new creation that heals the divorce of earth and heaven.

Renewal movements throughout the 1700s and 1800s zeroed in on personal experience. This was their strength and appeal. But the focus on personal experience veered into individualism (*my* experience, largely self-validating) and tended to eclipse a broader vision of God and his kingdom purposes. Here again the church's hymnody provides clues. Christianity's great "churchly" hymns, many of them ancient, are generally Trinitarian in structure, ending with a stanza praising the Trinity. In contrast, gospel songs of the Evangelical awakenings typically climax with an individualistic focus on heaven "in the sweet by and by." Trinitarian hymns are in short supply.[9]

Some renewal movements—notably Methodism and Pietism—offset the individualism and otherworldliness through structures of accountable community. The Pietist

9. The church desperately needs new hymns that express full biblical hope—not just the hope of heaven—as a counterweight to the hundreds of unbiblical or sub-biblical ones. Once you start looking, it is shocking to discover how many popular hymns and songs are misleading or unbiblical in some stanzas. Such songs reinforce the earth-heaven divorce and a very private salvation. In addition to ones already noted, these hymns and songs (from dozens that might be cited) are theologically problematic:

Are You Washed in the Blood?: "When the Bridegroom cometh . . . will your soul be ready for the mansions bright?"

Must Jesus Bear the Cross Alone: "then go home my crown to wear"; "Ye angels, from the stars come down and bear my soul away."

My Faith Looks Up to Thee: "When ends life's passing dream, . . . O lift me save above, a ransomed soul!"

Love Divine, All Loves Excelling: "Till in heaven we take our place."

Away in a Manger: "fit us for heaven, to live with Thee there."

Christ the Lord Is Risen Today: "Soar we now where Christ has led, . . . following our exalted Head . . . Ours the cross, the grave, the skies" (not the earth).

The Day of Resurrection: "From death to life eternal, from earth unto the sky."

Rejoice, the Lord Is King: "Our Lord the Judge shall come and take His servants up to their eternal home."

O Zion, Haste: "He stooped to save His lost creation, and died on earth that man might live above."

My Jesus, I Love Thee: "In mansions of glory and endless delight . . . in heaven so bright."

I Would Be Like Jesus: "All the way from earth to glory"; "That in heaven He may meet me."

Abide with Me: "Shine through the gloom, and point me to the skies. Heaven's morning breaks, and earth's vain shadows flee!"

He Keeps Me Singing: "Soon He's coming back to welcome me far beyond the starry sky; I shall wing my flight to words unknown, I shall reign with Him on high."

collegia pietatis (small growth and discipleship groups) and the Methodist class meetings and bands nurtured community that neutralized spiritual narcissism to a significant degree. When both U.S. and British Methodists abandoned the class and band system in the 1800s, they lost their key defense against an overly subjective individualism.

Typically renewal movements of the 1700s and 1800s were optimistic about the personal experience of God's grace, but not very optimistic about the transformation or healing of earth and its problems. That varied, though, in part mirroring the larger mood of society. It was generally less true of Methodism, with its "optimism of grace."[10]

Christianity in the United States enjoyed a burst of optimism during the pre-Civil War revivals of the 1820s and 1830s, and again with the rise of the Social Gospel in the 1880s and 1890s. Christians believed God's kingdom really could be substantially manifested on earth. But this optimism was soon killed—by the bloody Civil War in the first instance, and later by the theological weakness of the Social Gospel and the rise of dispensational premillennialism (Darbyism, Scofieldism). Much of the church, and especially North American conservative Protestantism, shifted from optimism to pessimism about the present order. Naturally this pessimism reinforced the earth-heaven divorce.

More broadly, two other dynamics further widened the earth-heaven split. The Industrial Revolution, undergirded philosophically by the European Enlightenment, saw the earth not as God's land but as mere "real estate"—"natural resources" to be exploited for personal and corporate gain. Another factor was that the vast North American continent, its indigenous inhabitants decimated by European diseases introduced in the 1500s, appeared empty and inviting. Here was a vast God-given treasure chest to be exploited—not a fresh Eden to be protected. Ironically, Native Americans had a better sense of the ecological importance of the land than did Christians.

The revivals of the 1800s that accompanied America's expanding frontier were thus filled with paradox and ambiguity. God's Spirit brought vital faith to the masses, yet the narrative was flawed. The vision of God's redemptive plan suffered many of the maladies of medieval Christendom, including a worldview that emptied the earth of its divine significance and robbed heaven of its full biblical meaning and eschatological promise.

This disembodiment of heaven continued, and continues to this day. Popular images of "streets of gold," "pearly gates," fancy "mansions," and so forth, have more to do with medieval Christendom than with biblical Christianity. The images are biblical, sort of, but the translation of these images into the standard furniture of heaven is the fruit of the Middle Ages, not of Scripture or the early church. An over-spiritualized, static idea of heaven has largely displaced the biblical image and promise of the kingdom of God.

10. John Wesley's optimism about what God could do in human experience through Jesus Christ by the Spirit tended to carry over into a measured optimism about the reform and eventual transformation of society, and ultimately of the whole creation. A similar optimism of grace was found in the Pietist leader Philip Jakob Spener and the Moravian leader Nikolaus von Zinzendorf. See Snyder, *Signs of the Spirit*, 155–57, 221–22, 233–34.

Biblically, heaven's "mansions" are temporary. They are not the end of the story.[11] The "rooms" or "dwelling places" Jesus promises in John 14:2 make up the interim guesthouse where the saints wait for Jesus to bring them back to earth, their true home, with their transformed bodies. This is, after all, the point of Jesus' return "with power and great glory" (Matt 24:30, Luke 21:27); "the time . . . for God to restore everything," as promised (Acts 3:21 TNIV), the time when God's will truly is done on earth as in heaven. Presumably this resting place (described figuratively in Revelation as "under the altar") is where God's people who have passed from this life rest and wait, and where the martyrs cry out to God, "How long?" (Rev 6:9–11).[12] Many Christians may be shocked to learn that "there is not one single reference" in the Bible "to 'heaven' as the eternal destiny of the believer," Richard Middleton writes.[13]

This collapse of the biblical vision of God's kingdom into the idea of disembodied souls in heaven is now enshrined in many popular hymns and gospel songs, as we have seen. When we sing about praising God "with the saints in glory, gathered by the crystal sea," and so forth, we behave as though the book of Revelation ended with chapter 4 or chapter 15, rather than with chapters 21 and 22 and the vision of the renewed heaven and earth.

The Church Visible. All this brings us back to the question of the *visibility of the church.* How was the body of Christ "seeable" during times of renewal?

On the one hand, the church continued to be visible mainly through its structures and institutions—church buildings and an expanding array of educational institutions, hospitals, and philanthropic organizations. But it was visible also in the changed lives of people touched by revival and renewal.

In England and North America, "the people called Methodists" were notable for their devout and holy lives. The same was true for early Quakers and Moravians and many Christians in other traditions who were touched by the Spirit through renewal movements. If most low-church Evangelical religion was less visible in its liturgies, sacraments, and stately temples, it was increasingly visible in its multiplying simple chapels and tabernacles, in visible committed community, and in the ethical quality of people's lives.

To summarize: The seventeenth, eighteenth, and nineteenth centuries were stirred by renewal currents that continue to shape the Christian faith to this day. Historically, renewal and mission are often interconnected, and we see this here. The global

---

11. Contemporary biblical translations now have "rooms" or "dwelling-places" rather than "mansions" in John 14:2 (TNIV, "plenty of room"). "Mansion" meant "room" in 1611 when the KJV was issued, not a big luxurious private house.

12. It is impossible to know how much this imagery is an accommodation to the limitations of present human knowledge, language, and experience. It is not clear that *time* means the same thing after we pass from this earthly life; possibly at death the Christian immediately "wakes up" at the resurrection, even though people on earth experience a long passage of time. There are complex issues of dimensionality here. In any case, many Scriptures do speak of the conscious and blessed life of departed saints between physical death and the final consummation.

13. Middleton, "New Heaven," 86.

Protestant missions movement of the nineteenth century was birthed in the Pietist, Moravian, Methodist, and other revivals of the previous two centuries.

Thus from 1500 to the early 1800s, much of the church was on a journey of renewal and expanding global mission.[14]

GOSPEL GLOBALIZATION, 1600–2000

The next act in the drama carries us to the present. This is the age of gospel globalization. For Protestants the period runs roughly from 1800 to 2000, but for Roman Catholics it starts two centuries earlier with Catholic global missions, as noted earlier. For Pentecostals, it begins about 1900.

The great missions historian Kenneth Scott Latourette called the nineteenth century (specifically, 1815 to 1914) the "Great Century" of Christian missions. It was an amazing period of the global expansion of the Christian movement.[15] Even more amazing, however, was the dramatic growth of Pentecostal and Charismatic Christianity in the twentieth century.

The Book of Revelation speaks of "a great multitude that no one could count, from every nation [and] from all tribes and peoples and languages" (Rev 7:9). In the 1800s, for the first time in history, that picture began to describe the actual visible church—Christians worldwide in hundreds of nations and cultures. This was the fruit of remarkable Protestant missionary outreach from Europe and North America, especially, added to the earlier and continuing Roman Catholic and Orthodox missionary enterprise.[16]

The gospel proved to be remarkably winsome and adaptable throughout virtually all the cultures of the world. Always, of course, syncretism lurked as a danger. Yet the gospel has been a transcendent transforming reality in very diverse "tribes, peoples, and languages" worldwide—and still is.

What then of the narrative, the redemptive plan, and the church's visibility during this period?

The Narrative, the Plan, the Visible Church

The Christian family grew dramatically during this period. It became amazingly diverse. Christians now worship in the languages not just of Europe and Russia and North America, but also in Cantonese, Korean, Hindi, Bantu, Guarani, Arabic, Japanese, Tamil, Telugu, Hausa, Tagalog, Creole, and hundreds of others. For the first time the gospel truly reaches "to the ends of the earth" (Acts 1:8, 13:47). The key point is that the

14. During this period a number of renewal movements occurred within Eastern Orthodoxy and Roman Catholicism as well as within Protestantism. Judaism also experienced significant renewal movements.

15. Latourette, *History of Christianity*, 1061–1345. Latourette calculated the "Great Century" from the end of the Napoleonic wars in Europe in 1815 to the outbreak of World War I in 1914. Although his designation has been critiqued as too much an expression of nineteenth-century Western optimism, the global growth of Christianity during the 1800s was indeed unprecedented.

16. A competent and very readable overview is Tucker, *From Jerusalem to Irian Jaya*.

narrative is moving precisely in the direction Jesus and the biblical prophets foresaw. In some sense, the story is now reaching a climax.

But that is not the whole story. The tale also includes the drastic decline of Christianity in Europe and North America, the global growth of Islam, Buddhism, and Hinduism, the expansion of secular and economic humanism and materialism, and the rise of global Internet culture.

We do see positive signs. The Christian faith is being reborn in secularized Europe through ethnic and immigrant churches, and Christian mission itself is being globalized. This is new. Dedicated missionaries from Korea, China, India, Africa, and Brazil now minister in all the North Atlantic nations. By the year 2000, more missionaries were being sent into the world from what used to be called the "Third World" than from the North Atlantic nations.

Note especially the church's increasing cultural diversity. This is unprecedented. Of course, the church has engaged and interacted with different cultures from the start—that's always been part of the story—but today quantitative growth has produced a qualitative shift. Now the church's influential leaders, theologians, and institutions are arising as much in Asia, Africa, and Latin America as in the North Atlantic nations. The full flowering of this will hit us when we see most Christian publications, new theological insights, and fresh initiatives coming not from the West, but from remote corners of the earth largely unknown to Western Christians except perhaps as far-flung dots on a missions map.

This remarkable gospel globalization is part of God's redemptive plan. "All the ends of the earth shall remember and turn to the Lord; and all the families of the nations shall worship before him" (Ps 22:27). God's salvation is "the hope of all the ends of the earth and of the farthest seas" (Ps 65:5). "All the ends of the earth shall see the salvation of our God" (Isa 52:10).

We do not yet see the full promise. The kingdom of God has not yet fully come. We do not witness the earth being "full of the knowledge of the Lord as the waters cover the sea" (Isa 11:9; Hab 2:14). We still await thorough renewal of the church and the coming of the kingdom in fullness.

The Visible Fruits of Globalization

The church's global engagement with diverse cultures has been overwhelmingly positive. Yes, there are too many stories of exploitation, syncretism, and unholy compromises. Yet gospel globalization has brought four great benefits.

First, gospel globalization has proved that *the gospel can flourish in diverse cultures and environments*. We have proof that Jesus' gospel both transcends and takes root in the world's diverse cultures.

Second, church globalization *helps the church distinguish between gospel and culture*. It helps the church recognize and engage the difference. Everywhere it occurs, this globalization raises the critical question: How much of what we believe and practice is really Christian, and how much is mere cultural tradition? How do we know the difference?[17]

Third, the church's globalization *underscores the difference between Christian identity and national identity*. Christians are citizens of the kingdom of God, not just of the United States or Korea or Lebanon. Gospel globalization relativizes issues of patriotism, national security, and national sovereignty, for God's kingdom is a global, supranational reality and the church is the worldwide people of God and body of Christ.

Fourth, gospel globalization *raises the issue of culture itself as a key theological concern*. It forces the church to develop a theology of culture based on Scripture, theology, mission practice, ecology, and anthropological insight.

For these reasons, the church's globalization could prompt a fresh understanding of the church, the gospel, and God's kingdom—in short, the entirety of God's redemptive plan.[18] Theologically, it may hold the key to the reconciliation of earth and heaven—the healing of creation—as Christians globally rethink God's salvation plan.

The globalization of the church also dramatically affects the *visibility* of the church. Globalization gives the church new faces, in several ways: First, *the church is now visible in many more places*. It is actually globally visible—seeable in most nations and cultures of the world. Yet it also remains remarkably invisible to many people and in some areas.

Second, *the church's visibility is now much more diverse*. Christians don't all look alike. Even if most of their church buildings look like they were transported from Europe or America, other elements empirically demonstrate the church's new diversity.

Third, *the church now has internet visibility*, something unimaginable fifty years ago. This has both positive and negative potential, and a significance which so far is unfathomable.

Fourth, *in many places the church is still visible primarily through its buildings and institutions* rather than in visible communities of discipleship. In some societies the church's visibility is static—inert buildings and creaking institutions. In other places its visible presence is much more dynamic, seen primarily in visible disciples and communities that look like Jesus—most notably in China's multiplying house churches. In many places the church's visibility is a confusing mix of living and dead images. In some places the church is actually *invisible* in terms of buildings, institutions, and physical symbols, yet is clearly seen in godly character and caring, those "deeds of love and mercy" through which "the heavenly kingdom comes."

AN AGENDA AWAITS

Looking back over seven hundred years from about 1500, we see an amazing story of the church's growth, expansion, and increasing diversity. We trace many highways and

17. These are not new questions in Christian missions, but they are now global and inescapable as never before.

18. This is another reason why the church's first three centuries should not uncritically be taken as normative.

byways of renewal. The promise of the gospel continues to become more visibly real and more geographically and culturally spread. Today there is truly a global Christian church that, despite its failings, gives empirical testimony to the power of the gospel and the fulfillment of biblical prophecy.

But an agenda remains. The church has spread throughout the earth—but often doesn't really *see* the earth. The church is still far from realizing its potential to renew and heal the land. Millions of people have been and are being reconciled to God. Yet the full promise of salvation as creation healed is yet to become real and visible worldwide.

At heart, what is at issue here is a worldview problem. Our historical overview shows that the gospel is as powerful as ever. Yet its full healing power will not be unleashed until the gaping hole in the Christian worldview is healed.

William Blake, *The Reunion of the Soul and the Body* at the resurrection (1808)—a vision of the marriage of earth and heaven? Engraving after Blake by Louis Schiavonetti for Robert Blair's poem, "The Grave": "the Body springs from the grave, the Soul descends from an opening cloud; they rush together with inconceivable energy; they met, never again to part!" The image is in the public domain.

4

The Hole in the Christian Worldview

The earth will be filled with the knowledge of the Lord,
as the waters cover the sea.

(Hab 2:14)

TWICE IN THE SPACE of a five-minute talk the children's pastor told the kids, "Jesus is going to come back some day and take us to heaven." Is this what we're teaching our children? Where do we find *that* in the Bible? We don't. The Christian story has gotten mixed up as it has drifted away from its biblical roots. We saw in previous chapters how this happened.

And yet the logic of this popular Christian mythology is compelling, isn't it? Jesus came to earth to take us to heaven. If Jesus is going to take us there, then heaven is important; earth isn't. Heaven is permanent; earth is temporary.

That is not historic Christian orthodoxy. It is unorthodoxy.

Heaven is popular today, and not just among Christians. According to a 2007 Gallup poll, 81 percent of Americans claim to believe in heaven—up from 72 percent just ten years earlier.[1] Books on heaven abound, from Ann Graham Lotz's *Heaven: My Father's House* and her forthcoming *Heaven: God's Promise for Me*, to the popular *Heaven* by Randy Alcorn ("a leading authority on Heaven"), to Mitch Albom's *The Five People You Meet in Heaven* and many more.[2] As historian Jeffrey Burton Russell puts

---

1. Miller, *Heaven*, xix.
2. In stark contrast is Wendell Berry's classic, *Gift of Good Land*.

it in *Paradise Mislaid*, "Heaven, despite centuries of attack and ridicule, survives and flourishes in the early twenty-first century."[3]

Perhaps this is unsurprising; "For many Americans, heaven is the kingdom of ultimate personal fulfillment."[4] But belief in heaven and belief in the Christian gospel are two different things. The New Testament focuses more on resurrection than on heaven. Among Americans, however, Lisa Miller notes that "resurrection belief is fading" even as heaven becomes more popular.[5] Only about a quarter of Americans expect to have bodies in heaven, and nearly a third believe in reincarnation—including one out of five professing Christians! Says Miller, a religion professor at Boston University, "It seems fantastic and irrational that we're going to have a body in heaven."[6]

These trends highlight the problem this book tackles. Many Christians seem not to notice how *little* emphasis the Bible puts on heaven, and how much it focuses on earth and the restoration of creation (as we show in the coming chapters).

Clearly, Christianity today has a big worldview problem. If we compare the *biblical* gospel with the one shared by many Christians, we find a disconnect that distorts the good news. We discover a hole in the Christian worldview—a gap that explains the theological divorce between earth and heaven.

In the Bible, "heaven and earth" means *one whole*—the entire physical creation, not two different realms.[7] In Christian thinking, however, that one whole has been split in two. As we have seen, a divorce happened. What God joined together the church has split apart.

A hole in our gospel? Can it be? In his prophetic book *The Hole in Our Gospel*, Richard Stearns (president of World Vision U.S.) decries the "limited view of the kingdom of God" found in many churches. We teach "a gospel with a gaping hole," Stearns writes, not the whole gospel. He shows how "focusing almost exclusively on the afterlife reduces the importance of what God expects of us in this life. The kingdom of God [in us] was intended to change and challenge everything in our fallen world in the here and now. It was not meant to be a way to leave the world but rather the means to actually redeem it." Stearns shows biblically that the "gospel—the *whole* gospel—means much more than the personal salvation of individuals. It means a *social revolution*" based on the work of Jesus Christ and the power of the Spirit.[8]

Look carefully at Scripture and you will see that Stearns is right. But *why* has the church so reduced the scope of the good news? The reason is theology. The hole in

3. Russell, *Paradise Mislaid*, 157.

4. Miller, *Heaven*, 216.

5. Ibid., 216.

6. Ibid., 107, 109.

7. While in the Bible "heaven" or "heavens" often means the skies, and sometimes designates God's throne or dwelling beyond our earth (Ps 11:4), most often "heaven" is paired with "earth" to mean the whole created order, as in Gen 1:1; 2:1; 4; 4:19; 14:22; 24:3; 27:28; Exod 20:11; 31:17; Deut 4:26; 30:19; 31:28; 2 Kgs 19:15; 2 Chr 2:12; Ezra 5:11; Pss 69:34; 113:6; 115:15; 121:2; 124:8; 134:3; 146:6; 148:13; Isa 24:21; 37:16; Jer 23:24; 33:25; Dan 6:27; Matt 5:18; 11:25; 24:35; 28:18; Mark 13:31; Luke 10:21; 21:33; Acts 4:24; 14:15; 17:24; Eph 3:15; Phil 2:10; Col 1:16; 1 Pet 3:7; Rev 5:13; 14:17.

8. Stearns, *Hole in Our Gospel*, 17, 20 (emphasis in the original).

our gospel is not just the failure to practice the whole gospel. It is our neglect of biblical teachings about creation, the beautiful world God made. At root, the issue is the doctrine of creation.

Biblical teaching on creation is clear enough. But the disease of sin has so thoroughly wormed its way into all human cultures that people persistently misunderstand creation—its nature, its purpose, and God's plan its healing. And *to misunderstand creation is to misunderstand the gospel.*

Biblical teachings can get distorted by philosophies and ideologies, by economics and politics, to the point that Christians miss the meaning of basic biblical truth. This chapter shows just how biblical teaching on creation became twisted over time. We look first at the idea of "nature," then explain more fully the hole in our worldview.

"NATURE": FOUR WARPED VIEWS

English speakers tend to talk more of *nature* or *the natural order* than of *creation* or *the created order.* But for Christians, the issue is *creation,* not what is "natural."

Popular thinking typically distorts the biblical view of creation in four ways. This makes it difficult for Jesus-followers to grasp the biblical meaning. And without that, the idea of creation healed makes little sense.

Romantic Nature

Romanticism is the first distortion. It has shaped Western ideas especially since the 1800s. Romanticism sees nature as the great source of all beauty and truth. Through creative, imaginative engagement with nature we find meaning, even transcendence. Nature lifts our thoughts and feelings to the sublime—to the truth.

As a movement in Western culture, Romanticism had its start in Europe in the late 1700s. Its tools were poetry, music, and the visual arts. This was a reaction against Enlightenment rationalism, the dominance of aristocratic power structures and, later, the Industrial Revolution. Nature in its power and beauty—and the power and beauty of language as it engaged with nature—was the deepest source of truth and real enlightenment.[9]

Christians were not immune to this mood and mode. Romantic notions wove their way into the Christian worldview to the point that, today, many Christians have a more romantic than biblical view of creation.

Isn't this good? Shouldn't we appreciate and enjoy nature; shouldn't we have our emotions stirred? Doesn't this give some relief in an industrial, technical world?

The problem is that romanticism contains both truth and error. Since all creation reflects God's beauty and creativity, we do and should enjoy the beauty of nature. We revel in the colors of flowers and sunsets; we marvel at the complexity of life forms and

---

9. In *Age of Wonder,* Richard Holmes points out that the second wave of the scientific revolution in the 1700s actually combined romanticism and scientific investigation, creating "romantic science" (Holmes, *Age of Wonder*).

the vast structure of the universe. We hear "the music of the spheres." We enjoy the great art and literature of Romanticism.

But this is only half the story. Nature is not always a pretty thing. It is "red in tooth and claw," as Tennyson wrote.[10] The animal kingdom is full of violence, predation, and death—billions of creatures great and small devouring and being devoured. Scripture is very frank about this. The biblical worldview is not romantic. It recognizes the fallenness and transitoriness of nature. "The grass withers, the flower fades; but the word of our God will stand forever" (Isa 40:8).

Yes, the created order is a source of beauty and of truth—the beauty that comes from God's rich creativity and the truth that comes from such beauty. But nature also shows us the truth of violence, fallenness, and bondage to death. We can enjoy and glory in the beauties of nature and yet see that something is deeply wrong in the created order—a creation-wide disease that only God can heal. So whatever we learn from "nature," we need the higher revelation of God's Word.

Commodifying Nature

A second distortion of the biblical worldview is commodification: turning everything into a product. Today, the romantic view of nature is largely overshadowed by this second dynamic.

If poets are romantics, capitalists are commodifiers. Nature means "natural resources" and the created order is mere raw material for profit-making. Today, a new irony of contemporary globalizing society is the marketing of the romantic; the commodification of culture itself. The way indigenous art and music are being sold as products on the world market is but one example. Global capitalism has discovered that romanticism has commercial value as a commodity.[11]

Like romanticism, commodification contains both truth and error. Yes, nature does richly provide "commodities," "raw material" and "natural resources." Yes, the earth is rich and bountiful in resources to sustain human life (though not limitless). God has set this good earth under our dominion (Gen 1:26, 28), and it is proper to use it prudently.

But earth belongs to God, not us. It's not the property of private individuals or nations. It doesn't belong to corporations, whether local or transnational. "The earth is the Lord's, and the fulness thereof; the world, and they that dwell therein" (Ps 24:1 KJV). Dominion means holding the earth in trust for all people, including unborn generations. Scripture nowhere grants unfettered rights to exploit creation for profit;

10. Man . . .

Who trusted God was love indeed
And love Creation's final law—
Tho' Nature, red in tooth and claw
With ravine, shrieked against his creed.

Alfred, Lord Tennyson, "In Memoriam A. H. H." (1850). Stephens et al., *Victorian and Later English Poets*, 65.

11. Rifkin, *Age of Access*.

to turn the whole earth into an assembly line. The universe belongs to God, so *all* humans are responsible to God for their use or abuse of the earth. God holds humanity accountable for the common good. We are all accountable before God for sustainable stewardship of the created order.

Commodification is ungodly exploitation—ultimately a dangerous delusion. It is not the way the Bible sees the created order.

Worshiping Nature

Some people worship nature. They divinize the created order; it becomes their god. This is romanticism gone to seed.

And it is not new. The Apostle Paul pronounced judgment on those who have "exchanged the truth about God for a lie and worshiped and served the creature rather than the Creator, who is blessed forever!" (Rom 1:25).

Worship of nature is in fact ancient. Today it is making a comeback in New Age mysticism, various flavors of pantheism, even in pantheistic forms of Christian theology. The biblical line drawn between Creator and creation is being erased. Nature, God, and ourselves become pretty much the same thing.

There is a small grain of truth here. Nature *is* sublime in the sense that it can open our minds to the spiritual and the transcendent, as romanticism teaches. But nature is not God. Idolatry is always tempting. It may mean out-and-out nature worship, but it can take subtler forms: worshiping ourselves, another person, our cars or houses or books or pets, our culture, our music, our tech toys, our land, our "right" to use and abuse earth solely for our own purposes.

Worship is whatever really centers our lives; whatever is our ultimate, captivating concern. If our main focus is our own rights, our own stuff, our own land, even our own culture or nation—we are worshiping the creation rather than the Creator.

What do we worship? What are our idolatries? Do we worship God alone, treating his good creation as gift *through which* we can worship and serve more fully? The Bible says not to worship nature. More common among committed Christians, perhaps, is a different distortion: not worshiping but over-spiritualizing nature.

Christians can succumb to any of these distorted views of creation. But for many the biggest temptation is spiritualization—failing to see that God loves and will restore the physical world he made. So let's look at this squarely.

Spiritualizing Nature

Spiritualization is the view that creation has no value in itself; it just points us to spiritual truth. When we spiritualize what is physical and material, we veer from the biblical path and fall prey to romanticism and commodification. Romanticism: we enjoy nature, but only because it "lifts" us to "higher, loftier," spiritual truths. And thus commodification: since the material world has no value in itself, we do with it what we will, using and abusing it for our benefit, disregarding its own integrity and well-being. Clearly this is dualism—cutting apart that which Scripture welds together.

A spiritualized understanding of the material world has become the reigning worldview of popular American Evangelicalism. It is what enables Billy Graham, for instance, to write, without qualification: "Because of the Cross and the resurrection of Christ, we can look forward with confidence to an eternal home in Heaven."[12] In this view matter has value only to the degree that it (1) sustains our physical and economic life and (2) teaches us spiritual lessons, reminding us of what is "really" important. As we saw in previous chapters, the roots of this plague go way back in church history, well before the rise of Evangelicalism.

Such spiritualizing is simply not what the Bible teaches. God did not degrade himself in creating material things. He honored and dignified matter by bringing it into existence through his own power—and supremely by becoming incarnate within the material creation.

So there is truth and error in spiritualization. The truth is that all creation is shot through with spirit, spiritual reality, spiritual significance. This is "natural" and, of course, inevitable, since the very existence of matter comes from God's creative power. This is why biblical figures and metaphors, including the parables of Jesus, in fact, work! Material things can teach us spiritual lessons.

But this is only half the biblical story. The other half is that the created order has its own reality, its own integrity, its own purpose, dignity, and destiny. Physical things and life forms have their own "right to exist" because they come from God's hand and are overseen by him. Jesus Christ "sustains all things by his powerful word" (Heb 1:3).

Jesus-followers should shun all four of these unbiblical distortions—romanticism, commodification, worship, spiritualization. We should see the created order as Scripture presents it. We should inhabit the physical world of space, time, and matter as it truly is. We should view it from the biblical standpoint: God's creation of, continuing involvement with, and ultimate plans for the universe.

We will not *romanticize* nature, but recognize its beauty *and* its violence. We will not *commodify* the material world, exploiting it and disregarding God's ownership and the common good. We will not *worship* nature, erasing or eroding the line between Creator and creature. And we will not *spiritualize* the material world, either. We will remind ourselves that the earth in its materiality and physicality is good. Even more: we will see how creation plays a key role in God's whole plan of salvation—the healing of creation.

EVANGELICALISM'S WORLDVIEW HOLE

Spotting these four distortions helps us identify a huge problem in popular Christianity. We now understand why Christians so easily accept the divorce of heaven and earth.

---

12. Billy Graham, Foreword in Lotz, *Heaven*, ix. We will show later the incoherence of the view that Jesus Christ rose *physically* in order to save us only *spiritually*. The new creation must be as physical as Jesus' resurrection—or else Jesus only *seemed* to rise physically, which is a heresy.

Consider, especially, American Evangelicalism. Why haven't Evangelicals taken stewardship and creation care more seriously? Why are efforts to confront pollution, climate change, species depletion, and the protection of lakes, forests, and rivers often viewed as politically misguided or even morally subversive? Many Evangelicals think concern about environmental stewardship springs from a wicked political agenda that is anti-God, anti-American, and anti-free enterprise.

This is a puzzle. Evangelicals claim to believe the full authority of the Bible. Yet in the United States especially (less elsewhere), most Evangelicals read the Bible in a strange way. Either they positively exclude creation care, or they give it such a low priority that it effectively gets lost. Our impression from lives spent mainly in the Evangelical community is that most American Evangelicals simply *do not believe* that the Bible teaches creation care as an *essential* part of the good news. Most Evangelical Christians do not accept environmental concern as an indispensable part of faithful Christian witness.

This aversion to creation care is caused by a gaping hole in the Evangelical theological ozone layer. Unbiblical views of the environment have rushed in and the biblical perspective has been shoved out.

This hole in the Evangelical worldview comes into clearer focus when we retrace the path Western Christianity has traveled. The story of the divorce of heaven and earth told in the previous chapters explains a big part of the problem. Looking back from the early twenty-first century, we can identify a series of historical shifts that, step by step, led to our twisted contemporary worldview. Taken together, these changes explain the four distortions noted above. They show how we got to where we are.

Today we face a sevenfold barrier—a distorting thick window that obscures the biblical worldview, especially with regard to creation. The key elements in this barrier are: (1) the theological inheritance from Greek philosophy, (2) the impact of the Enlightenment, (3) the ideology of capitalism, (4) American individualism, (5) uncritical patriotism, (6) neglect of the biblical doctrine of creation, and (7) premillennial dispensationalism.

Let's look at each briefly. Once we identify the pieces and see how they fit together, the puzzle of Evangelical resistance to creation care is solved.

The Inheritance from Greek Philosophy

As we saw in chapter 1, the Christian church of the second and third centuries wrestled with the ideas of Greek philosophy, then popular in the Roman Empire. Early Christian thinkers did a masterful job of defending the reasonableness of the Christian faith, viewed from a Hellenistic perspective. They also struggled against that perspective as they clarified basic matters of Christian belief. The fruit of these efforts included several breakthroughs—especially the Nicene Creed and other early declarations that nailed down basic consensus on Christology and the Trinity.

A price was paid, however, for these interactions. In a step away from biblical teaching, Christian theology began to view the material world as separate from and strictly inferior to the spirit world. Since it participates in change and decay, matter is tainted; something to be escaped. Human changeability, including physical passions, must be overcome or transcended.

The problem is that this view is more that of Plato, four hundred years before Jesus, than it is of the New Testament. It is not the Old Testament picture, either. Plato taught that at death our souls fly off to an invisible, spiritual heaven where they live forever, free from the fears and follies and wild passions of a physical body. This is perfection.[13] In the church's early centuries, a Christianized version of this view emerged as part of classic orthodox theism. God was seen to be pure spirit—unchangeable, impassive, almost Stoic. The Christian ideal came to mean denying or escaping the physical world, seeking a world of the pure spiritual contemplation of God, as we have seen.[14] In ancient Christian spirituality, this perspective is most clearly seen in the radical, body-rejecting asceticism of the Desert Fathers.

We saw in chapter 2 how the unbiblical "spirit is perfect, matter is imperfect" idea got deeply imbedded in Western theology. The ideal life in medieval Christianity—though not the *actual life* of the great majority—was to escape the world with its changes and passions. The natural world was mere symbol or shadow, a vain show, a metaphor pointing towards higher, eternal spiritual reality. It had little value in itself. For many, the ideal life—though unattainable by most—was the saint who left the world and all its possessions and lived in pure contemplation of God.

This tradition offers much that is good and true. It produced profound devotional writing that still feeds us. But it upset the biblical balance, with disastrous consequences. The inclusive biblical understanding was replaced by a split-level, hierarchical worldview with pure immaterial spirit on top and changing, decaying matter at the bottom. Spiritual growth therefore meant a journey upward from matter to spirit, from the material world to the spiritual one.

This inheritance is still with us, especially in our hymns and devotional writing. The book *Longing for God: Seven Paths of Christian Devotion,* by Richard Foster and Gayle Beebe, is unfortunately typical. Though excellent in many ways, the book essentially concerns "the soul's journey from earth to heaven" rather than the healing of creation through Jesus Christ.[15]

13. Miller gives a succinct summary of Plato's ideas in *Heaven,* 43–46. "Plato's rationalistic approach to questions of God and heaven has influenced every important Christian theologian since Clement of Alexandria" in the second century (ibid., 115). Randy Alcorn calls the "unbiblical belief that the spirit realm is good and the material world is bad" *Christoplatonism.* This view "looms like a dark cloud over the common view of Heaven" and "has had a devastating effect on our ability to understand what Scripture says" about heaven and earth. Alcorn, *Heaven,* 52; cf. 476–78. The book does not adequately confront sub-Christian views of heaven and earth, however, or seriously challenge premillennial dispensationalism. In other words, it is not fully free of Christoplatonism.

14. This view, which gave rise to classical Christian theism, has been roundly critiqued by much of contemporary theology, including the "open theism" of Clark Pinnock and others.

15. Foster and Beebe, *Longing for God,* 21. Symptomatic of its acceptance of Greek philosophical dualism, the book begins with an exposition of the spirituality of Origen of Alexandria.

This is split-level Christianity, and it is unbiblical. In fact, it is un-Christian. It's more like something you might find in Hinduism or other religions. The collection of ancient classical Hindu tales known as the *Mahabharata,* for instance, tells of mortals ascending from earth to heaven, sometimes by climbing the Himalayan Mountains.[16]

For Western Christians, however, the influence comes primarily from the ancient Greeks. As N. T. Wright says, "Our minds are so conditioned . . . by Greek philosophy, whether or not we've ever read any of it, that we think of heaven as by definition nonmaterial and earth by definition as nonspiritual or nonheavenly. But that won't do. Part of the central achievement of the incarnation, which is then celebrated in the resurrection and ascension, is that heaven and earth are now joined together with an unbreakable bond and that we too are by rights citizens of both together."[17] This inheritance from Greek philosophy twists our biblical interpretation and distorts the Christian worldview.

The Enlightenment: The Triumph of Reason

The European intellectual movement of the 1600s and early 1700s known as the Enlightenment made a break with the traditional authority of church and state. Enlightenment writers promoted reason as the key to human life and understanding. The Enlightenment is therefore often called "The Age of Reason."[18]

Orthodox Christian theology rejected many Enlightenment claims, particularly its over-reliance on reason. Nevertheless, Christian thinking was leavened by it. Endorsing science and the scientific method, Protestant Christians largely accepted the subject-object split introduced by René Descartes (1596–1650) and others. Human beings were "subjects" examining "objective" evidence. The natural world was increasingly objectified—something to be studied, "rationalized" through analysis, and used for human purposes.

This legacy produced rich benefits. It yielded the scientific, technological, and material advances we enjoy today. But here also, a price was paid theologically. Since the material world was already viewed as secondary and transitory, people saw no ethical problem in dominating and using it—exploiting it—for human purposes. Nature was "here" objectively to serve us. It was the God-given natural resource for human higher purposes, Christians thought. Virtually no ethical limitations were put on exploiting the earth.

And a price was paid socially, as well. Air and water pollution created by industrialization poisoned the urban poor. Such social ills were seen as a small price to pay for the benefits of new technologies and inventions. Environmental issues were not moral questions unless they directly and observably threatened human health, especially the health of the wealthy. They were merely technological challenges to conquered.

---

16. Chaturvedi, *Tales from the Mahabharat*, 167–68. Cf. Uberoi, *Mahabharata*.

17. Wright, *Surprised by Hope*, 251.

18. Hampshire, *Age of Reason*; Durant and Durant, *Age of Reason Begins.*

Such thinking produced a two-fold legacy: over-confidence in reason and technology on the one hand, and a devaluing of the earth on the other.

The Ideology of Capitalism

Capitalism is another part of our inheritance from Europe. As an economic system, its roots go back well before the Enlightenment. It grew out of the rise of cities in late-medieval Europe and also from the successful economic innovations of a number of Christian monastic communities, as Rodney Stark and others have shown.[19] The rise in the 1200s of banks and other financial institutions in cities like Venice and Florence, Italy, also played a key role. Later capitalism was fueled by European global colonialism and the British Industrial Revolution in the 1700s. Adam Smith published his *Wealth of Nations,* the Bible (almost literally) of capitalism, in 1776.[20]

Capitalism became the engine of economic growth and prosperity in the Western world. It brought tremendous material, economic, and often political benefits. Combined with science, technology, and industrialization, it led to today's global economy. It is a key reason for the high standard of living in so-called "first-world countries."

Western prosperity did not come solely from the genius of capitalism, however. Other fortuitous factors played a key role. U.S. economic success, for example, arose not only from free enterprise and democracy but also from a host of other things Americans often forget: nearly unbounded natural resources, the suppression of Native American peoples and cultures, slave labor, a nearly constant flow of immigration, and the legacy of European empire and colonialism. Additionally, American military power and covert operations worldwide, government sponsorship and protection of business, unequal trade arrangements, and intellectual property laws favored the economic rise of the United States. American Christians should therefore be cautious about claiming that God has uniquely "blessed" America. It is a mixed and often morally muddy history.

So here again, a price was paid for the benefits. From the beginning, critics of capitalism warned of two main faults: its power to enslave and exploit the poor (especially laborers) who had no capital and therefore little economic clout, and the power of wealth to enslave the wealthy. Marxism made the most revolutionary critique of capitalism, but many Christians have also raised their voices over the centuries, pointing out the moral dangers of capitalism. In our time, one of the most prophetic voices was that of Pope John Paul II.

For Christians, the primary *biblical* critique of capitalism should be obvious. Human beings are corrupted by sin and will therefore use whatever freedom and power they possess for selfish ends and to exploit others. Capitalism is the world's most effective way to "store up treasures on earth"—the very thing Jesus warned against. But Jesus' warnings and prohibitions regarding wealth are seldom heard in our churches. Preachers denounce sins of personal and sexual behavior but overlook greed and laying up treasures on earth. Some even promote getting rich as a sign of God's favor.

19. Stark, *Victory of Reason,* 57–63.

20. An excellent overview is Ferguson, *Ascent of Money.*

Surprising numbers of Christians have bought the central myth of capitalism: that the self-centered pursuit of profit inevitably works for the common good. This is very difficult to defend biblically. Most thoughtful Christians writing on the subject argue that this myth is true *only* if there are effective mechanisms, through government and/or the church, to limit the subversiveness of greed and the worst effects of capitalism.

Partly because of Greek philosophy and Enlightenment rationalism, noted above, Evangelicals have tended to view economics as a separate world, operating according to its own laws. The economy is allowed to have its own morality, walled off from normal considerations of Christian ethics. Economic growth is by definition good, and the pursuit of wealth can never be questioned, for it is the engine that drives the economy.

In this view the "invisible hand" of the market is perceived to be practically sacred, and must never be denied or restricted. In conversations with Christian businessmen over the years, we have been surprised that ethical issues are *never raised*, except for concerns about individual morality and "sin industries" like alcohol, tobacco, and pornography. Almost never is environmental exploitation raised as a moral issue, and those who raise it are generally dismissed as "tree huggers," crazies more concerned about spotted owls and snail darters than about human beings, who are what *really* matter. Fortunately, thanks largely to growing climate and energy concerns, this is starting to change.

"Invisible hand" economics is not biblical morality or authentic Christian ethics. It contradicts Jesus' teachings and violates the biblical worldview. Biblically speaking, *nothing* operates outside God's sovereignty or the ethics of God's moral law and the Sermon on the Mount. All economic systems—capitalism as well as communism and socialism—must be subject to thorough Christian critique. Like the prophets of old, Christians should be particularly outspoken in exposing forms of exploitation that are most dominant in our age.

The uncritical acceptance of capitalism—giving it a moral pass—undermines the healing of creation. Capitalism requires the use of natural resources. This was true of early industrialism, which relied heavily on coal and steel, and it is just as true today. All the key ingredients of the information age—plastics, silicon, copper, uranium, petroleum—come from the earth.

At this point, most North Americans use a simple moral equation: since economic growth is good, the exploitation of natural resources is morally necessary, not to be questioned. Most corporations simply do not factor in the depletion of natural resources as an economic cost, though it really is. Even worse, the tax system often rewards industries with tax credits for their consumption of natural resources (the so-called "depletion allowance"). A true economic accounting would require companies to pay for the depletion.

Many conservative Christians oppose protecting the environment because they think this would place an unfair burden on business and stunt economic growth. Since spiritual, not material, things are what really count, and since the material world has no real value in itself (the inheritance of Neo-Platonism and Enlightenment rationalism), no theological red flags pop up in defense of the earth.

Biblically speaking, something is painfully wrong with this picture. Responsible capitalism can be a blessing, but unfettered capitalism becomes inhumane and can destroy us and the earth.[21] North American society has long recognized the truth of this in some areas—for instance, protecting the public through interstate commerce regulations, pure food and drug laws, limitations on the exploitation of workers, and minimal regulation of air and water pollution. The raping of God's good earth, however, has been largely ignored.[22]

American Individualism

Individualism is a fourth reason for Evangelical dis-ease with talk about healing creation. The "rugged individualism" of North American culture undermines a sense of interdependence, shared responsibility for the common good, and earth stewardship. Nature is something to be conquered, subdued, fought against, overcome—not something to be nurtured or cared for.

Here also we find plusses and minuses. The strength of U.S. society owes much to the freedom of individual initiative. America provides space for the entrepreneur, the innovator, the "self-made man." But as many studies have shown—for example, Robert Bellah, et al., *Habits of the Heart* and Robert Putnam, *Bowling Alone: The Collapse and Revival of American Community*—the downside to such individualism is the lack of a sense of social solidarity and mutual responsibility.[23]

Today individualism is further diseased by consumerism and materialism. We live in a world devoted to promoting, buying, then quickly replacing brand-name products whose prices bear little relationship to the actual cost of manufacture. Such society daily contradicts Jesus' words that a person's life "does not consist in the abundance of possessions" (Luke 12:15).

Individualism wedded to consumerism undermines a vision for healing creation. Although American individualism sometimes celebrates living simply with nature (Henry David Thoreau, for example), today it insulates us from nature so that we have little sense of our *actual* dependence on the earth's well-being. And since material wealth in our day depends on the limitless production of goods, many American Christians resist any environmental restrictions that would (hypothetically) put a brake on or add cost to the production of those goods.

A biblical theology of creation and the environment must squarely address the problem of individualism if it is to be persuasive.[24] The Bible teaches the mutual interdependence of the human family and its dependence on the well-being of the earth.

---

21. See for example Baumol et al., *Good Capitalism, Bad Capitalism*.

22. See Snyder and Runyon, *Decoding the Church*, 143–46, 175–78.

23. Bellah et al., *Habits of the Heart*; Putnam, *Bowling Alone*.

24. Genuine Christian community, of course, affirms the importance of personhood. The biblical ideal is not to lose or submerge individuality in the collective but rather responsible mutual community in which Jesus-followers find their true personal identity, freedom, and responsibility. See "Mind of Christ," chapter 9 in Snyder, *Problem of Wineskins*; chapter 10 in Snyder, *Radical Renewal*.

Uncritical Patriotism

A fifth ingredient in the mix that explains the hole in the Evangelical worldview is uncritical, unreflective patriotism.

Whatever the country, nationalistic patriotism leads to arrogance, empire-building, and disdain for other nations and peoples. This seems to be a constant of history. When nations become dazzled by their own supposed greatness, they go blind to God's concern for all earth's peoples and the welfare of creation. They in fact come under God's judgment. The Bible gives many examples of God judging arrogant, self-worshiping nations. Ezekiel 31 and Revelation 18 provide great examples.

The United States naturally saw a big upsurge in patriotic fervor after the September 11, 2001 terrorist attacks. But unreflective patriotism in the U.S. didn't begin then. Uncritical patriotism is a long-standing dynamic in American history—as it is many places in the world.

Love of country is good and proper, of course. But when it leads to disregard for the welfare of other lands and peoples, it becomes a plague. When patriotism or nationalism turns into ideology, and when criticism of our own government becomes unpatriotic, we are in grave danger. Uncritical nationalism leads to idolatry.

Christians should see uncritical patriotism as a theological problem—even a sin. The Bible teaches that Christians are part of a new humanity, citizens of a new nation: the kingdom of God. The New Testament is very explicit about this. Christians are "citizens" and "members of the household of God" (Eph 2:19). "You are a chosen race, a royal priesthood, a holy nation, God's own people, in order that you may proclaim the mighty acts of him who called you out of darkness into his marvelous light" (1 Pet 2:9).

Christian identity thus trumps national or political identity. Biblical Christians understand that they are first of all citizens of the kingdom of God. Allegiance to one's own nation necessarily comes second to kingdom allegiance. True Jesus-followers understand that Christians in other lands—including Iran, Afghanistan, and North Korea—are their own brothers and sisters in Christ, nearer and dearer to them than their fellow Americans who do not acknowledge Jesus. They care just as much about the welfare of people in these lands as they do for the prosperity of the United States.

Consequently, genuine Christians see the whole earth in global, not just national, perspective. They are concerned about creation healed for the sake of the health of all peoples and nations. They don't see the world simply through the lens of what benefits their own country. This broader perspective—based on a sense of kingdom-of-God citizenship and a sense of God's love for all nations—is key to closing the hole in the Evangelical worldview.

Missing the Biblical Doctrine of Creation

Sixth: biblical teaching about creation. A really biblical worldview demands that we pay attention to what the Bible teaches—not only about God's original creation, but about the place of the created order in God's saving plan.

Popular Christianity focuses mostly on *personal* new creation—salvation through the blood of Jesus Christ. Yet Evangelicals often neglect the underlying meaning and purpose of creation itself. To some degree this is true of other Christian traditions, as we have seen. However, any doctrine of redemption that does not take into consideration God's purpose in creating and sustaining the world is deficient.

Evangelical theology typically lacks a robust biblical theology of creation. A striking example is the otherwise brilliant book, *Let's Start with Jesus: A New Way of Doing Theology*, by the distinguished Wesleyan theologian Dennis F. Kinlaw. Kinlaw makes a strong case for basing theology on the Trinitarian Personhood of God as revealed in Jesus Christ. But the physical creation and its role in God's economy is nearly invisible in the book. "Creation" generally means the human creation only. Kinlaw writes, for example: "God wants a closeness that means *actual personal identification with the creation*. . . . Since the creation cannot cross the chasm to him, God crossed the chasm to it" through the incarnation.[25] Clearly only the *human* creation is in view here.

Similarly, the book notes that "persons by definition always come in webs of relationships," and that these relationships give persons their "own identity and fulfillment"—but there is no mention of the key relationship between humans and the nonhuman creation, so prominent in Scripture.[26] The *land*—the physical earth and the whole nonhuman created order—are nearly absent from the book. In this sense, the whole argument is two-dimensional rather than three-dimensional.

Kinlaw does mention the suffering of the created order. In a key passage he writes, "The physical world has its counterpart in human birth. We are all here because someone else carried us in her body until we were born. . . . Of course, the physical is only analogical to the spiritual. There is a mystery in both arenas—the physical and the spiritual."[27] Precisely here is the worldview gap so popular in many churches. The physical world becomes only an analogy or symbol of the spiritual world.

Biblically there are three problems here, as in much similar writing: spirit and matter are viewed dualistically; spirit is seen as more "real" and ultimately more important than matter; and—crucially—the biblical and empirical interconnection between humans and the created order is lost. This cuts the nerve of creation stewardship and diminishes the full scope of the biblical economy of salvation as pictured in Ephesians 1:10 and many other passages in both Testaments. Such biblical interpretation is clearly tainted with Neo-Platonism.

The whole argument of *Let's Start with Jesus* would be much richer, and not at all compromised, if it affirmed that salvation is about God's people and God's land—the *whole* creation, in fact, as Scripture teaches.

Kinlaw writes from a Wesleyan perspective, but we find the same problem in much popular Calvinist and Reformed writing. In *Let the Nations Be Glad! The Supremacy of God in Missions*, John Piper makes a strong case for reaching all the world's people groups with the gospel. He talks at length about the biblical hope "that God would one

25. Kinlaw, *Let's Start with Jesus*, 71 (emphasis in the original).

26. Ibid., 127.

27. Ibid., 135.

day be worshipped by people from all the nations of the world."[28] Yet he says virtually nothing about the redemption of the earth itself. Here also a fully biblical doctrine of creation, and thus of creation healed, is missing.

For Evangelicals, a big part of the problem is the tendency to view God's salvific plan almost exclusively through the lens of Paul's letter to the Romans. Much Evangelical theology suffers from this "hermeneutical inversion." The whole Bible is interpreted by the book of Romans, rather than the other way round. The glorious promise of creation liberated in Romans 8 gets misinterpreted because it is severed from the larger biblical picture of God's plan for the whole earth. The result is a diminished view of salvation—thus even of God's glory!

We find this hermeneutical inversion in Piper's 2007 book, *The Future of Justification*. "God's purpose in the universe," writes Piper, "is not only to *be* infinitely worthy, but to be *displayed* as infinitely worthy."[29] This summarizes God's basic intent. Aside from the question of how it could be God's purpose to be what he already is (infinitely worthy), it is hard to find biblical support for the idea that being "displayed as infinitely worthy" is God's central motive in salvation. God is already so "displayed" in the created order and in the lives of those who faithfully serve him. "The heavens declare the glory of God; and the firmament shows forth his handiwork" (Ps 19:1 KJV). God's purpose, biblically speaking, is more than this. It is "to bring all things in heaven and on earth together under one head, even Christ" (Eph 1:10 NIV). Then indeed will the Triune God be "displayed as infinitely worthy" in the new creation that is finally established.

Piper does give a more biblically balanced view in his book *Future Grace*. Here he writes, "Christianity is not a platonic religion that regards material things as mere shadows of reality, which will be sloughed off as soon as possible. Not the mere immortality of the soul, but rather the resurrection of the body and the renewal of all creation is the hope of the Christian faith. Just as our bodies will be raised imperishable for the glory of God, so the earth itself will be made new and fit for the habitation of risen and glorified persons."[30] Precisely. The problem is that this full biblical hope is often assigned to an eschatological footnote, or understood in totally non-material ways— rather than being part of the essential structure of God's whole plan of salvation.

Theologies which fail to articulate the full biblical hope are deficient in their teachings about creation. Evangelicals have rightly emphasized God as the *source* of the created order. But most have not reflected deeply on the *nature* of the created order as an interdependent system.[31] Too often we are blind in our views of creation to the built-in mutual interdependence between humanity and the physical environment. Nor have we reflected deeply enough on what *creation* tells us about *new creation*—

28. Piper, *Let the Nations*, 181.

29. Piper, *Future of Justification*, 185 (emphasis in the original).

30. Piper, *Future Grace*, 374.

31. This is true for example of Donald G. Bloesch's much-used *Essentials of Evangelical Theology*. In using this work as a textbook I found I had to substantially supplement the material on the doctrine of creation in order to be biblical and to relate creation to new creation in Jesus Christ.

God's plan of redemption. Biblically speaking, the doctrine of new creation depends upon a clear understanding of the original creation.

In practice, Evangelical theology often begins with Genesis 3 rather than Genesis 1. All are sinners in need of God's saving grace. But biblical theology does not begin with sin; it begins with creation and God's goodness. Human beings—man and woman together—are created in God's image and placed in a garden that also reflects God's nature. In their unique creation, man and woman embody the image of God in a primary sense. But the whole created order portrays God in a secondary sense. The beauty, order, coherence, and intricate design of the universe reveal something true and essential about God himself (Rom 1:20).

Scripture consistently grounds God's glorious work through Jesus Christ by the Spirit in both creation and redemption. Jesus is both "the firstborn of all creation" and "the firstborn from the dead"—affirmations that unite creation and redemption (Col 1:15, 18). In the book of Revelation, God is praised in hymns celebrating both creation (Rev 4:11) and redemption through Jesus' blood (Rev 5:9). In the Old Testament, the Sabbath, so full of eschatological portent, is grounded both in creation (Exod 20:11) and redemption from Egyptian slavery (Deut 5:15). In Genesis, God establishes covenants both for the preservation of creation (Gen 9:8–15) and for redemption (e.g., Gen 17:1–8).

In multiple ways Scripture weds the themes of creation and transformation—new creation. The biblical doctrine of redemption through the cross presupposes the doctrine of creation. Redemption can never be understood in a fully biblical way unless the full story of creation, and not just human creation, is kept in view.

Premillennial Dispensationalism

Finally, we come to a modern theological quirk that, mixed with the other currents traced above and in previous chapters, threatens to sink the whole biblical hope of creation healed.

In the 1800s a new theory was hatched: premillennial dispensationalism. This novelty, though lacking real biblical or historical support, became wildly popular in conservative Christian circles—the capstone of the whole skewed edifice of popular Christianity, especially in the United States.

Oddly, most Christian theologians have given scant attention to the radical nature and pervasive impact of this doctrinal innovation. It strikes us as strange that more Christian thinkers haven't exposed the ways premillennial dispensationalism branches off from the Great Tradition of Christian doctrine. Oddly, few have questioned its eccentric biblical interpretations and asked whether the theory is heresy. Instead, this view has been treated as a mere minor variation within historic orthodoxy.[32] Nevertheless, the implications of premillennial dispensationalism must be

---

32. I (Howard) confess that the oddness of this has only recently struck me with force. As a child I occasionally heard the pre- and post-millennial debates, but these were considered peripheral, at least in my context. In recent decades I've become more and more aware how much the shift to premillennial dispensationalism marks a major watershed in history—what was really at stake in the debates.

understood if the biblical hope of creation healed is to capture the heart of American Christians today.

In the twentieth century, major popularizers of premillennial dispensationalism included Hal Lindsey's *The Late Great Planet Earth* (1970) and the *Left Behind* series of novels. But the infection started a century earlier.[33] Sadly, millions of Christians today believe that premillennial dispensationalism is simply what the Bible teaches!

Relatively few denominations officially adopted premillennial dispensationalism, but the new ideology colonized much of the Evangelical mind. The plague is fed today by "Christian" radio and television, popular books, political commentators, and educational institutions that explicitly or implicitly teach the theory.

The Roots of Dispensationalism

Dispensational theories are not new, as we saw earlier. But today's premillennial dispensationalism has little connection with earlier views. It is a sharp departure from historic Christian doctrine, tracing back mainly to the Anglo-Irish evangelist John Nelson Darby (1800–82) and the American Fundamentalist theologian Cyrus Scofield (1843–1921). The *Scofield Reference Bible* (1909), still widely used, popularized premillennial dispensationalism worldwide through the global missions outreach of American Fundamentalism.

Darby himself invented the hallmark premillennial doctrine of the "rapture" of the saints. Misinterpreting 1 Thess 4:16–17, Darby came up with rapture theology. The Thessalonians passage says Jesus will return to earth "with the sound of God's trumpet . . . and the dead in Christ will rise first." This prophesies Jesus' second coming to earth, but Darby said it meant a "secret rapture" of Christians to heaven.[34]

The Darby-Scofield theory is "premillennial" because it says Jesus will return to earth *before* the "millennium," Christ's thousand-year reign described in the book of Revelation. Until then, society and world conditions will simply deteriorate. Since this is God's predestined plan, there is little point trying to improve things now. Our exclusive focus should be on rescuing souls for the eternal future. As Randall Balmer puts it, the shift from postmillennial to premillennial theology "has had enormous repercussions for the ways that evangelicals approach society." For if you "believe that Jesus will come for his followers before the millennial age, then the onset of the millennial kingdom" cannot happen now, "thereby absolving believers from responsibility" for manifesting God's kingdom now.[35]

This theory is "dispensational" because originally (there have been modifications to the theory in recent years) it divided all history into seven neat periods ("dispensations" or ages), keyed to the letters to the seven churches in Revelation 2–3. This use of the term "dispensation" is a distortion of the biblical idea of God's *oikonomia* or overall plan of redemption. The King James Bible renders the phrase "a plan (*oikonomia*) for

33. For a brief overview and sources, see Snyder, *Models*, 123–26.
34. Faupel, *Everlasting Gospel*, 98.
35. Balmer, *Making of Evangelicalism*, 29–30.

the fullness of time" in Ephesians 1:10 as "the dispensation of the fullness of times." Thus dispensational language in English is based on this and a few other references in the King James Bible, such as 1 Cor 9:17, Eph 3:2, and Col 1:25 ("according to the dispensation of God").

Darby's theology greatly reinforced the divorce between earth and heaven already afflicting Western theology. In fact, premillennial dispensationalism would very likely not have developed at all had the church from the beginning stayed true to biblical teachings about God's covenant with the earth. William Faupel notes that Darby, completely separating Old Testament Israel and the church, argued that "the unfulfilled prophecies of the Old Testament applied only to the Jewish nation. Israel, God's *earthly* people, by rejecting Christ as their promised Messiah, was cut off for a season, while the church, God's *heavenly* people, was called forth from the Gentile nations to be prepared as Christ's waiting Bride."[36]

Spreading the Theory

Faupel shows how premillennial dispensationalism captured the imagination of many North American Christian leaders. Darby visited the U.S. seven times between 1862 and 1877, and (together with George Müller, who also adopted Darbyism and visited the U.S.), triggered a "paradigm shift" from amillennial or postmillennial views to "the premillennial world-view."[37] The names of the early adopters of dispensational premillennialism read like a Who's Who of American fundamentalism, figures who in turn shaped Evangelical, Pentecostal, and some Wesleyan thought: Dwight L. Moody, A. J. Gordon, J. Wilbur Chapman, R. A. Torrey, A. B. Simpson, Billy Sunday, A. T. Pierson, and Henry Clay Morrison (president of Asbury College and founder of Asbury Theological Seminary). And this is just a partial list.[38]

The shift to dispensational premillennialism became an avalanche. Dwight L. Moody, for instance, converted to Darbyism in 1877 and began teaching it in his Northfield, Massachusetts, Prophecy Conferences. Moody declared, "I look upon this

---

36. Faupel, *Everlasting Gospel*, 97. Darby's theological move was clever: "The secret rapture, Darby's most distinctive teaching, [resolved] neatly the most perplexing problem faced by the millenarians. The secret event would restart God's prophetic time-clock. No longer would proponents have to struggle, trying to correlate biblical prophecy with history. They could hold that Christ may come at any moment without the embarrassment of subsequent disconfirmation" (ibid., 98).

37. Ibid., 98–105. See also Carpenter and Shenk, *Earthen Vessels*; Marsden, *Fundamentalism and American Culture*; Robert, *Occupy until I Come*; Sandeen, *Roots of Fundamentalism*.

38. Faupel, *Everlasting Gospel*, 98–105; cf. Balmer, *Making of Evangelicalism,* 32–35. Faupel documents the "widespread conversion from a postmillennial to a premillennial eschatology" within various branches of American Christianity. "On the surface this change appeared to be minor. In many ways premillennialism looked forward to a thousand-year period that was similar in character to that which was expected by postmillennialists. The one apparent difference was that premillennialists believed that Christ's second advent would take place *before* the inauguration of the millennium, whereas the postmillennialist position was that Christ would appear *at the end* of that period. Despite the apparent similarities, however, much more was at stake than a simple change in timetable. The new chronology disclosed a transformation in world-view." Faupel notes that premillennialism "emerged within the Reformed tradition" but spread rapidly to other branches of the church. Ibid., 91 (emphasis in the original).

world as a wrecked vessel. God has given me a lifeboat and said, 'Moody, save all you can.'"[39] Faupel notes, "Nearly every major American evangelist of the period followed Moody's lead. Countless journals were established, numerous Bible colleges were founded, rescue missions in urban centers were set up, missionaries were sent into the foreign field, and hundreds of local associations all articulating Darby's dispensationalism were formed. Through these interlocking forums, an informal network was created which enabled the millenarian movement to challenge the prevailing views of American Christianity."[40]

Not everyone was swayed. Methodists in particular, with a few exceptions like Morrison, were more resistant to this radical worldview shift because they had inherited Wesley's expansive view of God's grace. Methodist holiness leader Daniel Steele, for instance (reflecting Wesley and much of the church's historic consensus) wrote in 1887 that "as a Church we are by no means so discouraged with the progress of the Gospel as to pronounce the dispensation of the Holy Spirit as inadequate to the conquest of the world for Christ."[41] Another major exception was the Salvation Army, part of the holiness movement, which "managed to retain its twin emphases on evangelism and social reform" even after coming to the United States in 1880.[42]

But for the most part, dispensational premillennialism "raptured" popular American Christianity even farther away from a biblically earthed worldview. "The theological shift from postmillennial optimism to premillennial pessimism had ripple effects that shaped evangelicalism throughout most of the twentieth century," notes Balmer.[43] The most influential U.S. dispensational educational institution has probably been Dallas Theological Seminary, but fundamentalist-based liberal arts schools such as Virginia's Liberty University and Michigan's Cornerstone University also play a key role today. Cornerstone, for example, which grew out of dispensational Grand Rapids Bible Institute (founded in 1941), still reflects its Darbyite roots. The Cornerstone "Christian Worldview" statement, as well as its doctrinal statement (though now revised in a more culture-affirming way), holds out no hope for the earth's redemption or the healing of the divorce between heaven and earth.[44]

Premillennial dispensationalism continues to be popularized by noted Evangelical speakers such as Anne Graham Lotz, Billy Graham's daughter. Lotz says she doesn't recall her parents talking much about Jesus' second coming, but today wherever she goes worldwide, "people are expecting the return of the Lord." Lotz preaches a premillennial "rapture" theology (even though neither the term nor the idea of "the rapture"

39. Balmer, *Making of Evangelicalism*, 36.

40. Faupel, *Everlasting Gospel*, 99–100.

41. Steele, *Antinomianism Revived*, 195.

42. Balmer, *Making of Evangelicalism*, 36.

43. Ibid., 41.

44. Available online at http://grts.cornerstone.edu/about/confessions; http://www.cornerstone.edu/about/core_beliefs/worldview.

is found in the Bible[45]), with a major emphasis on heaven.[46] While there are increasing exceptions, especially among younger evangelicals, much of mainstream Evangelical theology at the popular level is still premillennial and dispensational.

Creation Destroyed or Restored?

Premillennial dispensationalism undermines the biblical worldview by locating the renewal of creation exclusively after the return of Jesus Christ. Since the present world is headed for inevitable destruction, any concern with saving it is a distraction from rescuing souls before Jesus returns. Frank Peretti's novel *This Present Darkness* gives a striking example of this view. In the novel, it turns out that anyone concerned with social justice or creation care is in league with the devil.

Premillennial dispensationalism popularized the view that the earth and the whole material creation is destined to be destroyed. This makes creation concerns pointless.[47] As Balmer puts it, the "evangelical penchant for dispensationalism" results in "lack of concern for the environment and the natural world. . . . If Jesus is going to return soon to rescue the true believers and to unleash judgment on those left behind, why should we devote any attention whatsoever to care of the earth, which will soon be destroyed"?[48]

This view hinges on a misinterpretation of 2 Pet 3:10 in the KJV: "But the day of the Lord will come as a thief in the night; in the which the heavens shall pass away with a great noise, and the elements shall melt with fervent heat, the earth also and the works that are therein shall be burned up." The NRSV translates, "the heavens will pass away with a loud noise, and the elements will be dissolved with fire, and the earth and everything that is done on it will be disclosed."

But, of course, this passage must be seen in light of the whole Bible. In Scripture, fire is a key image for God's refining or purifying judgment, particularly in the prophetic books where God's future action is pictured. Note especially Mal 3:2 ("For he is like a refiner's fire and like fuller's soap") and Zech 13:9 ("I will put this third into the fire, refine them as one refines silver, and test them as gold is tested"). Fire is a symbol of God's power and holiness (Deut 4:24, 9:3; Heb 12:29), which can destroy if disregarded but is intended to cleanse all impurities so that people may experience and exhibit the pure love of God.

Viewed in full biblical context, the heat and fire of 2 Pet 3:10 signify refining, revealing, and cleansing, not destruction or annihilation. This is how John Calvin saw it. He commented, "heaven and earth are to be purged by fire, that they may correspond

---

45. See the discussion in Wright, *Surprised by Hope,* 133–34.

46. Miller, *Heaven,* 62–64.

47. Premillennial dispensationalism holds that the function of the various covenantal dispensations was to prove the impossibility of humans saving themselves and thus show the absolute need of God's sovereign grace. But why does the same point need to be made over and over again? Wouldn't once have been enough?

48. Balmer, *Making of Evangelicalism,* 39.

with the kingdom of Christ."[49] Wesley wrote with regard to Rom 8:21, "Destruction is not deliverance; . . . whatsoever is destroyed, or ceases to be, is not delivered at all." Wesley suggested that in fact no "part of the creation" will "be destroyed."[50]

God is not in the destroying business; he is in the refining, recycling, and recreating business. "Creation will be cleansed and transformed, yet this new creation will stand in continuity with the old," writes David Field.[51] This is clear even from 2 Pet 3:6–10, for the writer says that in the flood the world was "destroyed" (TNIV)—but, of course, it was not physically destroyed or annihilated; it was judged and cleansed.

These and similar passages must be seen in light of Jesus' own death and resurrection. Scripture reveals a deep, shaping, underlying pattern here: as Jesus died in judgment for sin, the created order will be judged and refined. As Jesus rose again, the created order will be transformed through the power of Jesus' resurrection by the Spirit. We don't understand the mystery (1 Cor 15:50–51), but we trust in new creation after the pattern of what happened to Jesus. We trust God's promise.

Passages such as 2 Pet 3:10 must be viewed through the lens of the broad sweep of Scripture. Otherwise we easily misunderstand both the meaning of new creation and its present ethical and missional implications. Our controlling hermeneutic or method of interpretation should be the whole sweep of the biblical narrative. This provides a safeguard against misinterpreting Scripture through secondary theories such as premillennialist (or any other kind of) dispensationalism.

Premillennial dispensationalism is a potent virus that worked its way, largely undetected, throughout much of the body of Christ over the past century and more. This disease makes the church's witness anemic, hampering its healing role in creation. *But this would not have happened had it not been for other developments over centuries* that made the Evangelical church vulnerable to the new virus. Premillennial dispensationalism would probably never have caught on if the theological divorce between heaven and earth was not already in place.

HEALING A DAMAGED WORLDVIEW

Taken together, these seven historical trends—ranging from the ancient philosophical inheritance of Neo-Platonism to today's premillennialism—have produced the lopsided worldview so popular among most U.S. Evangelicals and Pentecostals today. These influences make it very difficult for Christians to understand *and feel* the full biblical hope of creation healed. Together, these developments shrink the full biblical meaning of salvation and of the cross of Jesus Christ. The cross and resurrection are reduced to an individual salvation to eternal life in the next world, rather than the restoration of fallen creation now and into the future.

49. Calvin, *Commentary on 2 Peter.*

50. Wesley, *Explanatory Notes New Testament*, comment on Rom 8:21.

51. David Field, "Confessing Christ."

So we find a gaping hole in the worldview of many, perhaps most, Christians. Often unconsciously, Christians deny or distort the full biblical promise of creation healed. Take 1 Pet 1:3–7, for example. Peter speaks of "new birth into a living hope" through Jesus' resurrection, guaranteeing Christians an imperishable "inheritance" that is "kept in heaven" for them until the time "when Jesus Christ is revealed" at his return to earth. Unfortunately, many understand these verses the way *The Message* paraphrases them. *The Message* renders "an inheritance . . . kept in heaven" until Christ's return as *"a future in heaven"* for Christians. As a matter of fact, 1 Peter says nothing about "a future in heaven." It speaks of Jesus having gone to heaven *until* he returns to earth.

How easy it is, then, for Christians to assume the divorce of heaven and earth. Many of us have unconsciously accepted a worldview that inverts the direction of salvation. We think salvation means going up to heaven rather than heaven coming to earth, as the Bible teaches. We have been taught that Jesus ascended to heaven so that our spirits could join him there eternally!—rather than what the Bible says: Jesus will come to earth to redeem all creation, including our own physical bodies. To a surprising degree, contemporary Christians are modern-day Gnostics.

Yet there are positive signs, as we will note in later chapters. Some Evangelicals and Pentecostals are starting to discover the broader biblical picture, and to rethink the doctrine of creation.

Biblical salvation means all creation healed. Grasping the power and wonder of salvation means affirming the biblical doctrine of creation, as well as the meaning of Jesus' death and resurrection for the healing and restoration of God's created order. In the biblical view, as Timothy Tennent notes, "creation is innately good apart from us. Before humans were created, God created plant and animal life and called them good (Gen 1:11, 21, 24). Creation has intrinsic value, not just instrumental value." Beyond this, the "very presence of God in the incarnation of Jesus Christ" testifies "to the inherent goodness of creation."[52]

In later chapters we will explore the meaning of this for our understanding of salvation and the church's mission. First however we need to understand more deeply how the disease of sin afflicts our world. The next section explores the biblical promise of creation healed by first examining sin and salvation—the disease, then the cure.

---

52. Tennent, *Christianity at the Religious Roundtable*.

Charles Anderson, *The Rapture* (1974)—a premillennial-dispensational interpretation of 1 Thess 4:16–17 and 1 Cor 15:51–52. Used by permission of the Bible Believers' Evangelistic Association: www.bbea.org.

PART TWO

The Disease and the Cure

5

The Ecology of Sin

The whole head is sick, and the whole heart faint. From
the sole of the foot even to the head, there is no soundness . . . but bruises and sores and bleeding wounds.

(Isa 1:5–6)

THE GOSPEL IS ABOUT healing the disease of sin—and the healing of all creation
through Jesus Christ by the Holy Spirit. Sin is the disease; salvation is the cure.

New creation is the final fruit—something greater and more glorious than healing sin's disease. But we, and all history, cannot reach that new creation without first
facing squarely the disease of sin and God's way of healing it. Healing sin is the necessary step toward a larger goal.

Earlier chapters of this book showed how developments in Christian history introduced, then reinforced, a radical and unbiblical theological divorce between heaven
and earth. We begin the book's second section with the strong affirmation that God
intends to heal and reconcile the divorce between heaven and earth. He is in fact doing
this *now* through Jesus Christ in the power of the Spirit. But we won't fully understand
what it means if we don't correctly diagnose the disease of sin.

At the root of the divorce between earth and heaven lies the vast moral disease
of sin. The theological divorce between heaven and earth leads us to ask about the
deeper fact of sin—the *cause* of the factual, historical divorce between heaven and
earth. This divorce is directly connected to the problem of sin, and the alienation,
suffering, degradation, and moral maladies that sin brings. This analysis will help us
gain a comprehensive biblical view of the good news of healing salvation that comes
through Jesus Christ (the focus of the third section of the book).

This chapter examines sin as a moral disease. In it, we survey the fourfold alienation that sin introduced into human history—the real ecology of sin.

To repeat a key theme of this book: We must understand the disease if we want to know the cure. Our understanding of salvation will be shallow, our discipleship weak, and our hope anemic and escapist unless we comprehensively grasp the disease that infects us all.

THE ECOLOGY OF SIN

In the biblical story, the salvation of human beings plays the central role in the redemption and transformation of creation—the full healing that Scripture promises and profoundly pictures. Salvation through Jesus Christ begins with "substantial healing" now (as Francis Schaeffer called it) and leads to total restoration, a new heaven and earth, when God's kingdom comes in fullness.

God created man and woman to live in complete harmony with him, with each other, and with the created world. They were at peace (*shalom*) with God, with themselves and each other, and with the plants and animals God had made. As Sandy Richter writes, "And so God's ideal is initiated—a world in which [humanity] would succeed in constructing the human civilization by directing and harnessing the abundant resources of the garden under the wise direction of their Creator. Here there would always be enough, progress would not necessitate pollution, expansion would not demand extinction. The privilege of the strong would not necessitate the deprivation of the weak. And humanity would succeed in these goals *because of* the guiding wisdom of God."[1]

This is the picture we find in Genesis 1 and 2 that is recalled occasionally throughout Scripture. It is also the seminal background of the stirring picture of the new creation—creation healed—that we find in Revelation 21 and 22. These twin pairs of chapters at the beginning and end of the Bible are the bookends of the meta-story of creation healed.

Then Genesis 3 introduces the problem of sin. Sin's curse and infection becomes a key theme in the biblical story. The man and the woman disobey God's command. The Bible does not explain precisely how and why the sin of Adam and Eve was transmitted to their offspring, and thus the whole human family. The key point is that, through human sin, the vital life-connection between humans and God was severed. We may think of the fall as the loss of God's animating Spirit that gave humans the capacity for open communion with God. The capacity for unhindered communion with God was lost, or deadened, "and so death spread to all because all have sinned" (Rom 5:12). The connection to God was broken but not totally lost, and so hope for healing remains, thanks to God's action through Jesus Christ.

"Sin" then is our word for this disruption between humans and God; this moral disease that entered human history because of the loss of life-giving communion with

1. Richter, "Biblical Theology," 69.

God. The Bible teaches that human sin traces back to the mystery of Satan's rebellion against God. But the biblical story focuses primarily on human sin and how it poisoned the relationship with God and with the whole world.

Sin is thus a poisoning of relationships that brings disorder and a deep moral disease. In this sense, "Sin is not attached to our nature as an alien substitute in the vacuum of lost righteousness. Sin is deprived human nature acting out of itself, rather than out of the Spirit. Without the Spirit, every human expression is bent; bent away from God and toward self."[2] That is the dismal dynamic of the disease.

Viewing sin as a deadly disease, a fatal infection, helps us grasp what sin is and how it affects humans and all creation. Disease is in fact one of the Bible's root metaphors for sin. God tells Israel, "Your wound is incurable, your injury beyond healing" (Jer 30:12 TNIV). "The whole head is sick, and the whole heart faint. From the sole of the foot even to the head, there is no soundness, . . . but bruises and sores and bleeding wounds" (Isa 1:5–6). The prophet Jeremiah asks, "Is there no balm in Gilead? Is there no physician there? Why then has the health of my poor people not been restored?" (Jer 8:22). King David laments in Psalm 38, "Because of your wrath there is no health in my body; there is no soundness in my bones because of my sin. . . . My wounds fester and are loathsome because of my sinful folly" (Ps 38:3, 5 TNIV). In the New Testament, Paul speaks of evil talk spreading "like gangrene" (2 Tim 2:17). And we recall Jesus' words, "Those who are well have no need of a physician, but those who are sick; I have come to call not the righteous but sinners" (Mark 2:17).

In the biblical narrative, Genesis 3 is key because it shows that sin disrupted the human story in four fundamental ways. Francis Schaeffer summarized the problem in his prophetic 1970 book, *Pollution and the Death of Man: The Christian View of Ecology.* Schaeffer identified four divisions or alienations that affect all humanity because of sin, all clearly indicated in Genesis 3. In the fall, Schaeffer wrote that "man"—that is humanity—

> was divided from God, first; and then, ever since the Fall, man is separated from himself. These are the psychological divisions. I am convinced that this is the basic psychosis: that the individual [person] is separated from himself as a result of the Fall.
>
> The next division is that man is divided from other men; these are the sociological divisions. And then man is divided from nature, and nature is divided from nature. So there are these multiple divisions, and one day, when Christ comes back, there is going to be a complete healing of all of them, on the basis of the "blood of the Lamb."
>
> But Christians who believe the Bible are not simply called to say "one day" there will be healing, but that by God's grace substantially, upon the basis of the work of Christ, substantial healing can be a reality here and now.[3]

Schaeffer's analysis is insightful because of its comprehensiveness. It opens some key insights into the ecology of sin. In the next chapters we will explore how the

2. Hynson, "Original Sin as Privation," 77.

3. Schaeffer, *Pollution*, 67.

gospel is God's way of providing "substantial healing . . . here and now" through Jesus Christ. First, however, we need to dig more deeply into the four divisions signaled in Genesis 3. Here is the initial diagnosis of the human problem, which is the whole problem of history.

In alienating man and woman from God, human disobedience introduced three other kinds of alienation that are with us still. Here is the ecology of sin: alienation from God, internal alienation within each person (alienation from oneself), alienation between humans, and alienation from and within nature. These are the spiritual, psychological, social, and environmental alienations that afflict the whole human family.

All these divisions derive from sin, and all distort God's good purpose in creation. Therefore they all cry out for a gospel of reconciliation and healing. Understanding this deep ecology of sin will in turn help clarify the church's mission agenda. *Faithful Christian mission focuses on healing the four alienations or divisions that result from the fall.* Working to heal and reconcile this fourfold alienation based on the provisions of the gospel is indispensable in Christian mission. This is the essential good news which Christians offer the world.

But we need to be sure we grasp the deep meaning, the ramifications of this multiple and complex alienation. Beyond the mere *fact* of this fourfold alienation, a key point is the way these multiple alienations interweave, interconnect, and mutually reinforce each other. In other words, we need to grasp the ecology of sin. If we treat these four alienations separately, we miss God's comprehensive way of healing his entire creation.

The key biblical passage is Gen 3:8–24. The fourfold alienation pictured here reveals key themes that remarkably interweave throughout the whole Bible, in both Testaments.

Alienation from God

Genesis 3 clearly shows the problem, the disease of humanity. The fundamental malady, the root of all the rest, is alienation from God. Sin brings estrangement between humans and their Creator—their source of life, sustenance, and health.

Genesis 3:8 puts it this way: "Then the man and his wife heard the sound of the Lord God as he was walking in the garden in the cool of the day, and they hid from the Lord God among the trees of the garden" (TNIV). Previously Adam and Eve lived in the garden in harmony with God, naked and unashamed (Gen 2:25). Now their first impulse on hearing God approach is to hide. This is humanity's basic estrangement. Because of sin we hide from God. An open, trusting relationship has been broken.

An analogy between parents and children makes plain what is happening here. A little boy is happy to see his mother. He runs to her for a hug. But if he has done something his mother sternly warned him not to do, he is more likely to run away and hide when she shows up. Because of sin we hide from God—which, of course, only compounds the problem.

Here is a key theme of the whole Bible: estrangement from God because of sin. Old Testament history is a chronicle of this estrangement and its results. "All we like sheep have gone astray; we have all turned to our own way" (Isa 53:6). "The Lord's hand is not shortened, that it cannot save; neither his ear heavy, that it cannot hear: But your iniquities have separated between you and your God, and your sins have hid his face from you, so that he will not hear" (Isa 59:1–2 KJV).

Ironically, this very alienation between God and humanity provides much of the richness and fascination of the biblical stories. Consider the tower of Babel, a Bible story that has become an icon in Western culture. In the book of Genesis it immediately precedes the call of Abram, another key turning point in the biblical narrative.

Babel is not only a story of human hubris—"Come, let us build ourselves a city, and a tower with its top in the heavens, and let us make a name for ourselves" (Gen 11:4)—it is also a story of alienation from God. The tower with "its top in the heavens" was a way to reach the gods, a technology for uniting heaven and earth. It testifies to the sense of distance and alienation from "heaven" that the people felt. Babel also stands in stark contrast with Jacob's (later) vision of "a ladder set up on the earth, the top of it reaching to heaven; and the angels of God . . . ascending and descending on it" (Gen 28:12). Here God takes the initiative to communicate with Jacob, another key part of the larger story.

Human alienation from God is suggested also in Gen 11:5, "The Lord came down to see the city and the tower, which mortals had built." Due to sin, God no longer walks in fellowship with Adam and Eve in the garden.

Alienation from God because of sin is thus a key theme of the biblical narrative. Sin creates a barrier between us and God. The relationship with God has been broken. The Bible uses many metaphors for this, including disease (Isa 1:5–6) and blindness (Deut 28:29). The metaphor of disease is particularly apt in grasping the ecology of sin because disease affects all aspects of life. The disease of sin must be healed, so humankind's deepest need is for "salvation"—which fundamentally means healing. (English still has an echo of this in the related word "salve.") Salvation, both in Scripture and in the English language, certainly includes the sense of *rescue*, but *healing* is the root meaning.[4]

This background enriches Paul's declaration about Jesus in Eph 2:14, "He is our peace." The biblical conception of peace is *shalom*, with rich connotations of health, well-being, flourishing, and "at-home-ness" with people and the land. In later chapters we will see more deeply how *shalom* and salvation are intertwined.

The deep alienation of humanity from God because of sin echoes through many of the Psalms and through much of Job and the Prophets. The Psalmist cries, "O God, do not be far from me; O my God, make haste to help me!" (Ps 71:12). David's prayer of repentance in Psalm 51 breathes his sense of alienation from God due to sin. We think of Ps 22:1–2,

---

4. "Salvation" traces to the Latin *salus,* whose root meaning is health or soundness. The word can also have the sense of safety, welfare, and a salutation (that is, a wish for well-being or good health). Simpson, *Cassell's New Latin Dictionary.*

> My God, my God, why have you forsaken me?
> Why are you so far from helping me, from the words of my groaning?
> O my God, I cry by day, but you do not answer;
> and by night, but find no rest.

This agonizing sense of separation from God will take on deeper meaning later as the New Testament writers wrestle with the meaning of Jesus' death on the cross.

The annals and archives of world history are filled with a sense of, or at least evidence of, our alienation from God. One striking example is the story of Pandita Ramabai, born into a high-caste Hindu home in India in 1858. Ramabai's father, a distinguished scholar in Sanskrit and Indian literature, took the controversial step of teaching his daughter the Hindu classics rather than letting her become a child bride. Ramabai's parents and sister died of starvation when Ramabai was only about sixteen, but she and her brother survived. In 1880 she married and the next year had a daughter, Manoramabai ("Heart's Delight").

Ramabai's husband soon died of cholera, leaving Ramabai to support herself and her infant. Brilliant like her father, Ramabai's classical Hindu education became her means of survival.

Hinduism left Ramabai spiritually unsatisfied, however. She yearned for the God she did not know. Eventually, through reading the New Testament and contacts with Anglican missionaries, Ramabai became convinced of the truth of the Christian faith. But she still had no sense of God's reality or presence. She went to England to study and there with her two-year-old daughter was baptized in the Church of England. She had now "found the Christian *religion,* which was good enough for me," she later wrote, "*but I had not [yet] found Christ, Who is the Life of the religion,* and 'the Light of every man that cometh into the world.'"[5] Still, this was a key step in healing her alienation from God after her disillusionment with Hinduism.

Then Ramabai encountered the story of Jesus and the Samaritan woman. This triggered Ramabai's spiritual breakthrough, a genuine encounter with the living Jesus Christ. She had asked one of the (Anglican) Sisters of the Cross to explain why they so selflessly cared for the poor and "fallen" women, and the sister read her the story in John 4. "I had never read or heard anything like this in the religious books of the Hindus," Ramabai wrote. "I realized after reading the 4th Chapter of St. John's Gospel, that Christ was truly the Divine Saviour He claimed to be, and no one but He could transform and uplift the downtrodden womanhood of India and of every land."[6]

Here was reconciliation with God, a healing of the alienation that sin brings. Ramabai's story shows how broadly sin has affected the whole human family.

Alienation from One Another

Alienation from God is not the whole story. If we focus solely on this alienation, we miss the deep ecology of sin and the full wonder of salvation. Genesis 3, and in fact the

5. Ramabai, *Testimony,* 309 (emphasis in the original).

6. Ibid., 309.

Pandita Ramabai (1858–1922) with her daughter Manoramabai.

whole Bible, is emphatic that sin has divided the human family in multiple ways. Sin alienates us from one another.

"The man said, 'The woman whom you gave me to be with me, she gave me fruit from the tree, and I ate'" (Gen 3:12). The first "fruit" of alienation from God is the man blaming the woman—and indirectly, God himself ("the woman *you* gave me"). Estrangement from God brings deep division in the human family, multiplied alienation in the whole web of human interrelationships. In Genesis 3, the sin of Adam and Eve disharmonizes their perfect relationship, and the consequences of that broken relationship lead to estrangement throughout the whole human family. The Bible gives us dozens of examples. If it were not so the Bible would be much shorter!

Alienation within the human family begins with the damaged relationship between man and woman and extends to parents and children, sisters and brothers, families, tribes, nations, and all the world's ethnicities. We see this already in Genesis: alienation between brothers: Cain kills Abel and tries to deny it, but God says, "Your brother's blood is crying to me from the ground!" (Gen 4:10);[7] alienation between sisters: Rachel and Leah compete for their husband Jacob's attention (Genesis 29–31); estrangement between Jacob and his twin brother Esau; not to mention Sarah and Hagar, Abraham and King Abimelech (Genesis 20), the whole story of Lot, Isaac and his brother-in-law Laban, and the entire lot of Jacob's children, from Dinah (Genesis 34) to Joseph to Judah.

And we see the same throughout Scripture, from the horrid examples in the book of Judges to disputes among Jesus' disciples, rivalry between sisters Mary and Martha—and even after Pentecost, the betrayal by Ananias and Sapphira (Acts 5).

But the deepest alienation in the human family appears to be that between man and woman. This is the relational "stem cell" of all human interactions. It is also the most powerful and volatile alienation because of the force of the sexual drive. The oppression and degradation of women by men in many cultures throughout human history stands as an often unseen and ignored witness to the alienation brought by sin. Clearly, this alienation is still with us, as we are reminded daily by sexual, emotional, and physical violence against women in virtually all societies. In the Bible, one of the most painful examples of this happens in King David's family. David's son Amnon violently rapes his beautiful half-sister Tamar, using the ruse of being sick in bed. Tamar's irate brother Absalom has Amnon murdered. But Absalom, bent on revenge, shows little real sympathy or understanding for his own sister. "Do not take this to heart," he says! (2 Sam 13:20). Tamar, now "a desolate woman," is soon forgotten (though Absalom later names his own beautiful daughter Tamar, 2 Sam 14:27). This is how sin compounds sin in its expanding, complex ecology.

In human history, the root alienation brought by sin mutates into conflicts between tribes, nations, and religions. It leads to the "clash of civilizations" described by historian Samuel Huntington[8]: Clashes between Jews and Arabs; between Christians, Muslims, and Hindus; "nation against nation and city against city" (2 Chr 15:6), all down through history. Yes, all kinds of cultural, philosophical, and religious factors are part of the mix. But the basic problem traces back to the human alienation brought by sin, which traces back to our alienation from God.

So pervasive is sin's alienation that every reader of this book can probably cite and *feel* examples from their own experience, their own families.

---

7. Implicit here in "from the ground" is the larger ecology of sin involving not only human beings but also the ground, or land—emblematic of the whole nonhuman created order and its interconnection with human beings.

8. Huntington, "Clash of Civilizations?"

But lest we lose hope, we are again reminded that Jesus "is our peace," our *shalom* (Eph 2:14), and that where God's narrative and economy is headed is "the healing of the nations" (Rev 22:2). Paul says that the very "mystery of God" (1 Cor 2:1) is the multifold reconciliation that God brings to the human family through Jesus Christ by the Spirit (Eph 2:2–6; Col 1:25–27)—"Christ in you all" (second person plural, the restored human family in Christ), "the hope of glory" (Col 1:27).

India's Pandita Ramabai illustrates this dimension of the ecology of sin—and, even more, its healing. As a woman, she suffered especially the alienation between the sexes, the alienations and oppressions of the caste system (though she herself was high-caste), and the British oppression of colonial India. She wrote about all of these. As a child she overcame the prejudices against educating girls. She saw the plight of child widows and famine victims and made them the special focus of her Mukti ("Liberation" or "Salvation") Mission near Pune, which still continues its ministry of hope.[9] Pandita Ramabai suffered these human alienations, overcame them through the gospel of Jesus, and herself become a healer.

We misdiagnose the malady of sin if we fail to see how its cancer has spread through all human society and history. This is a key aspect of the ecology of sin. We thank God for the healing Jesus Christ offers for our alienation from each other! Gospel healing means more than inner peace with God, important as that is—it touches all our relationships.

Alienation from Ourselves: Internal Division

Something terrible happened to humanity internally when the relationship with God was broken. Man and woman became diseased within themselves as well as in their relationship. This is no surprise, for we know—increasingly so—that humans are not isolated atoms or self-contained "individuals." We are intrinsically relational. We are social beings, so alienation from others and alienation from ourselves go hand-in-hand.

Genesis 3:10 reports the man's feeble but profound answer when God asked where he was. "I heard the sound of you in the garden, and I was afraid, because I was naked; and I hid myself." Such fear signals a divided self; an inner disease which, of course, has outward manifestations. "Perfect love casts out fear" (1 John 4:18), but here we have just the opposite. Before the fall there was only trust, no cowering fearfulness and anxiety. God's intent is that his children "serve him without fear, in holiness and righteousness before him all our days" (Luke 1:74–75). But sin's alienation makes that impossible. "I was afraid," says Adam. His new fear of God showed his internal dis-ease—his dis-ease with God because of his disobedience—and its effect on his psyche, his spirit, and his conscience. Adam was not only "objectively" afraid of God; he was inwardly, anxiously fearful.

Because of sin, people are not at home within themselves. They experience uneasiness, disquiet, inner conflicts, and fears. Sin brings that whole range of maladies and symptoms that psychology and psychiatry deal with.

---

9. For a summary and sources, see Snyder, *Populist Saints*, 895–909.

Clearly this internal dividedness, like the other dimensions of sin's disease, is a basic human problem. It is traceable straight through history, from ancient biblical stories to rising suicide rates today in materially prosperous nations.

This self-alienation is really a spiritual disease. It is not just a psychological problem. Because of sin we are alienated from ourselves, as well as from God and others. This is the root cause of what the Bible calls being "double-minded" (Ps 119:113; Jas 1:7, 4:8). Genesis 4 hints at this in the story of Cain killing his brother Abel. Cain was alienated from God, from his family, and from the land. God tells him, "You will be a fugitive and a wanderer on the earth" (Gen 4:12, or "restless wanderer," TNIV). But he was a fugitive also from himself. Earlier God had warned, "If you do well, will you not be accepted? And if you do not do well, sin is lurking at the door; its desire is for you, but you must master it" (Gen 4:7). The metaphor of sin lurking or crouching at the door may suggest Satan's temptation, but it also signals an internal struggle.

This alienation from ourselves brings a guilty conscience. In the beginning, humans were enjoying open fellowship with our Creator, but sin disrupted that sense of communion, bringing alienation and a guilty conscience. However, the New Testament promises us that "the blood of Christ, who through the eternal Spirit offered himself without blemish to God," can "purify our conscience from dead works to worship the living God" (Heb 9:14).

Internal alienation shows itself in the ambivalent desire to do both good and evil. People who have received God's self-revelation through Scripture and the law of God especially feel this ambivalence. Paul says eloquently in Romans 7:

> I do not understand my own actions. For I do not do what I want, but I do the very thing I hate . . . I can will what is right, but I cannot do it. For I do not do the good I want, but the evil I do not want is what I do. Now if I do what I do not want, it is no longer I that do it, but sin that dwells within me.
>
> So I find it to be a law that when I want to do what is good, evil lies close at hand. For I delight in the law of God in my inmost self, but I see in my members another law at war with the law of my mind, making me captive to the law of sin that dwells in my members. Wretched man that I am! Who will rescue me from this body of death? (Rom 7:15–24)

This internal dividedness is thus a key part of the ecology of sin. Today people spend billions of dollars every year trying to heal their internal divisions and find inner peace. This largesse goes to psychologists, psychiatrists, family and personal counselors—"spiritual advisors to guide your every move," as Bob Dylan sang in "When You Gonna Wake Up?"—and multiple forms of mindless entertainment. We are thankful, of course, for the legitimate ministry of counseling, and yet the development of counseling and entertainment into modern growth industries testifies to the deep self-alienation introduced into the human soul and psyche by sin.

No one escapes this internal alienation, though it may be suppressed. It manifests itself psychologically, emotionally, socioculturally, and even physically. Readers of this book can probably identify this alienation right now in their own lives, or see it in others who are close.

But there is hope. The restlessness and internal dis-ease produced by sin is addressed directly by the good news of Jesus Christ and proclaimed by his church. Healing comes through Jesus Christ and the fullness of the Spirit as God works to heal our brokenness. Because this internal estrangement undermines healthy community, the gospel brings healing through Christian community and the medicine of the sacraments.

The Apostle James wrote that the "conflicts and disputes" he saw in his day arose "from your cravings that are at war within you. You want something and do not have it; so you commit murder. And you covet something and cannot obtain it; so you engage in disputes and conflicts" (Jas 4:1–2). Here is clear testimony to *both* the internal and social divisions that spring from our alienation from God. So James writes, "Draw near to God, and he will draw near to you. Cleanse your hands, you sinners, and purify your hearts, you double-minded" (Jas 4:8). James is speaking here of finding healing within the Christian community through the work of the Holy Spirit.

God's Spirit brings not just a one-time change, a conversion experience, critical as that is for setting many on the path of healing. God continues working in people's lives as they respond to his healing grace. Consider again Pandita Ramabai.

Ramabai's life embodied both the problem and the cure. She continued growing in God's healing grace until her death in 1922 (and probably beyond). About 1892, as Ramabai's work with child widows was expanding, she had a deeper encounter with God. Faith became more profound and personal. She now felt Christ's presence daily. She wrote, "I have come to know the Lord Jesus Christ as my personal Saviour and have the joy of sweet communion with him."[10]

But in April 1895, Ramabai experienced a deeper work of the Spirit at a camp meeting established by American Methodists who were part of the holiness movement. Reading the autobiography of Amanda Berry Smith—the African Methodist Episcopal holiness evangelist and former slave—helped prepare Ramabai's heart for this deeper healing. "I found a great blessing to realize the personal presence of the Holy Spirit in me and to be guided and taught by Him," she wrote. "The Holy Spirit taught me how to appropriate every promise of God in the right way, and obey His voice."[11] Thank God for inner healing through Jesus Christ! This is a key part of the complete cure that the gospel offers, God's way of dealing with the ecology of sin.

But this leads to a question: does internal alienation bring alienation between humans, or is it the other way around? In ecological perspective, this is a foolish question. It is both, of course—simultaneously and in multiple ways. Influences flow both ways, as in any organic system. In particular instances, one might be able to discover a cause-and-effect sequence, but generally the interactions are so close and complex as to fall beyond our ability to discern. That's the nature of ecology, whether we're talking about sin or science. Ecologists speak of multiple feedback loops with multiplying effects and often-unforeseen ripples. So it is with sin.

---

10. Ramabai, *Testimony,* 314.

11. Ibid., 316.

Due to sin, then, we experience estrangement from God, from one another, and within ourselves. But that is not the whole story. If we miss the fourth alienating dimension we misdiagnose the disease and fail to experience the cure. That fourth dimension is alienation from the land.

Alienation from the Land

The Bible shows that at a deep level human beings are estranged from the land. This is our alienation from the created order (what we commonly call "nature") and is a basic theme of Scripture, especially of the Old Testament.

Scripture is emphatic that our estrangement from the earth arises from sin. God says to the man:

> Because you have listened to the voice of your wife, and have eaten of the tree about which I commanded you, "You shall not eat of it," cursed is the ground because of you; in toil you shall eat of it all the days of your life; thorns and thistles it shall bring forth for you; and you shall eat the plants of the field. By the sweat of your face you shall eat bread until you return to the ground, for out of it you were taken; you are dust, and to dust you shall return. (Gen 3:17–19)

God says, "cursed is the ground *because of you.*" This does not mean that God objectively put a curse on the earth so that it is under his disfavor. No, the Bible is describing *consequence* here. Humans cannot sin without it affecting their relationship both with their Creator and with the creation. God still cares for the land, as we shall see.

The land suffers from human sin in three ways: it suffers directly from human ill treatment of the land; indirectly it suffers the consequences of human violence; finally, it languishes from the lack of the proper stewardship care that was entrusted to humankind. At creation "the Lord God took the man and put him in the garden of Eden to till it and keep it" (Gen 2:15), or "to care for it and to maintain it" (NET).

The spoiling of the land is thus a consequence of human sin. Harmony between people and the rest of the created environment was broken. In the garden the man and his wife were not only naked and not ashamed; they were naked and not uncomfortable (as Sandy Richter comments). But now, due to sin, "the Lord God banished [them] from the Garden of Eden to work the ground from which [they] had been taken" (Gen 3:23 TNIV).

Now alienation from the land becomes a basic biblical theme, a key strand in the narrative tapestry, an essential part of the plot. The fact that in English versions of the Old Testament "land," "earth," and sometimes "ground" translate the same Hebrew word (ʾerets) underscores the significance of this whole theme. (In English versions "ground" often translates the Hebrew ʾadamah [ground/dirt/soil], and sometimes ʾerets.)

The biblical prophets repeatedly lament the earth's sufferings due to human sin. Perhaps the most poignant passage is Hos 4:1–3, "There is no faithfulness or loyalty, and no knowledge of God in the land. Swearing, lying, and murder, and stealing and adultery break out; bloodshed follows bloodshed. Therefore the land mourns, and all who live in it languish; together with the wild animals and the birds of the air, even the fish of the sea are perishing."

Under the Mosaic covenant, the Sabbath and Jubilee laws protected the land, specifying how Israel was to fulfill its earth stewardship. Here is what would happen, God said, if his people violated this covenant: "Then the land shall enjoy its sabbath years as long as it lies desolate, while you are in the land of your enemies; then the land shall rest, and enjoy its sabbath years. As long as it lies desolate, it shall have the rest it did not have on your sabbaths when you were living on it" (Lev 26:34–35).

Sin makes the earth suffer. So Paul says in Romans 8, "the whole creation has been groaning in labor pains until now." It was "subjected to futility" or frustration and is in "bondage to decay" (Rom 8:20–22).

Look at what we humans have done to the earth! We have been abusing and destroying it from the beginning. But the cumulative development of modern industry and technology without a proper sense of stewardship has vastly multiplied and magnified the human sin of creation misuse. Today the earth suffers from loss of biodiversity, air and water pollution that threaten the climate, and many other maladies. This is all part of the ecology of sin. It is part of the groaning of creation.

But God intends to heal and restore the land. He plans to restore the garden. If his people truly repent and follow his ways, God says, he will "forgive their sin and heal their land" (2 Chr 7:14). "The creation itself will be set free from its bondage to decay and will obtain the freedom of the glory of the children of God" (Rom 8:21). God promises through the gospel a "time of universal restoration" as he "announced long ago through his holy prophets" (Acts 3:21).

Down through history, many of the church's greatest saints have shown special sensitivity to living things and the general created order. We think of St. Francis speaking to the birds and to "brother sun and sister moon." John Wesley told his traveling preachers they should tenderly care for their horses, their fellow-creatures. At her Mukti Mission in India, Pandita Ramabai nurtured the land and taught her girls good gardening—responsible living on the land, in simplicity. Such examples show how, despite the theological divorce between heaven and earth that has infected much Christian thought and piety, God's love in human hearts tends to flow out to all God's creatures, all creation. That's the nature of love.

But love flows most fully and freely when not constricted by misunderstandings of the world and God's intent. That's why we need to fully understand the divorce of heaven and earth and the ecology of sin and salvation.

Alienation from the land, then, is another key aspect of the ecology of sin. Placing it fourth does not reduce its importance, for we are thinking ecologically. If we deal with only three of the four symptoms of a disease, we are still ill. We can still die.

Here is a simple illustration: I happen to meet Bill at a conference. We discover that we have some past experiences in common—we both grew up in southern Michigan. As the conversation develops, I can see that Bill is very stressed. Eventually he tells me his story—health problems, a strained marriage, pressures at work, increasing worry and anxiety. And he has no sense of God in his life.

Does Bill need Jesus? Definitely! So does his whole family (and probably his neighbors and his boss and everyone at work, as well). But what does needing Jesus mean concretely for Bill's situation?

I soon see that Bill is suffering from all four dimensions of sin. He lives in a world largely isolated from the restorative beauty of nature. The rhythms of his life are governed by work and email and television, plus his hour-long daily commute. His diet consists of processed foods that are mostly artificial, several steps removed from real farm-grown groceries. On top of all that, his job contributes nothing to human well-being. And so on and so on. In short, Bill's life is a mess. He sees this in part, but he doesn't see the whole ecology of his ills.

Coming to know Jesus Christ as his Savior will transform Bill's life. Maybe it will put his family back together. It will go a long way toward healing his internal issues. But Bill won't really be healthy until *all* dimensions of his life are healed. This will require healthy community (through the church, especially), life-pattern changes (maybe even a different job), and a sense of his own mission within God's healing mission.

However, here we face a key issue: because sin has become a "system-wide" problem, Bill can't be healed in isolation from his larger environment—family, neighborhood, city, nation, climate, world. This means he can't fully be made whole within the present order of things. *But he can make a start.* He can be (mostly) part of the cure rather than (mostly) part of the problem. He can be part of a healing community and family, and part of healing causes and currents on the earth. In so doing he will find his own health.

The goal is healthy living on a healthy planet, as God intended. But since you can't have healthy people on a sick planet—not spiritually, not physically—Bill will never be fully whole in this life. But *he can experience healing*—"substantial healing here and now." And that includes *becoming a healer* as he lives as a part of his community in the hope and power and promise of Jesus' resurrection.

Christians believe they are both saved and being saved. In this sense, God's people today are like those described in Hebrews 11: "All of these died in faith without having received the promises, but from a distance they saw and greeted them"; "God had provided something better so that they would not, apart from us, be made perfect" (Heb 11:13, 40). We now enjoy that "something better" through the work and resurrection of Jesus Christ and the presence of the Spirit. Yet presently, we still live in between the "It is finished" of John 19:30 and the "It is done" of Rev 21:6, when the "something better" fully comes.

SIN'S REAL ECOLOGY

The ecology of sin, then, has four key dimensions: alienation from God, from each other, from ourselves, and from the land. The whole human family, diseased in all its relationships—with God, inwardly, with each other, and with the land—suffers a fourfold ill that requires a fourfold cure. Or better: *an ecology of sin that cries out for an ecology of salvation.*

Both the diagnosis and the cure must deal fully with the nature of history and culture and the ongoing march of generations. Sin is generational because human ecology proceeds through time, creating history. Clearly this is part of the biblical diagnosis of sin.

"Generations" is a key biblical theme. God says to Abraham, "I will establish my covenant between me and you, and your offspring after you throughout their generations, for an everlasting covenant, to be God to you and to your offspring after you" (Gen 17:7). Earlier God spoke to Noah and his family about "the covenant that I make between me and you and every living creature that is with you, for all future generations" (Gen 9:12). In the Pentateuch, the phrase "throughout their generations" occurs ten times (in the New Revised Standard Version).

To understand the ecology of sin, Exod 20:5–6 is especially crucial: "I the Lord your God am a jealous God, punishing children for the iniquity of parents, to the third and the fourth generation of those who reject me, but showing steadfast love to the thousandth generation of those who love me and keep my commandments." And Exod 34:6–7 is like unto it:

> The Lord, the Lord,
> a God merciful and gracious,
> slow to anger,
> and abounding in steadfast love and faithfulness,
> keeping steadfast love for the thousandth generation,
> forgiving iniquity and transgression and sin,
> yet by no means clearing the guilty,
> but visiting the iniquity of the parents
> upon the children
> and the children's children,
> to the third and the fourth generation.

Here is one of the highpoints of all Scripture, for here Yahweh appears to Moses on Mount Sinai and reveals his deepest character. The revelation of God's character in both these passages illuminates the ecology of sin. God punishes sin "to the third and the fourth generation" but shows "steadfast love" for a thousand generations.

There is mystery here at several levels. Who can understand God and his ways? And yet three things stand out clearly: First, sin is an affront to God, and he responds righteously, consistent with his character and with the responsibility that is built into his God-imaged creatures.

Second, God's mercy and steadfast love reach further than his judgment. Using the figures of speech "to the third and fourth generation" and "to the thousandth generation" emphasizes how the Lord's mercy triumphs over judgment.

Third—and especially important for our discussion here—the effects of sin continue for generations. God "visit[s] the iniquity of the parents upon the children and the children's children, to the third and the fourth generation." This could be understood rather mechanically, as though God willfully and directly punishes people for their forebears' sin. However, it is more consistent with the biblical revelation of God, the image of God, and the ecology of creation, to understand this passage in terms of *consequence* rather than direct punishment. It is clear empirically that the sins of one generation get "visited upon" their descendents—often in multiple and ramifying ways. Society gives a bad harvest of examples: child abuse, drug use, the effects of crime and war. Abused children often grow up to be child abusers themselves, unless grace intervenes somehow. And so on. As with the "curse" on the earth, so with the "visiting" of human sinfulness through the generations: The consequences ripple down through time as well as outward in our immediate cultural space. This is the nature of sin, the ecology of the multidimensional alienation introduced by human rebellion against God. Salvation is the comprehensive cure that God offers through Jesus Christ.

In later chapters we will explore this fourfold cure—though not sequentially, since we are thinking ecologically. We will see how the gospel provides reconciliation with God, with one another, within ourselves, and with the land. We will focus especially on mission: the church's role in bringing God's healing into all these intertwined, ever-interacting dimensions. Christians responsive to God's Spirit really can help to launch a great epidemic of health in the world—of the healing of creation.

Hieronymus Bosch (1450–1516), "The Garden of Earthly Delights," center panel—the ecology of sin?

6

The Groans of Creation

We know that the whole creation has
been groaning in labor pains until now.

(Rom 8:22)

CCCREATION IS GROANING—WHETHER IN birth pangs, as Paul describes in Romans 8,
or in death throes, I am not sure," says Scott Sabin, executive director of Plant With
Purpose. We "live on a deeply troubled planet. And yet this crisis seems to have little
effect on our daily lives."[1]

In the past dozen years, books and reports have piled up fast that spotlight the
rising dangers to our physical environment. All the scientific studies not funded by
special interests point in the same direction. Good recent summaries include Mark
Hertsgaard, *Hot: Living through the Next Fifty Years on Earth* and Bill McKibben,
Eaarth: Making a Life on a Tough New Planet.[2] Hertsgaard dedicates his moving book
to his infant daughter Chiara, "who has to live through this."

This chapter builds a bridge between the current state of our planet and the
biblical theme of all creation groaning—an essential link for theology, mission, and
discipleship.

In explaining salvation, Christian theology has mostly stressed alienation from
God and each other. We need a corrective here, however, lest we fall short of biblically

1. Sabin, *Tending to Eden*, 85.

2. Hertsgaard, *Hot*; McKibben, *Eaarth*. McKibben intentionally uses the spelling "Eaarth" to under-
score his argument. See also Wheeler, *Magnetic North*. Wheeler argues that the Arctic is the "lead player
in the drama of climate change"; "survival of civilization as we know it hangs on what happens" there.

revealed truth. The alienation brought by sin is four-dimensional, not two-dimensional. The disease has multiple parts. The previous chapter showed how alienation from God, ourselves, one another, and the land are all essential strands of the ecology of sin, and thus of salvation.

We must now dig deeper into the disease of sin as it affects the earth. We are pressed to consider the groaning of creation under the disease of sin. We still misunderstand the gospel, and Christian mission, if we fail to see the depth of human alienation *from the land*. If we fail to hear creation's groanings, we haven't fully heard the good news. We stress this because of the gaping worldview hole described earlier. A full cure demands a fuller diagnosis. We must get specific, even scientific, about the symptoms. Otherwise salvation is not complete, not truly holistic.

It's not merely that we must see the place of the created order in the larger economy of salvation. There is a larger point: full reconciliation with God, ourselves, and one another *depends upon* reconciliation with the land. That's the way God made the world—it's the ecology of redemption. The biblical story is God, his people, and his land. Grasping the profound depth of salvation requires that we grasp the depth and meaning of creation's groaning, looking at both causes and symptoms.

GOD'S WORD, CREATION'S GROANING

God reveals in Scripture *how* God's people are to live "shalomistically" in and with the land—how they can flourish and be at peace, enjoying true *shalom*. In Genesis 9 God establishes an "everlasting covenant" with the earth (Gen 9:16).[3] Later he forms his special covenant people, and after the exodus gives them the Ten Commandments as part of the Mosaic covenant. This covenant shows Israel how to be God's people, preparing the way for the new covenant in Jesus Christ. Here is the complete cure for the disease of sin in all its deadly dimensions.

Creation is still groaning. God's people have deviated from God's way. Failing to care for the land, we have in fact broken every one the Ten Commandments—for all touch the land in one way or another.

God says, "You shall have no other gods before me" (Exod 20:3). But when we despoil the creation we are not honoring God; we are putting our own selfishness and comfort before God the Creator and his intentions for the creation. First commandment broken.

God says, "You shall not make for yourself an idol" (Exod 20:4). When we fail to care for God's creatures, we make an idol of ourselves. We put ourselves ahead of God and his glory and mission. Second commandment shattered.

God says, "You shall not make wrongful use of the name of the Lord your God" (Exodus 20:7). When people profess to be God's people, yet mistreat the earth and claim to own the land, they misuse the name of the Lord who says, "The earth is mine, and all that is in it" (Ps 24:1). So much for the third commandment.

---

3. We explore this more fully in chapter 8.

God says, "Remember the Sabbath day, and keep it holy" (Exod 20:8). The Sabbath principle is rest, acknowledging God as sovereign provider. God says the land must be allowed to rest, to rejuvenate itself; to be properly cared for. "The land will rest, and enjoy its Sabbath years" (Lev 26:34). Exploiting the land is one of the ways we fail to keep Sabbath and so break the fourth commandment.

God says, "Honor your father and your mother, so that your days may be long in the land" (Exod 20:12). God's economy ties together the honoring of family relationships and peaceful living in the land. Since our parents (and all future generations) depend on the land, we dishonor our father and mother if we exploit the land.

God says, "You shall not murder" (Exod 20:13). We are to nurture the life of others, not destroy it. Yet, we now know that polluting the climate raises the death toll, especially among the poor. Environmental exploitation and death are linked at multiple levels. Creation care is pro-life.

God says, "You shall not commit adultery" (Exod 20:14). Adultery springs from lust for someone or something that does not properly belong to us, and causes us to break faith with those to whom we have promised to be faithful—thus dishonoring God. So the Bible speaks much of spiritual adultery and prostitution. God's original intention was that we would be stewards and caretakers of the land, the land we were placed in to "husband." But our lust to serve ourselves has led us to abandon the land. Failure to nurture the land is ecological adultery.

God says, "You shall not steal" (Exod 20:15). Spoiling the land steals from God, who owns the land, and from the poor, to whom God gives special rights to the land and its produce (Lev 19:10, 23:22).

God says, "You shall not bear false witness against your neighbor" (Exod 20:16). But when we blame others, not ourselves, for the spoiling of creation (blaming politicians, for instance, or environmentalists, or other countries, or even God's will or providence) we bear false witness. We ignore our environmental interdependence and co-responsibility. If we say we have no clear God-given responsibility for local and global creation care, we bear false witness against God's Word!

God says, "You shall not covet your neighbor's house . . . or anything that belongs to your neighbor" (Exod 20:17). God says to practice mutual respect, especially with regard to those things that properly "belong" to us as God's creatures. The earth does not belong to us, but the right to the proper enjoyment of the land and its beauty and bounty does belong to us. This right belongs to the whole human family—certainly not just to ourselves or our family or nation or religion. Creation care means not coveting the land or the economic advantages or profits of others.

If we consider the ecological setting of the Ten Commandments, we see how our intentional actions as well as our unthinking habits actually defy God's Word. Loving God and keeping his commandments (Deut 7:9) means not putting our conveniences and customs ahead of following God's way. If we spoil creation and multiply its groaning, we daily break God's Word.

But there is a larger picture here: the whole sweep of the divine economy. The Apostle Paul puts the pain of creation in the largest possible context: "We know that the whole creation has been groaning in labor pains until now" (Rom 8:22). All creation groans, a groaning that traces back to the fall. But like a woman in labor, the whole "creation waits in eager expectation" for the full revelation of God's redemptive liberation and healing. "For the creation was subjected to frustration, not by its own choice, but by the will of the one who subjected it, in hope that the creation itself will be liberated from its bondage to decay and brought into the freedom and glory of the children of God" (Rom 8:19–21 TNIV).

This we know from Scripture: creation is groaning in its bondage to decay, but waiting . . . waiting . . . waiting in eager, hopeful anticipation for God's salvation to be fully accomplished. How is all creation groaning in bondage to decay? The Bible doesn't explain fully. God tells Adam, "Cursed is the ground because of you." But as we saw, this does not mean that the earth itself is evil or under a curse from God. It means rather that the whole creation is bound and restrained as a consequence of human sin. As John Wesley wrote, "The *ground* or *earth*, by the sin of man, is made *subject to vanity*, the several parts of it being not so serviceable to [our] comfort and happiness as they were when they were made."[4] Together earth's "several parts" constitute earth's physical ecology. Brian Walsh and Sylvia Keesmaat write, "From a biblical perspective, ecological brokenness is rooted in human sin. Creation groans in travail (Rom 8:22) because of the disobedience of the human steward of creation."[5]

Earth's "bondage to decay" is amply documented today. The created order is subject to entropy, the second law of thermodynamics. It is running down, moving from order to disorder. Scripture seems to teach that this is also the consequence of the fall, of human sin, though how this can be is not at all clear.[6]

Nonetheless, the groaning of creation is ever more audible today. Consider four key evidences of creation's groaning: climate change, increasing threats to the oceans, deforestation, and species depletion. Many other ecological issues confront us, but these especially deserve our attention because they interact with every other environmental malady.[7]

4. Wesley, *Explanatory Notes Upon the Old Testament*, comment on Gen 3:17 (emphasis in the original).

5. Walsh and Keesmaat, *Colossians Remixed*, 195.

6. The Bible does not specify precisely in what ways the created order was affected by the fall and the flood. Some would object to drawing any connection between the creation's "bondage to decay" and the scientific "law" of entropy. There clearly is at least a link analogically, and perhaps even more directly. Climate and weather were affected by the fall and the flood, according to Genesis, and these may be symptomatic of larger physical changes introduced into the created order through human sin. On the significance of (and debates about) entropy, see Nürnberger, *Prosperity, Poverty and Pollution*, 334–55. "Even social structures, cultures and convictions have a tendency to disintegrate" (ibid., 336). The certainty of creation's liberation and human ethical responsibility for creation care do not depend on the equation of entropy with creation's "bondage to decay," but it is empirically true that wasteful lifestyles speed up the process of entropy (deterioration). Entropy and gracious "extropy" are discussed in Snyder, "Energies of Church Renewal," chapter 9 in Snyder, *Yes in Christ*, 185–200.

7. See the excellent summary in Sabin, *Tending to Eden*, chapter 7, "The Global View." Sabin focuses particularly on deforestation, biodiversity, land degradation, oceans and water, and climate change. In his review of the evidence, Hertsgaard lists the effects of climate change as harsher heat waves (and more powerful blackouts), stronger storms, more disasters, more disease and pestilence, less water (except when there is more), less food, more fires, and mass extinctions. Hertsgaard, *Hot*, 51–60.

CLIMATE CHANGE AND GLOBAL WARMING

The most pressing large-scale threat to the earth today is human-induced climate change—now increasingly recognized by earth's nations.[8] As long ago as 1896 the Swedish chemist Svante Arrhenius worried that increased burning of coal, oil, and firewood was adding millions of tons of carbon dioxide to the atmosphere. "We are evaporating our coal mines into the air," he wrote. The result would be "a change in the transparency of the atmosphere" that could heat the planet to intolerable levels. Discovery of global warming in the late 1970s showed that Arrhenius likely was on the right track.[9]

Multiple UN and other scientific studies project a dramatic rise in global temperatures over the next century unless humans stop pumping greenhouse gases into the air. And even if that were to stop immediately, the effects will continue for decades, at least. A 1990 study by 250 leading climatologists predicted a rise in earth's average temperature of about one degree Celsius by 2025 and three degrees before the end of the twenty-first century. That would be the fastest increase in history. Recent studies vary in their results, but the trend line is clear. Earth is running a fever. Continuing temperature increases could raise sea levels about half a foot by 2030 and three times that by the end of the century. A rise of only five degrees Celsius (nine degrees Fahrenheit) is believed to have triggered the last ice age.[10]

Debates about climate change continue, especially among politicians and some Christians and professional commentators. The benign-sounding Global Climate Coalition, heavily funded by energy and automobile corporations, has spent millions on "a public disinformation campaign" designed to convince the public that global warming is "little more than a politically inspired hoax" and that climate change is just theory, not fact.[11]

But there is little debate among climatologists and oceanographers. Kevin Trenberth, head of the climate-analysis section at the National Center for Atmospheric Research in Boulder, Colorado, says, "There is no doubt that climate is changing and humans are partly responsible" so that now the "odds have changed in favor of more intense storms and heavier rainfalls."[12]

Already in August of 2004, a full year before Hurricane Katrina, *Business Week* ran the cover story, "Global Warming: Why Business Is Taking It So Seriously." The *Business Week* article noted that Republican Senator John McCain had concluded, "The facts are there. We have to educate our fellow citizens about climate change and

---

8. By way of definition, Hertsgaard points out that, "*global warming* refers to the man-made rise in temperatures caused by excessive amounts of carbon dioxide, ethane, and other greenhouse gases in the atmosphere. *Climate change,* on the other hand, refers to the effects these higher temperatures have on the earth's natural systems and the impacts that can result: stronger storms, deeper droughts, shifting seasons, sea level rise, and much else." Hertsgaard, *Hot,* 5.

9. Weiner, *Next Hundred Years,* 29.

10. Monastersky, "Global Warming," 391.

11. Hertsgaard, *Hot,* 6–7.

12. Kloberdanz, "Global Warming."

the danger it poses to the world." Carnegie Institution ecologist Christopher Field noted, "It's increasingly clear that even the modest warming today is having large effects on ecosystems. The most compelling impact is the 10% decreasing yield of corn in the [U.S.] Midwest per degree" of warming. In the past several years a number of far-seeing companies have begun to invest seriously in cleaner, more ecologically friendly sources of energy. These are absolutely necessary since the burning of fossil fuels is the major human source of global warming.[13]

Recent updated reports further confirm the climate-change peril. *New York Times* columnist Thomas Friedman notes "how insistently some of the world's best scientists have been warning—in just the past few months—that climate change is happening faster and will bring bigger changes quicker that we anticipated just a few years ago." Christopher Field of the Carnegie Institution's Department of Global Ecology at Stanford University said, "We are basically looking now at a future climate that's beyond anything we've considered seriously in climate model simulations." Similarly Joe Romm, climatologist at the Massachusetts Institute of Technology, warns that if present practices continue, by 2100 earth's surface temperatures will rise much higher than humans have ever known.[14]

Research by the Paris-based International Council for Science has shown that nitrous oxide (N_2O) is an even more potent greenhouse gas than is carbon dioxide (CO_2), which has been much more studied. The amount of nitrous oxide in the environment has grown dramatically due to widespread use of nitrogen-rich fertilizer in corporate farming. "Humanity has hijacked the 'nitrogen cycle,' as the passage of that gas into and out of the atmosphere is known, for its own use," notes *The Economist* in reporting the research. "What seems certain is that the nitrogen cycle is changing faster and more profoundly than the carbon cycle," speeding up global warming. Since corn and other crops used to make biofuels are rich in nitrogen, the manufacture and use of biofuels (burning food to run cars) further damages earth's climate, rather than preserving it.[15]

As climate studies pile up, environmental feedback loops become clearer. A *Washington Post* report on the annual meeting of the American Association for the Advancement of Science noted, "The pace of global warming is likely to be much faster than recent predictions, because industrial greenhouse gas emissions have increased more quickly than expected and higher temperatures are triggering self-reinforcing feedback mechanisms in global ecosystems."[16] An updated MIT report also highlighted new discoveries in the way multiple climate factors such as greenhouse-gas emissions and heat transfers jointly interact. The report notes, "No one of these effects is very strong on its own, and even adding each separately together would not fully explain the higher temperatures. Rather than interacting additively, [however,] these

13. "Global Warming: Why Business Is Taking It So Seriously."
14. Friedman, "Mother Nature's Dow."
15. "Biofools."
16. "Scientists: Pace of Climate Change."

different effects appear to interact multiplicatively, with feedbacks among the contributing factors, leading to the surprisingly large increase in the chance of much higher temperatures."[17]

For this reason, we might better speak of *climate chaos* than climate change, says Hans Schellnhuber, director of the Potsdam Institute for Climate Impact Research in Germany. Climate change and its effects are "nonlinear," he notes. "I'm not so concerned about a gradual climate change" to which we can adapt; "I'm worried about triggering positive feedbacks that, in the worst case, could kick off some type of runaway greenhouse dynamics."[18]

Multiple effects and multiple feedbacks—this is the way ecology works, whether we're talking about science or sin. As Christians, when we hear of climate change we don't think only of science and economics. We think of the groaning of creation, and we think ecologically.

OUR THREATENED OCEANS

Earth's oceans are so vast that they were long thought immune to any significant damage from human civilization. However, recent decades have shown just how intimately connected land, air, and water really are—and therefore how mutually vulnerable. The huge oil spill in the Gulf of Mexico in 2010 is dramatic proof of the ocean's fragility.

A key factor is the Great Ocean Conveyor Belt that helps sustain the ecological balance which makes earth habitable. Only in recent decades have scientists confirmed the existence of this great circulating "ocean river" that nourishes earth's ecosystem. The global circulation of warmer and cooler ocean currents, it turns out, is a major cause of earth's moderate climate, as well as bringing other benefits. (Search "ocean conveyor" on the Internet and in two seconds you find abundant sources!)[19]

The Great Ocean Conveyor is powered largely by melting ice, so the melt rate of the Arctic ice mass is a major issue for climate. This is where global warming comes in. With excessive melting, "the conveyor belt will weaken or even shut down," oceanographers say, bringing disastrous global climate change.[20] Should that happen, *Business Week* notes, "Europe and the Northeastern U.S. would be far colder. . . . This isn't science fiction: The conveyor has shut down in the past with dramatic results."[21]

This is the science that lies behind the melodramatic 2004 movie, *The Day After Tomorrow*. Though the movie was overdone and the timeline unrealistically compressed, the science behind it is real.

17. MIT Joint Program on the Science and Policy of Global Change, "Greenhouse Gamble."

18. Quoted in Hertsgaard, *Hot*, 68.

19. See for example http://www.enviroliteracy.org/article.php/545.html and resources listed there.

20. United Nations Environmental Programme 2005.

21. "Global Warming: Why Business Is Taking It So Seriously," 68.

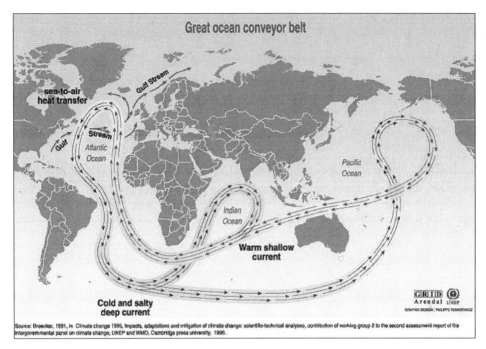

The Great Ocean Conveyor Belt

The Great Ocean Conveyor Belt is the oceanic parallel to the circulation of the air—with which it is ecologically linked. It is a life-giving flow, literally. But the burning of forests and of fossil fuels in our cars and SUVs, power plants, and industrial vehicles threatens it. When flowing normally, the conveyor belt demonstrates the harmony rather than the groaning of creation. Yet today it is part of the larger picture of earth's struggling ecology. It is a reminder both of the wonder of God's good creation and of the need for responsible creation care.

Important as the Great Ocean Conveyor is, it is only part of the story of ocean health and illness. The ocean's acid level is rising alarmingly, threatening marine life in new ways. A report by the National Research Council in the U.S. notes that the oceans are 30 percent more acidic than 200 years ago, now absorbing over a million tons of carbon dioxide every hour. James Barry, senior scientist at the Monterey Bay Aquarium Research Institute in California, testified before Congress in early 2010, "Acidification is changing the chemistry of the oceans at a scale and magnitude greater than thought to occur on Earth for many millions of years and is expected to cause changes in the growth and survival of a wide variety of marine organisms, potentially leading to massive shifts in ocean ecosystems."[22]

Another issue is the new international race to exploit the ocean's rich mineral resources. As polar ice caps melt, many nations—Canada, the United States, Russia, Norway, Denmark—are staking claims to the North Pole and its resources. Attempts at

22. Blumenthal, "Group Sounds Alarm."

deep-sea mining are expanding. A global mineral "gold rush" is heating up. All of this adds to the deep groaning of creation.[23]

DEFORESTATION

Deforestation usually gets less media attention than do climate and weather issues, but it is a major contributor to famine, poverty, and migration. Haiti and several countries in Africa are critical examples. This is doubly an ethical issue since it's both a matter of responsible creation care and of compassion for the poor. When trees disappear people suffer not only in the short run but for generations.

Klaus Nürnberger notes that population growth naturally "leads to an increased impact on nature: forests are chopped down, grazing is overstocked, agricultural lands are over-utilised, footpaths change into gullies, soil erosion takes away the topsoil, and water is polluted. The deterioration of the natural resource base again increases misery, thus leading to further population growth, further pressure against the system, greater security needs of the system, greater impact on nature, and so forth [in] a vicious circle, or rather a vicious network."[24] Deforestation, combined with desertification and related factors, leads "to the large scale migration of 'ecological refugees' in search of grazing, agricultural land or urban sources of income."[25]

These ecological and social impacts of deforestation are hugely aggravated by the large-scale destruction of forests by transnational agribusinesses and other corporations. This is a burgeoning part of the global economy. The forests of poorer nations are being ravaged in order to fuel the world's economic growth.

This is why planting trees is a creative act of creation care. Reforestation, both through small local projects and on large scales that deal with the political and social realities involved, is a key way to attend to creation's groaning. Think of the cycle of the life of a tree, from seed to seedling, to the seed-producing mature growth. Deforestation and reforestation are opposing acts that represent cycles of death and cycles of life.

SPECIES DEPLETION

God fills the earth with an amazing array of creatures and seems to delight in the profusion. "God created the great sea monsters and every living creature that moves, of every kind, with which the waters swarm, and every winged bird of every kind. And God saw that it was good" (Gen 1:21). "God made the wild animals of the earth of every kind, and the cattle of every kind, and everything that creeps upon the ground of every kind. And God saw that it was good" (Gen 1:25). Later when God ordered up the ark he told Noah, "Of every living thing, of all flesh, you shall bring two of every kind into the ark, to keep them alive with you; they shall be male and female" (Gen

---

23. "Suddenly, A Wider World below the Waterline" and "Seabed Mining."

24. Nürnberger, *Prosperity, Poverty and Pollution*, 29.

25. Ibid., 88.

6:19). God decreed an everlasting covenant with the earth (Gen 9:13). Specifically this is a covenant, God tells Noah, "between me and you and every living creature . . . for all future generations" (Gen 9:12). It is important to note that this three-dimensional covenant (God, humans, creatures) has never been revoked, and largely defines human stewardship on earth.

God delights in his creatures and wills their protection as part of the well-being of the created order. Given creation's complex earth-heaven ecology, human destruction of species violates the covenant in respect to all three parties. The creation groans.

Genesis 9 values all living things and "places them just as squarely under God's direct provision and protection" as human beings, say Fred Van Dyke and his coauthors in *Redeeming Creation: The Biblical Basis for Environmental Stewardship*: "What is the fate of those who set out by design, by ignorance or by selfishness to destroy what God has pledged himself to protect? What will be the outcome of having been on the wrong side of God on an issue of covenant preservation, the fate of the world's endangered species? It is on the basis of God's covenant protection of his creation, consistent with the value he has already imparted to it and with his determination to redeem it, that we believe it matters very much."[26]

Species depletion may seem a remote concern. We don't see it and don't really feel it. It is such a low-pitched groaning, we don't hear it. Yet it actually touches human well-being in multiple ways. Disappearing species are often the first signs of potentially lethal environmental changes. Still undiscovered plants and animals may yield cures to deadly human diseases.

Genetic diversity is, in fact, key to planetary health. In the long run, genetic depletion probably poses as great a threat to humankind as does climate change. Every living thing has its ecological niche and role. True, one vanished species might be replaced by another, but in the process, overall ecological richness is diminished.

These, however, are human-centered arguments. From a biblical standpoint, the reason we pay attention to earth's creatures is that they belong to God, not to us. Life forms are not to be destroyed, abused, or patented. Whether we fully understand why or not, diverse species exist, first of all, for God's glory and pleasure, and only secondarily for our benefit. Kingdom Christians help protect endangered species as part of their service to God, as well as for their own flourishing. The more we are attuned to God's heart and purposes the more we also hear this part of creation's groaning. Global warming would not have happened if Christians had read their Bible more carefully and more literally in what it says about the earth.

These four meta-issues—climate change, threatened oceans, deforestation, and vanishing species—represent a whole world (literally) of concerns that fall within the circle of creation's disease and healing. The point is that all these issues interlock. They all fit together in a vast ecology. Biblically speaking, they are all part of *God's* ecology and economy, of God's *oikos* and *oikonomia*. We are talking about more than science here.

---

26. Van Dyke et al., *Redeeming Creation*, 77.

Again we see how creation groans from human sin. And not only because of Adam and Eve's sin, but because of the ongoing infidelity of God's covenant people right up to today. Jesus' followers either amplify the groaning—thus further burdening the earth—or respond healingly, embodying by their actions the hope and assurance of all creation healed through Jesus Christ, in the power of the Spirit.

Romans 8 sets the groaning of creation within a larger story of hope. In view of Jesus' resurrection, Paul says, "I consider that the sufferings of this present time are not worth comparing with the glory about to be revealed to us" (Rom 8:18). Paul—in fact, all of Scripture—is very realistic about the pain and the suffering. But Paul sees creation's suffering as "labor pains" (Rom 8:22)—a hopeful image.

Paul identifies a threefold groaning in Romans 8: All creation groans (vs. 22). "We ourselves, who have the first fruits of the Spirit, groan inwardly while we wait for . . . the redemption of our bodies" (Rom 8:23). And God himself in his Spirit intercedes for us "with groanings which cannot be uttered" (Rom 8:26 KJV); "with sighs too deep for words" (NRSV). This profound threefold groaning shows again that the Bible is the story of God, the people, and the land. Through Jesus and the Spirit, God is deeply engaged in salvation—a comprehensive healing of sin's disease. The good news of Jesus Christ is the complete cure for the disease of sin in all its ecological dimensions, all its cancerous fibers and filaments. Creation healed, indeed.

7

The Gospel

A Complete Cure

> On either side of the river is the tree of life with its
> twelve kinds of fruit, producing its fruit each month; and
> the leaves of the tree are for the healing of the nations.
>
> (Rev 22:2)

SOMETHING ASTOUNDING HAPPENED IN Seoul, Korea, on New Year's Day, 2005. David Yonggi Cho, founding pastor of the world's largest church, made a public confession. Cho told his congregation,

> The Bible says, "For God so loved the world that he gave his only Son, so that everyone who believes in him may not perish but have eternal life." All these years, I misinterpreted it. I understood that God so loved *human beings*, not *the world*, that he gave his only Son. What is the world? In the world, there are all things such as people, society, sky, land, ocean, plants, insects and animals. The Bible says that God so loved the *world* that he gave his only Son; it does not limit the scope of the world to human beings.[1]

---

1. Lee, "Christian Spirituality," 9–10. We should make clear that Cho's conclusion—that the God of the Bible loves the whole created order—can be upheld *even if* his interpretation of John 3:16 is incorrect (i.e., if it is only concerned with humans). For, as this book has sought to show, Cho's conclusion can be given a far broader biblical basis.

Cho concluded, "Salvation without including our commitment to care for the ecosystem cannot be considered holistic salvation." His previously "limited understanding of the scope of God's plan for salvation had kept [Cho] from participating in God's integral salvation ministry in personal, social and environmental dimensions," says Young-Hoon Lee, who has now succeeded Cho as senior pastor at the Yoido Full Gospel Church.[2]

Yoido Full Gospel Church is awakening to salvation as creation healed. Perhaps Christian churches worldwide will come to affirm the really full gospel: the good news of complete redemption and transformation through Jesus Christ.

This chapter examines the good news of Jesus from the perspective of God's plan to heal creation, to overcome the multiple alienations arising from sin—and even more. We note how the gospel launches cycles of health and healing in a world that is otherwise spiraling toward death. The new creation we presently experience through Jesus Christ (2 Cor 5:17) is the firstfruits not only of our own salvation, but of all creation healed.

"It is good news that God cares about all that he has created," says Scott Sabin.[3] Scripture presents salvation as an immense divine plan for the redemption of all creation, "the restoration of all things" (Acts 3:21 ASV). We read in Ephesians 1:10 that God has a plan (*oikonomia*) for the fullness of time to bring everything in heaven and earth together in reconciliation under the headship of Jesus Christ—*all things,* things in heaven and things on earth; things visible and invisible. The plan of redemption is as broad as the scope of creation and the depth of sin, for "where sin abounded, grace [has] much more [abounded]" (Rom 5:20 KJV). The cure for the disease of sin in all its dimensions is salvation in all its reach. God is that big. Jesus' atonement is that awesome. God's Spirit, who "moved upon the face of the waters" (Gen 1:2 ASV) at creation, is still moving.

We have traced the depth of the disease, the deep ecology of sin. Now we ask: What does the Bible tell us about its cure? Here is what we find: Jesus "himself bore our sins in his body on the cross, so that, free from sins, we might live for righteousness; by his wounds you have been healed" (1 Pet 2:24). Here Peter refers to the messianic passage in Isa 53:5, "But he was wounded for our transgressions, crushed for our iniquities; upon him was the punishment that made us whole, and by his bruises we are healed."

The Apostle Paul writes, "If the Spirit of him who raised Jesus from the dead dwells in you, he who raised Christ from the dead will give life to your mortal bodies also through his Spirit that dwells in you" (Rom 8:11). Here is the promise of physical resurrection after the pattern and by the power of Jesus' rising. God's "incomparably great power" that "raised Christ from the dead and seated him at [God's] right hand in the heavenly realms" is the same power now at work among "us who believe" (Eph 1:19–20). What's more, "the creation itself will be set free from its bondage to decay

2. Ibid., 10.

3. Sabin, "Whole Earth Evangelism," 29.

and will obtain the freedom and glory of the children of God" (Rom 8:21). This is precisely the Old Testament promise—the "universal restoration that God announced long ago through his holy prophets" (Acts 3:21).

THE GOSPEL OF HEALING

This is the full scope of salvation, as revealed in Scripture. An illustration from history shows what this means practically. John Wesley (1703–91), the Anglican scholar-evangelist whose ministry birthed the Methodist movement, was passionate about medicine and health. He carried a small bag of remedies along with his Bible. He thought British doctors charged too much and didn't really help the poor, so he compiled his favorite remedies in a cheap handbook that went through twenty-three editions. He called it *Primitive Physick: Or, An Easy and Natural Method of Curing Most Diseases*. Today we would call it something like *Home Medical Advisor*. It was Wesley's most popular book, though his journals and sermons also went through many editions.

Wesley's journals are full of surprises. We read for instance of Wesley visiting someone who is sick. Will he pray for the person's healing or whip out his satchel and give medicine? Often he did both. He believed God was concerned for both body and soul; soul and body.

Wesley was also fascinated by how soul and body *interact*. He could see that they did. In fact, his whole life long he was fascinated by the interplay of body, mind, emotions, and the world around us. Wesley began his *Primitive Physick* this way: "When man came first out of the hands of the Great Creator, clothed in body, as well as in soul, with immortality and incorruption, there was no place for physic, or the art of healing. As he knew no sin, so he knew no pain, no sickness, weakness, or bodily disorder. . . . The entire creation was at peace with man, so long as man was at peace with his Creator."

Sin upset this harmony, Wesley noted. Even so, through exercise, healthy eating, and simple remedies, people can still enjoy a good measure of health. Wesley noted that most cultures have a long history of useful traditional medicine: "[E]very father [passed] down to his sons what he had in like manner received, concerning the manner of healing both outward hurts and the diseases incident to each climate, and the medicines which were of the greatest efficacy for the cure of each disorder. It is certain this is the method wherein the art of healing is preserved among the American Indians to this day."

So Wesley prescribed a variety of medicines, "several remedies for each disorder," not only because one might be easier to get than others, but also "because the medicine which cures one man will not always cure another of the same distemper. Neither will it cure the same man at all times." Variety and experimentation were necessary.[4]

John Wesley knew the gospel was for body and soul, for communities, and in fact for all creation. He focused primarily on healing the alienation between people

---

4. Wesley, *Primitive Remedies*, 9–11, 17.

and God through Jesus Christ, because he knew that was the deepest need. But he was concerned for the whole person, and especially the poor. This broad concern was a major reason for Methodism's remarkable worldwide growth, as ably documented by David Hempton in *Methodism: Empire of the Spirit*.[5]

Living three centuries ago, Wesley could not foresee how creation would be groaning today—with groans like those described in the previous chapter. But due to his constant immersion in Scripture and the lives he saw changed, he knew the gospel offered a complete cure. That is precisely what both the church and the world need today: a sense of the full hope and power of the good news and its promise for our intricately intertwined world. The church needs a new sense that the gospel of Jesus Christ is "soul therapy," as Wesley put it, "God's method of healing a soul which is *diseased*." Using "soul" in the biblical sense of the whole person, Wesley wrote:

> Hereby the great Physician of souls applies medicine to heal *this sickness*; to restore human nature, totally corrupted in all its faculties. God heals our atheism by the knowledge of himself, and of Jesus Christ whom he hath sent; giving us faith, a divine evidence and conviction of God and of the things of God—in particular of this important truth: "Christ loved *me*, and gave himself for *me*." By repentance and lowliness of heart the deadly disease of pride is healed; that of self-will by resignation. . . . Now this is properly religion, "faith thus working by love," [bringing] conformity to the whole will and Word of God.[6]

The gospel really is good news about creation healed, and it reaches every area of need.

REALLY GOOD NEWS!

We proclaim our faith in the Triune God, maker and sustainer of heaven and earth. God sent his Son into the world in the power of the Holy Spirit to bring redemption and the new creation that is the kingdom of God. Jesus sent the Spirit to continue and multiply and complete the work he began. This is the "mission of God"—the *missio Dei*. The Holy Spirit acts in his world to achieve God's saving purpose. "God is still at work in this creation and not just [as] its maintenance engineer," Eugene Peterson notes.[7]

The church is in mission *because God is in mission*. God loved the world so much that he sent his only Son to give us eternal life through faith in him. Therefore the church is to love the world and bring the good news to people everywhere. Biblically speaking, this good news is the healing of creation. Faithful mission therefore encompasses not only personal evangelism, compassion, and social justice; it includes proclaiming and living out God's intent for all creation. The ecology of salvation matches the ecology of sin.

---

5. Hempton, *Methodism*. See also Snyder, *Radical Wesley*.

6. Wesley, Sermon 44, "Original Sin," *Works*, 2:184 (emphasis in the original). Wesley uses the Greek for "soul therapy," meaning "therapy" not in the modern psychological sense but in the original, more comprehensive, sense of healing.

7. Peterson, *Christ Plays*, 93.

This grand portrayal of Jesus Christ both honors our Savior and makes the good news more persuasive and winsome. Here is a gospel of total healing: the healing of creation, the restoration of all things—truly the whole gospel for the whole world.

Salvation through Jesus Christ by the Spirit is thus the story of how God is redeeming and transforming his creation. He calls his disciples to partner with him to bring creation's healing. This really good news can be summarized in five points:

1. *God created the universe.* "By faith we understand that the worlds were prepared by the word of God, so that what is seen was made from things that are not visible" (Heb 11:3). Therefore the world belongs to God, not to private individuals, corporations, or governments. We have no right individually or corporately to mistreat it or claim it solely for our own interests. Human beings are stewards of what God has made and loaned to us.

The created order has unique value because it comes from the hand of God—from the very life of God. Life is sacred because its source and sustainer is the Holy Trinity. Jonathan Merritt points out, "The Bible doesn't teach the sanctity of human life, but the sanctity of all life. Although plants and animals—from flowers to frogs—are not equivalent to humans, they remain creations of a God who loves them and has placed value on them."[8]

Creation is good because God is good. "The Lord is good to all, and his compassion is over all he has made" (Ps 145:9).

2. *The created order is in some deep sense diseased because of sin.* Although earth's nonhuman biosystems cannot sin, the created order suffers the "enmity" that human rebellion brought into the world (Gen 3:14–19). As we have seen, "the creation was subjected to futility" and is in "bondage to decay" (Rom 8:20–21). This complex spiritual-physical-moral-ecological disorder is pictured graphically in the Old Testament prophets.

Disorder, disease and disharmony cry out for healing through the Word of God.

3. *God has acted in Jesus Christ to reconcile the creation to himself.* God is bringing transformation and re-creation through the God-Man. In the biblical vision, God acts in Jesus not to save men and women *out of* their environment, but *with* their environment. We are environed beings. Just as God will not ultimately save us without our works, so God will not ultimately save us without his good creation—his great good work, human and nonhuman.

The New Testament makes clear the tremendous cost of Jesus' reconciling work—his life of obedience and suffering, his death on the cross. Precisely because Jesus "humbled himself and became obedient to the point of death," God "highly exalted him and gave him a name that is above every name," and all will bow before him (Phil 2:8–11). All will submit, and the time will come "for destroying those who destroy the earth" (Rev 11:18).

Jesus—in all his functions as prophet, priest, and king—is the great healer. As Richard Foster writes, "The threefold office of Christ is the divinely revealed solution

8. Merritt, "Keeping an Eye on the Sparrow," 32.

to the threefold disease of sin: ignorance, guilt, and corruption. Christ by prophetic light overcomes our ignorance and the darkness of error. Christ by priestly merit takes away our guilt and reconciles us to God. Christ by kingly power removes our bondage to sin and death. The prophet enlightens the mind by the spirit of illumination; the priest heals the heart and soul by the spirit of compassion; the king subdues our rebellious affections by the spirit of sanctification."[9]

These are some of the dimensions of Jesus' great healing work. In gratitude and by the Spirit, Christians are able faithfully to fulfill their mission-and-stewardship mandate: to work out the implications of Jesus Christ's prophethood, priesthood, and kingship in all areas of culture and creation.

As both Savior and Model, Jesus calls all who believe in and follow him to a life of discipleship and stewardship, marked by the cross. True disciples of Jesus are to "walk as he walked" (1 John 2:6). Jesus forms a community marked by the cross, participating in the birth pangs of the new creation. Later we will see what this means in practice.

4. *God has given the church a mission for this world and the world to come.* The redemption God is bringing promises a new heaven and a new earth. What does this really mean? Biblically, it *does not* mean two common but extreme views: it does not mean only saving the earth from oppression or ecological collapse, nor does it mean disembodied eternal life in heaven and the annihilation of the material universe. Rather, it means reconciliation between earth and heaven, the heavenly city descending to earth (Revelation 22), the reign of God that in some way reconstitutes the whole creation through God's work in Jesus. The model for the new heaven and earth is the actual, historical, flesh-and-blood resurrection of Jesus.

5. *As Jesus-followers, we are called to live our lives as members of churches, communities, and economies in harmony with the biblical principles of justice, mercy, truth, and responsible interrelationship.* We thus learn to think interdependently and ecologically in all areas, including the church and our relationship to the earth. Christians—in fact all humanity—have a God-given responsibility to "care for the garden." According to the Bible, good news for the earth (and "all creatures great and small") is an integral part of redemption and new creation in Jesus Christ through the Spirit.

CREATION HEALED THROUGH JESUS BY THE SPIRIT

God brings salvation through the work of Jesus Christ—his incarnation, life, death, resurrection, ongoing reign, and eventual return. Jesus' redemptive work is pictured in broadest scope in John 1, Hebrews 1, Colossians 1, Ephesians 1, and similar passages. These key texts are a window into salvation as creation healed. "The restoration of God's creation was the reason for the incarnation of the eternal Son and Word of God in Jesus Christ," notes Thomas Torrance in his great study, *The Trinitarian Faith.*[10]

9. Foster and Beebe, *Longing for God,* 119. Foster is here reflecting on John Calvin's discussion of the three "offices" of Jesus Christ.

10. Torrance, *Trinitarian Faith,* 102.

Ephesians 2:8–9 states, "For by grace you have been saved through faith, and this is not your own doing, it is the gift of God—not the result of works, so that no one may boast." This truth expands on Eph 1:10, God's "plan [*oikonomia*] for the fullness of time to gather up [literally, to join together under one head] all thing in [Jesus Christ], things in heaven and things on earth." This is God's "economy"—the literal translation of *oikonomia* and a key term in Pauline and early Christian theology.[11] It is God's "plan" or "administration" that he is accomplishing through Jesus, an economy that is by definition ecological.[12]

The plan (economy) of salvation pictured in texts like Ephesians 1, Colossians 1, and Hebrews 1 is this: *that God may glorify himself by reconciling all things in Jesus Christ*. The biblical vision is of all earth's peoples, and in fact all creation, united in praising and serving God (Ps 67:3–5; Rev 7:9–12; 19:6). This is another way of speaking about the kingdom of God in its fullness.

The key idea and dynamic here is *reconciliation*—a reconciliation that heals earth's multiple alienations. God's plan is to restore his creation, overcoming in judgment and glorious fulfillment the damage done to persons and nature through the fall. This plan includes not only the reconciliation of people to God, but the reconciliation of "all things in heaven and on earth." As Paul puts it in Colossians 1:20, it is God's intention through Christ "to reconcile to himself all things, whether on earth or in heaven, by making peace through the blood of his cross." Jesus brings peace, not only in the sense of forgiveness of sins but in the full biblical richness of *shalom*.

Central to this plan is the reconciliation of persons to God through the blood of Jesus. The reconciliation won by Christ reaches to all the alienations that result from our sin—alienation from God, from ourselves, between persons, and between us and our physical environment. The biblical picture therefore is at once personal, ecological, and cosmic. As mind-boggling as the thought is, Scripture teaches that this reconciliation even includes the redemption of the physical universe from the effects of sin, as everything is brought under its proper headship in Jesus (Rom 8:19–21).

In all these passages, Paul begins with the fact of individual and corporate personal salvation through Christ. But he places personal salvation within a picture of cosmic transformation. The redemption of persons is thus the *center* of God's plan, but not *the circumference* of that plan. Paul switches between a close-up shot and a long-distance view. He uses a theological zoom lens, mostly taking a close-up view of personal redemption, but periodically zooming out to a long-distance, wide-angle view which takes in "all things"—things visible and invisible; things past, present, and future; things in heaven and things on earth; all the principalities and powers—everything in the cosmic-historical scene. To God be the glory in heaven and on earth!

---

11. Prestige, *God in Patristic Thought*, 57–68; Reumann, *Stewardship*, 11–24. The fact that *oikonomia* is often translated "dispensation" in the KJV is not unrelated to the rise of dispensational theories of various sorts (as noted in chapter 4), though such theories distort the biblical meaning of the term.

12. The biblical meaning of "economy of God" is more fully elaborated in Snyder, *Liberating the Church*, chapter 2, "Economy of God."

Although this comprehensive picture of salvation is most fully elaborated in Paul's writings, it is also the larger biblical view. All the promises of cosmic restoration in the Old Testament apply here, reaching their climax in Isaiah's sublime vision (Isa 11:6–9; 35:1–10; 65:17–25). Here is "the peaceable kingdom" pictured so poignantly by the American primitivist artist and Quaker preacher Edward Hicks (1780–1849), visualizing Isa 11:6–9:

> The wolf shall live with the lamb,
>> the leopard shall lie down with the kid,
>> the calf and the lion and the fatling together,
>> and a little child shall lead them.
> The cow and the bear shall graze,
>> their young shall lie down together;
>> and the lion shall eat straw like the ox.
> The nursing child shall play over the hole of the asp,
>> and the weaned child shall put its hand on the adder's den.
> They will not hurt or destroy
>> on all my holy mountain;
> for the earth will be full of the knowledge of the Lord
>> as the waters cover the sea.

The main message of the book of Revelation is the harmonious uniting of all things under the lordship of Christ as all evil and discord is destroyed (Rev 1:5–7; 5:5–10; 11:15; 21:1—22:5). In a somewhat different context, this same "summing up" perspective is pictured in Hebrews 1–2. Jesus' parables of the kingdom point in this direction. And Isaiah, Peter and John speak of God creating a new heaven and a new earth (Isa 65:17, 66:22; 2 Pet 3:13; Rev 21:1).

The testimony of Scripture is consistent: the same God who created the universe perfect, and sustains it in its fallen condition (Heb 1:3), will restore all things through the work of Jesus in the power of the Spirit.

Christians know therefore that the gospel of Jesus Christ offers the essential necessary resources for facing all earth's problems, including care of the earth. Here the bold claim of Scripture that in Jesus Christ all things cohere (Col 1:17) takes on deeper and broader meaning. As Charles Colson writes, "Every part of creation came from God's hand, every part was drawn into the mutiny of humanity against God, and every part will someday be redeemed. This means caring about all of life—redeeming people and redeeming culture."[13] Yes, and in fact all creation.

According to the gospel, the decisive act in history was Jesus' resurrection. This was God's dramatic triumph over death and despair, the reversal of discord and incoherence. This is the practical source of our practical hope. Jesus' resurrection *in fact* makes and is making everything new. "Jesus' resurrection is the beginning of God's new project not to snatch people away from earth to heaven but to colonize earth with the life of heaven. That, after all, is what the Lord's Prayer is about."[14]

13. Colson, "Reclaiming Occupied Territory."
14. Wright, *Surprised by Hope*, 293.

Meanwhile, a battle rages. There will yet be many casualties. But we are energized by the assurance that the one who won the decisive victory over evil in his resurrection at a precise point in history *will* bring the story to final, glorious fulfillment. The goal of history is final harmony and reconciliation, justice and moral symmetry—the ultimate triumph of justice, mercy, and truth. The Apostle Peter called it "the time of universal restoration" (Acts 3:21).

PREDATION AND ATONEMENT

Jesus' atoning death and resurrection in the power of the Holy Spirit thus has cosmic significance. It accomplishes our redemption and starts us on the path of new creation.

In his earthly ministry Jesus freed some people from the physical and demonic predation of sin. He showed his power over nature—most notably in his sign miracles and in calming the sea. Yet in his life and in his cross he submitted to sin's predatory powers—then decisively triumphed over them in his rising.

Jesus' victory inaugurates the new creation *now*, in the Spirit's power. But this occurs only in God's way, not according to the wisdom of the world (1 Cor 1:20). Thus we wait for—but also live in—the new creation in expectant hope that "the creation itself will be set free from its bondage to decay and will obtain the freedom of the glory of the children of God" (Rom 8:21). Thus the new creation through Jesus' death and resurrection means the end of death and predation. "The last enemy to be destroyed is death" (1 Cor 15:26).

The fourfold alienation brought by human rebellion against God not only broke the harmonious relationships, the healthful ecology, of creation as it came fresh from God's hand. Sin turned God's creatures into predators rather than partners. The self-centeredness introduced by sin means that God's creatures are now ready to sacrifice each other's well-being in order to satisfy their own desires—even if that means harm or even death to the other.

In some sense, all sin is predation. Perhaps predation in fact goes to the heart of sin.[15] At least in terms of its behavioral manifestations, all sin is predatory. It is the willingness of God-imaged persons (and the proclivity of all creatures) to sacrifice the life of another for their own (perceived) benefit.

From this view, the essence of sin may not be pride so much as the desire and willingness to exalt oneself, or prefer oneself, over another. Humans prey on each other and on God's creatures—on the earth itself. Foolishly (for sin blinds), humans even try to practice predation on God, using God for selfish ends.

There is hardly a more horrid and yet more illuminating example of the predatory power of sin than so-called "ethnic cleansing," exterminating whole groups—whether Jews, Gypsies, or native tribes—as a matter of policy. In his book *Ordinary Men,* Christopher Browning shows how, step by step, ordinary folks can become vicious predators with seared consciences. The Nazis sent Reserve German Police Battalion

---

15. We use predation here as a heuristic theological model, recognizing its limitations and the importance of other models.

101 into Poland to help massacre the Jews. Gradually most of these common citizens became mindless killers—though, significantly, a few resisted.

Very few of these men had ever "fired a shot in anger or even been fired on, much less lost comrades fighting at their side," Browning notes. "Once the killing began, however, the men became increasingly brutalized. As in combat, the horrors of the initial encounter eventually became routine, and the killing became progressively easier."[16]

Browning shows how ideology and war intensify the predatory power of evil. "War, a struggle between 'our people' and 'the enemy,' creates a polarized world in which 'the enemy' is easily objectified and removed from the community of human obligation. War is the most conducive environment in which governments can adopt 'atrocity by policy' and encounter few difficulties in implementing it." War in the service of ideology is even more vicious, Browning notes; he quotes Stanley Milgram's observation that "ideological justification is vital in obtaining willing obedience, for it permits the person to see his behavior as serving a desirable end," thus deadening the conscience.[17]

Such organized, corporate predation shows how cultural mechanisms can multiply and intensify the effects of sin. This is a key dynamic of the ecology of sin. It is not an either/or, however—*either* sin in the heart *or* in society—clearly it is both/and, as the very concept of ecology suggests, with multiple layers of reinforcement.

But sin and predation begin in the heart. They spring from a ruptured relationship with God, and thus a derangement of human character. Because of sin humans become predators, "human sharks," as John Wesley put it.

The Bible explicitly teaches that God's purpose is to put an end to *all* predation. "The wolf shall live with the lamb, the leopard shall lie down with the kid, the calf and the lion and the fatling together, and a little child shall lead them. . . . They will not hurt or destroy on all my holy mountain" (Isa 11:6, 9). If the created order will indeed be "liberated from its bondage to decay," then this promise in Isaiah is not just metaphor or allegory. It is a picture of the new creation; the promise of deliverance from earth's bondage to decay and predation—and a signpost for how we are to live today.

Is the extermination of all predation really possible within the ecology of the created world? This is a legitimate question. Some say no; that the very existence of earth's life forms requires that some creatures devour others.

We don't know, and probably can't explain scientifically, how God could end all predation. How could all carnivores become vegetarians, for example, feeding on non-sentient life forms? But we do have the promise of Scripture and the powerful wonder of Jesus' resurrection. Jesus was not a predator in his relations with others. The whole creation will one day be like him. The risen Jesus did eat fish and meat, for the creation had not yet been fully healed. But we still have the promise of healing. So when we read "the wolf shall live with the lamb," we may find ourselves echoing John Wesley: This promise "may be literally as well as figuratively understood."[18]

16. Browning, *Ordinary Men*, 161.

17. Ibid., 162, 176, quoting Milgram, *Obedience*, 142.

18. Wesley, Sermon 64, "The New Creation," in Wesley, *Works*, 2:509.

SALVATION AS TRINITARIAN DRAMA

Predation in fact gives us profound insight into the meaning of salvation. The predatory nature of sin illuminates Christ's atoning sacrifice for us. God's offering up of his own Son in Jesus' death could look like predation. Some have even called it "divine child abuse." But what turns this argument on its head is that Jesus offered himself freely, and that Jesus' death and resurrection is a Trinitarian drama. God gave himself, refusing to follow the world's and Satan's way of predation.

This was the only way to break the cycle and disorder of predation and set humanity and human history on the right course, the divine course of self-giving and loving concern for the other, with cycles of life and healing rather than death. Colin Gunton puts it this way: "It is for the redemption of this world, to restore and perfect its capacity to praise its maker—in other words, to bring it into true otherness and relation in its various dimensions—that the Father 'gives up' the Son into that relation with the world which involves his bearing its disorder and stain; and the incarnate Son reciprocates, in the Spirit, the Father's sacrifice by giving up his life as a perfect offering of human praise and obedience."[19]

Jesus died for our sins and rose in the power of the Spirit. He is the firstfruits of the new creation, and by the Spirit we already with Christ become firstfruits of the new creation (1 Cor 15:20; Rom 8:23; Jas 1:8; Rev 14:4).[20] Jesus' resurrection brings healing and deliverance to both the human and the nonhuman creation. Presumably Jesus would not have died for the non-human creation if it had not been the home of his specially-imaged human creation.[21] So helping human beings come to transforming faith in Jesus is always a central focus of Christian mission. But this is no either/or, for God wills, now as always, to save his people *and* his creation and bring heaven to earth (Rev 21:1–2), not to take disembodied souls to a nonmaterial heaven. That would be Gnosticism or Neo-Platonism, not biblical Christianity.

In Romans 8, Paul *simply assumes,* without elaborating, the Old Testament view of salvation as involving both people and the land. This is an important and often overlooked point. When Paul begins talking about the whole creation in verse 19, he is introducing no strange or alien subject. He expresses the biblical worldview, the biblical "all things" perspective. Since salvation is all about God, God's people, and God's land, *of course* one must speak of the liberation of all creation itself from its "bondage to decay" when we speak of salvation and Jesus' resurrection! How could salvation mean anything else?

Jesus' atonement through his death and triumphant resurrection is a cosmic-historical act through which all creation is redeemed—potentially and partially now, and fully when the kingdom comes in fullness. "Justification is a trinitarian act of cosmic proportions that is based in the Father as the one who creates and elects, in

---

19. Gunton, *Promise of Trinitarian Theology,* 206.

20. On the rich biblical, eschatological significance of firstfruits, see "Pentecostal Renewal of the Church," chapter 12 in Snyder, *Yes in Christ,* especially 261–66, 275–79.

21. Biblically speaking, we do not know this for sure.

the Son as Redeemer, and in the Spirit as the giver of life," writes Frank Macchia. It is "the Holy Spirit's work to bring about justice through new creation." A fully Trinitarian understanding of God's work in Jesus Christ, Macchia suggests,

> would not confine the Spirit's role to the subjective or even interpersonal dimensions of the life of faith. . . . The Spirit's involvement as advocate and intercessor for creation is implied in the Spirit's groaning in and through us for the suffering creation (Rom 8:26). The divine will and judgment to justify and redeem may be seen as a response to an advocate and an intercessor already present in all of creation. If the "Father's" will to justify is expressed in the divine will to send the Son, and the Son's will is expressed in the willingness to be sent, the Spirit's will would therefore be in the cry from creation to receive the gift that will be sent and in the cooperation with the Son in the shaping of the christological answer.[22]

Atonement is not primarily about punishment, not most basically about penalty. It is fundamentally about overcoming the results of sin, the hurt of violation—which necessarily involves suffering the consequences. It is the death of predation. This is what Jesus, and Jesus alone, accomplished through the cross and resurrection. Jesus is thus the great healer, and by his Spirit he summons the church to join in both the suffering and the healing.

God the Trinity wills to heal all creation. The biblical promise is that radical, awesome, and hope-inspiring. New creation in Jesus by the Spirit births the firstfruits community that *lives now* the new-creation life in the fullness of biblical "all things" hope (Rom 8:28, 32; 11:36; Eph 1:10; Col 1:16–20).

Salvation is indeed a Trinitarian drama. Though the inner life of the Trinity is a mystery, it looks to us like the perfect instantiation of *symbiosis*—living together in mutual support for mutual benefit. Healthy symbiosis is God's way. Satan's way is predation. In true symbiosis, all the participants (two or more) gain. Each nourishes and is nourished by the other. However, predation crosses the line from good to evil; here the life of one means the death or harm of the other. Through predation, symbiosis becomes parasitism.

Here again we feel the deep ecology of creation and redemption. Creation healed means sensing the *connections* between things—because of who the Trinity is. It means seeing how total and complete God's redemptive plan really is.

All this is consistent with the biblical doctrine both of creation and new creation. For as N. T. Wright notes:

> in the Bible heaven and earth are made for each other. They are the twin interlocking spheres of God's single reality. You really understand earth only when you are equally familiar with heaven. Your really know God and share his life only when you understand that he is the creator and lover of earth just as much as of heaven. And the point of Jesus's resurrection, and the transformed body he now possesses, is that he is equally at home in earth and heaven and can pass

---

22. Macchia, "Justification," 207, 209.

appropriately between them, slipping through the thin curtain that separates us from God's blinding reality.[23]

CYCLES OF LIFE AND CYCLES OF DEATH

The Bible speaks of times and seasons, the rhythms and cycles of the created world. God placed "lights" in the sky, marking off "seasons and . . . days and years" (Gen 1:14). Though the good order of creation was damaged by the fall, God still promises: "As long as the earth endures, seedtime and harvest, cold and heat, summer and winter, day and night, shall not cease" (Gen 8:22). In the new creation we see the tree of life "producing its fruit each month," offering its leaves "for the healing of the nations" (Rev 22:2).

Cycles and seasons are built into the created order. God, of course, is still sovereignly and providentially engaged in this world. "He changes times and seasons, deposes kings and sets up kings" (Dan 2:21). In the biblical picture, history is governed by God's purposes. History has a goal, a *telos* (hence the word *teleological*). God is guiding the historical drama toward new creation in fullness, as we have seen.

Within this drama we trace the cycles of seasons and years and "the music of the spheres." This is how God put the world together. In this sense, history is both linear (tracing a line or trajectory) and cyclical (in some ways repeating itself—a theme of the book of Ecclesiastes).

Another way to say the same thing: God's plan is both *historical* and *ecological*. In this book we have already seen several ways in which both are true. We must however avoid the error of thinking that history is a force in itself, an autonomous fate or *karma* to which humans (or even God!) are in some way subject. There is no autonomous "force of history." God the Trinity is the author of history, the Divine Dramatist, and his work is both historical and ecological.

Human history is linear but also operates in the rhythms and cycles of nature. In today's fallen world, history is the interplay of cycles of life and cycles of death (violence, decay, entropy) over time. Through the resurrection and Pentecost, God's Spirit gives the church the power to live in, and multiply, cycles of life and hope. Faithful discipleship disrupts the cycles of death with redemptive cycles as we wait expectantly for final liberation, new creation in fullness.

People who run regularly learn that cycles can work either for them or against them. If you put on extra weight, you'll probably run slower. Yet if you push against the resistance and run faster, you'll likely lose weight. The more you run, the more fit you feel. The more fit you feel, the better you run. Run regularly and you tend to lose weight. Add more pounds, and you run slower. This is life. We live by cycles, and those cycles work either for us or against us.

23. Wright, *Surprised by Hope*, 250–51.

The same holds spiritually. The more we exercise ourselves spiritually (in biblically sound ways), the more we grow spiritually. The more we grow spiritually, the more disciplined we grow.

The same principle holds with the physical creation and the way we treat it. Humans have dominion over the earth—constructively or destructively. Cycles of life and cycles of death abound within the created order. The cycles of death have been introduced by sin, including the human sin of neglecting creation care. Cycles of life (including Sabbath, worship, and Jubilee) are God's way. They are living cycles of life in our ongoing discipleship on earth.

Through creation care and a fully earthed discipleship, we can change "vicious cycles into virtuous cycles, where each change makes the next change more effective," writes Scott Sabin. "A vicious cycle of deforestation and poverty can become a virtuous cycle of reforestation and economic empowerment. When the Holy Spirit is involved and kingdom relationships are modeled, a virtuous cycle can become a victorious cycle."[24]

Empowered by the Spirit and Christian community, such cycles of life are not just for our own good. They don't just make us "more spiritual." They *actually contribute* to the coming of the new creation in fullness. In our discipleship, we can learn to live by the rhythms of nature and the Spirit, not just the cycles of the workday or TV or the sports schedule.

This is one reason recycling makes so much sense. We'll say more about that later when we talk about the practicalities of creation care. But here is the larger point: Recycling works *against* cycles of death and *with* cycles of life. Fred Van Dyke and his coauthors hint at this in their prophetic book *Redeeming Creation*: "We extend a Christian response to God's creation when we begin to use less and save more. Those who recycle their own bottles and cans live with integrity. Those who persuade the city council to make recycling part of the normal garbage-collection procedure have changed their world. The reason to recycle materials or to compost leaves goes beyond compliance with local ordinances. It is within compliance of greater ordinances, cycles that God created for the world in which we live."[25]

Once we grasp the real ecology of life and death, we get a sense of the interconnection between, say, recycling Styrofoam and other plastics and the larger cycles of creation and of God's plan. Cycles of life and death are physically, materially, economically true for the created order just as much as they are for our bodies and spirits, our products and our plans.

God's Spirit is at work in all these dimensions. The Holy Spirit works against the death cycles, nurturing cycles of life and healthy living as we follow the Jesus Way. This is the biblical promise.

24. Sabin, *Tending to Eden*, 32.
25. Van Dyke et al., *Redeeming Creation*, 45.

THE GOSPEL OF FLOURISHING

"In fact Christ has been raised from the dead, the first fruits of those who have died. . . . for as all die in Adam, so all will be made alive in Christ. But each in his own order. Christ the first fruits, then at his coming those who belong to Christ" (1 Cor 15:20–23). Jesus Christ is the firstfruits of what is to come. In the end, the tree of life continually flourishes with nourishing fruit and with "leaves . . . for the healing of the nations" (Rev 22:2).

So Jesus is the prototype as well the redemptive basis of new creation. He is the point of coherence between the visible and invisible worlds (Col 1:17). "The final coming together of heaven and earth is . . . God's supreme act of new creation, for which the only real prototype—other than the first creation itself—was the resurrection of Jesus. God alone will sum up all things in Christ, things in heaven and things on earth. He alone will make the 'new heavens and new earth.'"[26]

If Jesus' body was recognizably the same after his resurrection, so also the earth will be recognizably the same after its renewal. To the degree that Jesus' resurrected body was and is physical, so also will be the earth and our bodies. To the degree that there was continuity in Jesus' body before and after his resurrection, so also there will be physical continuity between the old heaven and earth and the new.

The good news of Jesus Christ is God's complete cure for the whole ecology of sin. It heals our multiple maladies, all the alienations that flow from human rebellion against God. It is the certain basis for the full healing of the divorce between heaven and earth.

The gospel has released forces of healing into the world which even now are bringing transformation—often out of sight, like a hidden seed that sprouts and grows, even if we do not know how (Mark 4:27). These hidden healing changes often occur silently in thoughts and attitudes, or in family relationships, or personal reconciliation between people who have been at enmity with one another. They occur in the long radiating influences of kindness, truth, and intellectual insights, perhaps over years and generations. While invisible, they are often more real and transformative than the news that gets reported in the communications media.

Salvation means creation healed—and it means even more. It means creation flourishing. Consider the composer Ludwig von Beethoven. Tragically, he grew deaf even as he was writing his greatest symphonies. At the end he could no longer hear the orchestra playing his greatest works.

What might we have wished for Beethoven? The healing of his deafness? Certainly—but much more! We would wish for his healing *so that his creativity could flourish.* Healing is not an end in itself. It is the means toward something greater and grander.

When we are ill, we hope to be healed—not just so we can survive, but so we can continue to develop, to create, to grow in wisdom, to help others, to more fully glorify God—to flourish in all the ways God intends.

---

26. Wright, *Surprised by Hope*, 208.

So also in the larger picture of God's plan and purpose: God's economy is more than salvation as commonly understood, more than creation healed. It is creation *flourishing* unendingly to God's glory. God's work is not just restorative; it is creative, generative, beautifully bountiful. Salvation is not just reversing the direction, not just returning to the starting point. The plan is to liberate all creation for God's original and unending project. Rather than just a return to square one, salvation means freeing creation to move and expand everlastingly in the opposite—that is, the right, good, beautiful, and bountiful—direction.

Salvation means creation healed, but *shalom* in its fullness means ongoing health, beauty, creativity, and even more—with many wondrous surprises. It means all creation reaching its full good, glorious, pure, and poetic potential—which no one knows except the Holy Trinity. "No eye has seen, no ear heard, no mind has conceived what God has prepared for those who love him" (1 Cor 2:9 NIV).

The larger picture, then, looks like this:

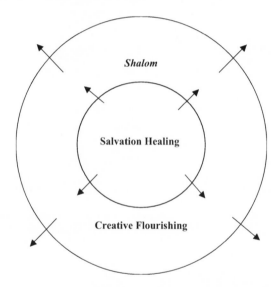

From Creation Healed to Creation Flourishing
How big is God's *oikos* and *oikonomia*?

The gospel is a complete cure—and more. Colin Gunton expresses this beautifully in his little book *Christ and Creation*. He writes, "What is the end of creation? That all things may through being perfected praise the one who made them."[27] Gunton elaborates:

> If creation is to an end, namely that all that is should within the structures of time and space come to be perfected in praise of the creator, what we call redemption is not a new end, but the achievement of the original purpose of creation. It only takes the form of redemption—of a "buying *back*"—because of sin and evil. . . .

27. Gunton, *Christ and Creation*, 96.

What is realized in the incarnate involvement of the Son in time and space is the redirection of the creation to its original destiny, a destiny that was from the beginning *in Christ*, for all creation is through and to the Son.[28]

What then is the human role within the present order? "The human race is given on earth the task of realising this perfectedness, through our relation to God, through our relation with each other, and through our care of the non-personal creation, which cannot be perfected without us."[29]

Here through Jesus Christ by the Spirit is true good news: Total healing, full flourishing, and strategic mission for God's people.

Edward Hicks, *The Peaceable Kingdom*

In *The Peaceable Kingdom*, Edward Hicks (1780–1849) visualizes the prophecy in Isaiah 11:6–9 in which predators and prey exist harmoniously, as a child leads them in peace. A Quaker, Hicks is often viewed as America's greatest and most influential American Primitivist artist. He painted dozens of versions of the same scene. The painting illustrates N. T. Wright's comment, "Art at its best draws attention not only to the way things are but also to the way things will be, when the earth is filled with the knowledge of God as the waters cover the sea. That remains a surprising hope, and perhaps it will be the artists who are best at conveying both the hope and the surprise" (Wright, *Surprised by Hope*, 224–25).

28. Ibid., 94.
29. Ibid., 96.

Interlude

God Works in Cycles and Seasons

God works in cycles and seasons,
God works in rhythms and years.
God moves through long generations—
God guides through joys and through tears.

"For everything there's a season,"
Time for all things in God's plan.
God works in exquisite freedom,
God has the cosmos in hand.

God works through lines and through circles,
God works in things small and great.
God renews life and guides history;
He is no prisoner of fate.

God works through ways straight and crooked;
God works in both time and space.
God owns both order and chaos;
God works in judgment and grace.

God works in ways of his choosing;
Fashioning goals quite his own.
His ways to us seem mysterious;
They are like seeds that are sown.

God worked through cycles of Mary,
Hannah, Melchizedek, Paul;
God works through rhythms and seasons,
Sagas of kings' rise and fall.

God works supremely in Jesus—
Broken the bread; spilled the wine—
God works through his gracious Spirit;
God works in Pentecost time.

He guides the days and the seasons,
He guides the birds through the air.
God works his gracious redemption—
We are but dimly aware.

God has his own eco-logic;
God has his own kingdom plan.
God works in Trinity wisdom;
God holds the world in his hand.

Cycles of cloud and of water;
Cycles of wind and of rain;
Deep-moving flows of the ocean,
Circling, returning again—

Cycles of love and of spirit;
Cycles of seasons of grace;
Times of refreshing revival,
Gaining fresh light from his face.

God is the world's great Composer,
Dramatist, Architect, King—
Rhythms of art; sounds melodic—
God gives us music to sing.

God simplifies deepest mysteries;
God complicates best-laid plans.
We walk in wonder before him,
Trusting our ways in his hands.

God in our own lives recycles—
Physically, through blood and cell;
Spiritually, through prayerful rhythms;
Stewardly, as we serve well.

We are a part of the story;
We have our key roles to play—
If we but follow the Master,
Spirit-led, day after day.

We are God's keepers of nature;
We are his stewards of grace.
We live the Spirit's commission;
Stewarding both time and space.

God makes us all his recyclers—
This is no secular whim.
This is no plot of the devil—
God makes us stewards for him.

God is the Lord who recycles,
Bringing forth things old and new.
God even makes evil serve him,
Turning the false to the true.

God is the perfect Recycler—
No wastage; nothing is lost—
Whether in storm, wind, or fire,
God wins the world through the cross.

"Praise God in his sanctuary!
Praise him for his mighty deeds!
Praise him with loud clanging cymbals!
Praise him, all that lives and breathes!"

(Psalm 150; Ecclesiastes 1–3; Genesis 9; Ps 18:26; Eph 1:10, 2:10;
1 Pet 4:10)

PART THREE

The Healing Mission of God

8

Mission

God, People, Land

Ask the animals, and they will teach you;
the birds of the air, and they will tell you;
ask the plants of the earth, and they will teach you;
and the fish of the sea will declare to you.

(Job 12:7–8)

T HE MISSION OF GOD is to heal all creation. God will indeed fulfill his promise of a "new heaven and a new earth."

The church is on mission because God is on mission. Paul says that "if anyone is in Christ, there is new creation."[1] And so God "has given us the ministry of reconciliation"; we are to "work together with him" in sharing God's grace of reconciliation and healing. "Now is the day of salvation!" (2 Cor 5:17—6:2).

John Piper famously wrote, "Missions exist because worship doesn't."[2] That is true, but it is not the whole story. Mission also exists because worship is often too weak, too limited—more otherworldly than God is.

---

1. The Greek does not say "a new creation" or "he is a new creation." It says simply: "new creation." Consequently the indefinite article "a," included in most translations, has been deleted in this quotation from the NRSV.

2. Piper, *Let the Nations*, 11.

This book's first section showed how the church over time suffered a theological divorce between heaven and earth, seriously shrinking its sense of mission and its practice of discipleship. The biblical vision of creation healed was lost. By viewing sin as disease and salvation as the cure, Section Two laid the groundwork for the recovery of a vision of salvation as creation healed. We expanded traditional views of sin through the concept of ecology, showing how God's creation, and therefore its illness, is deeply ecological. The gospel is the complete cure for the dreadful disease of sin.

The final two sections of the book apply the healing medicine of the gospel to the church's understanding and practice of mission. In the present section (chapters 8–10) we examine the relationship between God, people, and land as revealed in Scripture, showing how this enriches a biblical theology of the kingdom of God. We elaborate the meaning of mission as healing. The final section of the book then reconceives the church as God's community on earth for the sake of healing creation.

This chapter (1) explains the significance of God's covenant with the land in Genesis 9, (2) shows how the mission of God concerns both people and the land—that is, all creation, and (3) issues a new invitation to mission that takes seriously these biblical teachings and redemptively, "healingly," engages today's challenges.

GOD'S COVENANT WITH THE EARTH

The human race is sadly and lethally alienated from the land. We are estranged from Nature (as we often call it). This is a key dimension of the ecology of sin, as we saw in chapter 5. Sin separates us from the land as well as from God.

Remarkably, one of the first things God does in the history of salvation is to make *covenant* with the land. Why is this, the first of all the biblical covenants after the flood, so often overlooked?

God brings salvation through a series of covenants, climaxing in the new covenant through the blood of Jesus (Luke 22:20; Heb 12:24). These covenants are key markers in the biblical narrative. They are all linked, all essential in the ecology of the story. We won't fully understand the later story if we miss the significance of this first covenant. This "everlasting covenant" with the earth is beautifully and powerfully pictured in Gen 9:8–17.

God says to Noah after the flood, "I am establishing my covenant with you and your descendants after you, and with every living creature that is with you, the birds, the domestic animals, and every animal of the earth with you, as many as came out of the ark" (Gen 9:9–10). All covenants have a "sign," and the sign of this one is the rainbow.

Yahweh is a covenant-making God. He takes the initiative to bring healing and restoration, starting with this covenant with Noah and the land. A covenant is a form of contract or agreement; the word literally means "a coming together." In the Bible, covenant has special meaning because it expresses God's character and initiative. The biblical covenants reveal and bring about God's purpose and plan for salvation—the restoration of fallen creation.

The Meaning of the Genesis 9 Covenant

Three things stand out when we examine the covenant God makes in Genesis 9. First, it is *a three-dimensional covenant*. It is multidimensional, ecological. The covenant includes not only God and Noah's family, but "every living creature of all flesh that is on the earth" (Gen 9:16).

It is fascinating to see whom God includes in this covenant, and what this passage says about God, Noah, and earth's creatures. God is the initiator: "I am establishing *my* covenant" (Gen 9:9). God both establishes and sustains this covenant, the rainbow being the sign. So the covenant is first of all God's, not ours. It is beyond human manipulation. The passage is emphatic—three times God refers to "my covenant."

The second party is Noah and his family—that is humankind, all the human family that descends from Noah. It is not just Noah's immediate family, but "your descendants after you," God says, "for all future generations" (Gen 9:9, 12). Again, this is emphatic: A covenant between God and all humanity. Here is the theme of *generations* again—and so a covenant that reaches clear to our day.

The background here is the creation account in Genesis 1–2, with its emphasis on the good earth and all the creatures God made. Now, after fall and flood, Genesis 9 marks a new beginning. The plan of salvation really begins here, not with the calling of Abraham. This covenant is important in specifying the post-fall relationship between God and all humanity. God is the sovereign Creator and Sustainer; humans are his creation and his stewards of the earth.

The text emphasizes also the earthly dimensions of this covenant. All earth's creatures are included. Genesis 9 is surprisingly comprehensive here:

> "every living creature that is with you" (vv. 10, 12)
> "every animal of the earth with you" (v. 10)
> "every living creature of all flesh" (v. 15)
> "every living creature of all flesh that is on the earth" (v. 16)
> "all flesh that is on the earth" (v. 17)

The references become increasingly broad and inclusive throughout the passage. In verse 13 God, in fact, speaks of his "covenant between me and the earth"!

Why this stress on "*every* living creature"? This echoes the full variety of creatures God made at the beginning. It also recalls God's words to Noah to take "every kind" of creature into the ark (Gen 7:2). The "every creature" emphasis is also practical and ecological, a matter of human sustenance, because robust human health requires an abundance of creatures in wide variety, all in relative ecological balance. It reminds us too of God's care and concern for all creatures for all generations. Most amazingly, the "every creature" emphasis signals God's concern for *all* the creatures he has made, showing that God himself has a covenant with every creature, with every species! So Jesus says of sparrows, "not one of them is forgotten in God's sight" (Luke 12:16).

The Genesis 9 covenant is thus a three-dimensional covenant, not a narrow contract between God and humans only. It is a covenant between God, all people, and all the earth.

Second, this is a *covenant of preservation.* "Never again," God says, will he destroy the earth by flood. "As long as the earth endures, seedtime and harvest, cold and heat, summer and winter, day and night, shall not cease" (Gen 8:22).[3]

Four times God says, "Never again!" (Gen 8:21; 9:11, 15). This is God's promise to humanity, to the earth, and to himself. God promises to preserve the earth, working out his saving plan through the subsequent covenants he will make, culminating in the new covenant in the blood of Jesus. This covenant of preservation is thus also a *covenant of preparation.* God intends not merely to preserve but to create something greater. This first covenant with the land prepares the way for God's plan of salvation and new creation through Jesus Christ.

Third, this is *an everlasting, ongoing covenant.* It is not temporary, not interim; rather, it's a covenant "for all future generations" (Gen 9:12). Significantly, the phrase "everlasting covenant" here (Gen 9:15) is the same phrase used to describe later biblical covenants. The Bible uses the same language of the Genesis 9 covenant that it does of later ones. *God's covenant with the earth is unending.*

This may come as a surprise. Perhaps we assumed God's covenant with the earth was temporary, until Jesus' return. Not so. In fact, the *Septuagint* (the Greek version of the Old Testament) uses the word "eternal" here, the same word the New Testament employs for "eternal life."

Does God really have an eternal covenant with the earth and all its creatures? The Bible says yes—suggesting that the promised new heaven and new earth in some sense means the renewal, not the extinction, of God's creatures.

John Wesley, pondering this in his later years, concluded that God's covenant with his creation definitely is everlasting. He wrote a sermon on the subject, "The General Deliverance." Reflecting on his own long life and ministry, the whole sweep of history, the science of his day, and biblical revelation, Wesley wrote, "something better remains after death for these poor creatures [which like us] shall one day be delivered from this bondage of corruption, and shall then receive an ample amends for all their present sufferings." And so we ourselves should "imitate him whose mercy is over all his works." God's merciful plan of final restoration should "soften our hearts towards the meaner creatures, knowing that the Lord careth for them." It should "enlarge our hearts towards those poor creatures to reflect that, as vile as they appear in our eyes, not one of them is forgotten in the sight of our Father which is in heaven."[4]

In the Genesis 9 covenant, then, God acts to *preserve* the earth, limiting his judgment (the flood) so he can fulfill his larger purposes. Here again we see the constant

---

3. It has sometimes been suggested that seasons as we now know them, with the annual alteration of "cold and heat, summer and winter," is a defect introduced into earth's ecosystem by the fall and flood. Whether this is true (or plausible) or not does not change the significance and relevance of God's present covenant with the earth.

4. Wesley, Sermon 60, "General Deliverance," *Works,* 2:449.

biblical focus on God's concern for people and the land, the environment we inhabit—the earth God has given us to enjoy and care for, helping it to flourish. We see again God's plan to save people *with* their environment, not *out of* their environment.

GOD'S EARTH COVENANT TODAY

God's covenant with the earth is "everlasting," so clearly it was not cancelled by God's later actions. The rainbow sign ever reminds us that God's earth-covenant still holds. God says, "Whenever the rainbow appears in the clouds, I will see it and remember the everlasting covenant between God and all living creatures of every kind on the earth" (Gen 9:16). The rainbow is God's cupped hand over the earth. It shines forth his care and concern for the world and its creatures. God sees the rainbow—and *remembers* his covenant. Do we? Enjoying the rainbow, do we recall God's covenant with all his creatures?

The fact that the Noahic Covenant of Genesis 8–9 still holds is important for three reasons. First, *the Genesis 9 covenant teaches us the true relationship between God, people, and the earth.* God's earth covenant clarifies the *actual relationship* in effect right now between God and all his creatures. God continues as Creator and Sustainer. Human beings and the earth continue to be under his care. All people without exception depend moment-by-moment both on God and on the earth, God's gift. This is not theory; it is fact. The earthly side of this multidimensional covenant—that is, the interdependence between people and the physical environment—is now fully documented by the natural sciences, as well as being taught in Scripture.

Much confusion reigns here. On the one hand, many non-believers deny or are blind to our dependence upon God. On the other hand, many Bible-believing Christians deny or are blind to our fragile dependence upon the physical environment. Focused on spiritual things, Christians easily forget our dependence upon earth and miss the place of the earth in God's plan.

So Genesis 9 is important both to our physical wellbeing and to our understanding of salvation. Both are part of God's economy, the plan of salvation. Genesis 9, and in fact the whole biblical worldview, teaches us that the nature of the created order is *interrelationship* between God, humans, and the earth. It continues to be true that:

- God is the Creator and we and the whole earth depend upon him.
- Humans are dependent *both* on God *and* on the earth—on God for life and salvation; on the earth for life in all its physical dimensions, including food, oxygen, water, and space.
- The earth and all its creatures depend on humans for their wellbeing and even their survival.

In the larger sweep of the biblical narrative, the Noahic covenant is foundational for the new heavens and earth that Scripture promises. The new creation is not a second creation *ex nihilo*; it is the restoration and enhanced flourishing of the original creation. This becomes clearer as we examine Genesis 9.

Note again that the God-people-earth connection is a *covenant* relationship. Its source is God's sovereign action and initiative; his grace and mercy. Here the biblical worldview clashes sharply with two common distortions. Some views blur the distinction between humans and the rest of creation. New Age philosophies and some environmentalists and eco-theologians do this. On the other hand, many people are blind to God's concern for the earth and all its creatures, so are oblivious to our shared responsibility to care for the earth. This also is a serious distortion. Biblically, it is wrong *either* to elevate the environment over human beings *or* to stress human uniqueness to the point that we miss our utter earth-dependence. The biblical way is not to place one over the other, but to see the *interdependence* built into God's order. Here we think ecologically if we think biblically, rather than assuming a clashing hierarchy of priorities.

Since this interdependence is covenant-based, earth's abundance is not just "raw materials" for industry. It is not just "natural resources" or "real estate." The fruit of the earth is not just "commodities." It is God's good, morally valued creation—a partner in a covenant pact with God that still holds. Since God is in covenant with the earth, we sin against God when we fail to care for the earth. "The earth that nourishes me has a right to my labor and my strength. It is not for me to despise the earth on which I live. I owe it my trust and my thanks," wrote Dietrich Bonhoeffer.[5]

Second, *the Genesis 9 covenant is important today because it reminds us of God's concern for all living creatures.* Earth's life forms exist *for God,* not just for human use or enjoyment. The creatures have their own right to exist and flourish, because they were created by God. They are God's, not ours.

The Bible speaks repeatedly of God's concern for earth's creatures. This is a major theme of the Psalms, especially. "O Lord, how manifold are your works! In wisdom you have made them all; the earth is full of your creatures" (Ps 104:24). This is a key theme in Job, as Job finally learns the full wonder of God and his creation, with God addressing him "out of the whirlwind" (Job 38:1). "Have you entered the storehouses of the snow, or have you seen the storehouses of the hail, which I have reserved for the time of trouble, for the day of battle and war?" (Job 38:22). God goes on to speak of lions, ravens, mountain goats, deer, wild donkeys, ostriches, horses, hawks, great water creatures—and of the clouds and weather and the stars.

A sign of Solomon's wisdom was that he "spoke about plant life, from the cedar of Lebanon to the hyssop that grows out of walls. He also spoke about animals and birds, reptiles and fish" (1 Kgs 4:33).

The last thing God says to Jonah in the book that bears his name is: "Should I not be concerned about Nineveh, the great city, in which there are more than a hundred and twenty thousand persons who do not know their right hand from their left, *and also many animals*?" (Jonah 4:11). The city's "many animals" do not escape God's notice. They are the final echo of the book.

"The righteous care for the needs of their animals, but the kindest acts of the wicked are cruel" (Prov 12:10). These reminders undergird the larger biblical theme of the healing of the land (2 Chr 7:14) and "the healing of the nations" (Rev 22:2).

5. Bonhoeffer, *Meditations on Psalms,* 90.

A third key implication of the Genesis 9 covenant follows: *Here is the biblical basis for a theology of creation care.* In the biblical view, earth's creatures and species are to be "stewarded" for four key reasons: God created them; God delights in them; we depend on them; they are part of God's larger plan.

This abiding commission for all humanity has particular meaning for Christian mission, as we will see in later chapters. Creation care is important for our discipleship, our spiritual growth in all dimensions. It enriches Bible study (God's plan for the earth), prayer (meditating on God's wonders; interceding for earth), witness (telling and showing God's love and concern), life patterns (living lightly, in harmony with the earth).

Christians are countercultural precisely at this point. We have a different basis for looking at environmental issues. God the Creator and his everlasting earth covenant are the touchstones. We see the Noahic Covenant as part of the larger biblical story of creation, the disease of sin, and the healing restoration that comes through Jesus by the Spirit. We see creation care in light of the story of Jesus—his incarnation, life, teachings, death, resurrection, reign, return, and final triumph. We think of Jesus' literal, physical, flesh-and-blood resurrection and the promise of our own resurrection, "the redemption of our bodies" (Rom 8:23), not just our spirits. This is a renewed heaven and earth, not a disembodied heaven. The resurrection of Jesus renders incoherent the idea that salvation means living eternally in heaven.

In other words, we see Genesis 9 in light of Romans 8, and vice versa. We see the line that connects them. We see also how Genesis 9 illuminates the remarkable promise in Revelation 11:18, "The time has come for judging the dead, and for rewarding your servants the prophets and your people who revere your name, both great and small—and for destroying those who destroy the earth" (TNIV).

The Genesis 9 covenant opens the door to a comprehensive view of the mission of God, the *missio Dei.*

MISSION: GOD, PEOPLE, LAND

Since World War II, especially, Christian theology has wrestled with the idea and reality of the "mission of God." The missions of Nazism and Communism were pretty clear. Nationalism easily became an idolatrous mission in both East and West, and free-market capitalism quickly became the renewed mission of the West. But what of *God's* mission, the mission that transcends all human ideologies and idolatries?[6]

Mission of God means this: God the Father sends the Son into the world in the power of the Holy Spirit to bring salvation in all its dimensions, including the ultimate reconciliation of all things: the kingdom of God in its fullness. The church's mission

---

6. Good summaries of the development of *missio Dei* theology are found in Bosch, *Transforming Mission,* 389–93; Yates, *Christian Mission,* 127–32, 163–64, 196–97; Leffel, *Faith Seeking Action,* especially 18–23; Christopher Wright, *Mission of God,* 62–68; Bevans and Schroeder, *Constants in Context,* 289–304.

derives from this action of the Triune God. It is to embody and proclaim the "good news of the kingdom"—of salvation through Jesus Christ.[7]

Biblical Basis

Key dimensions of the mission of God, and thus of the church's mission, are revealed— in fact, often assumed—throughout Scripture. Take this instructive example in Deut 8:10. Moses says to Israel, "When you have eaten and are satisfied, praise the Lord your God for the good land he has given you" (TNIV). This simple statement is profound. In the first chapters of Deuteronomy, God reveals to Israel what it means to be his people as they enter the promised land. Moses reminds Israel of all he had taught and all that had been revealed at Sinai and through the desert wanderings. Moses is about to depart, and he carefully reinforces the revealed truth about who God is and what it means to be God's people in God's land. This one small verse holds all the seeds of the biblical understanding of wholistic or comprehensive mission.[8]

See the structure of the verse. It speaks of three realities: God, the people, and the land. And it shows the proper relationship between the three:

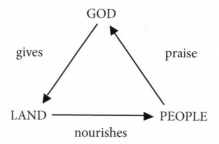

The story in Deuteronomy—in fact, throughout the Old Testament—is the story of God, people, and the earth. It is the story of God's action through a chosen people to restore harmony to creation by their being a blessing to all earth's peoples (Gen 12:3). This is the larger narrative underlying Deut 8:10, and also echoes the Genesis 9 covenant.

---

7. Noting the key influence of Karl Barth, especially, Bosch describes the initial formulation of *missio Dei* theology in 1952: "The classical doctrine on the *missio Dei* as God the Father sending the Son, and God the Father and the Son sending the Spirit was expanded to include yet another 'movement': Father, Son, and Holy Spirit sending the church into the world. As far as missionary thinking was concerned, this linking with the doctrine of the Trinity constituted an important innovation. . . . Our mission has no life of its own: only in the hands of the sending God can it truly be called mission, not least since the missionary initiative comes from God alone" and therefore cannot be "seen in triumphalist categories" but must be seen as "solidarity with the incarnate and crucified Christ. . . . Thus, next to the affirmation that the mission was God's, the emphasis on the cross prevented every possibility of missionary complacency" or hubris. Bosch, *Transforming Mission*, 390.

8. Though "holistic" and "wholistic" mean the same thing, the preference here is for the latter spelling (except in quoted material) as more obviously signaling the sense of "whole." At times we use the phrase "comprehensive mission" in view of the fact that in some circles "holistic mission" is becoming a mere cliché.

This verse specifies the *relationship* God intends between these three realities, these key "subjects." Three fundamental actions are indicated: (1) God *gives the land* to the people; (2) the land *provides food for* or nourishes the people; and (3) the people are to *praise* or worship the Lord. These actions form a perfect triangle, the relationship God intends between himself, his people, and his land. God gives the land, the land sustains the people, and the people are to praise God in response. The arrows move from God to the land, from land to the people, then back to God, completing the wholistic relationship—perfect *shalom.*

In other passages the arrows point the opposite way. God forms and blesses his people; the people are to enjoy and faithfully care for the land (Leviticus 25 and many other passages); and the land shows forth the glory of God (Ps 19:1 and many other passages). The model is this:

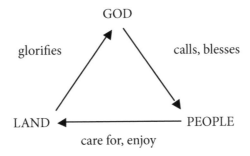

Here is *the God-intended relationship between Yahweh, his people, and the land.* Since in Hebrew, "land" and "earth" are the same word, this is actually a picture of the God-intended relationship between God, humankind, and the created order. This is the relationship, the *shalom,* which God intends but which has been disrupted by sin.

In the Old Testament, we learn that through Israel God begins a plan to restore creation. God intends *shalom,* a harmonious, reconciled interrelationship between himself, his people, and the land. Now the arrows point both ways, in perfect ecology. Here then is God's intent:

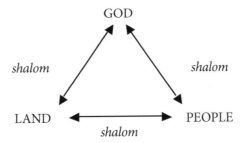

In the biblical narrative, God creates "the heavens and the earth" (Gen 1:1); he creates humans and places them on earth; and God plants a garden for the enjoyment and sustenance of the human community. This is a perfect picture of *shalom,* of the proper mutual relationship between God, humanity, and the earth.

This perfect ecology of *shalom* is beautifully captured in a key Old Testament image of Israel at peace: "They shall all sit under their own vines and under their own fig trees, and no one shall make them afraid" (Mic 4:4). In a measure this happened under King Solomon, when "Israel lived in safety, . . . all of them under their vines and fig trees" (1 Kgs 4:25). But this didn't last. Later, with Israel's destruction and exile, the image becomes an eschatological promise of the kingdom of God in fullness, as in Micah 4:4 and also Zechariah 3:10, "'On that day,' says the Lord of hosts, 'you shall invite each other to come under your vine and fig tree.'" Here is true *shalom*, peaceful and fruitful harmony between God, people, and the land. Sitting under your own vines and fig trees is a basic biblical image of creation healed.[9]

The story of the Bible is thus the story of God's perfect intent, then the disruption caused by human rebellion, and finally God's way of restoring the harmonious relationships that were disrupted and diseased by sin.

How does God undertake this mission of healing? We see in the Old Testament that God forms a special redemptive people and gives them a special land—the promised land. God's concern, however, is not just his chosen people, Israel, but in fact all the nations of earth. "The nations" is a key theme in the Old Testament, for God's plan is to bless all nations and include them in his redemptive work. Israel is chosen in order to show forth the truth of God and thus be a blessing to all the nations. God tells Israel, "If you obey me fully and keep my covenant, then out of all nations you will be my treasured possession. Although the whole earth is mine, you will be for me a kingdom of priests and a holy nation" (Exod 19:5–6 TNIV).

So Israel is to be God's priestly people among the nations, a contrast society to show who God is and what God intends. The mission of Israel, then, involves not only Israel's relationship with God but also her relationship with the earth and all its peoples. God is not just the God of Israel; he is the God of all the nations, of the whole earth.

The larger Old Testament picture, then, looks like this:

---

9. Similarly, the devastation of vines and fig trees becomes an image of judgment: The enemy "shall eat up your vines and your fig trees" (Jer. 5:17); "I will lay waste her vines and her fig trees" (Hos 2:12)—which in turn illuminates some of Jesus' actions and parables. See also 2 Kgs 18:31; 1 Macc 14:12.

As the plan of salvation unfolds in the Old Testament, we come to understand four essential things:

1. The Lord God is God of all peoples, not just of Israel.
2. God's plan includes the whole earth, not just the land of Israel.
3. God's plan includes all nations and peoples, not just the Hebrews.
4. God has chosen Israel in order to bring *shalom* to the whole creation.

We thus see how comprehensive God's plan is. And yet we do not yet see the fulfillment of this plan.

Israel's prophets promised that God would in time send a special servant-king, the Messiah, who would actually accomplish God's healing plan. Through the Messiah, God would himself bring perfect *shalom*, as pictured so beautifully in Isaiah 11 and many other passages. The first covenant would be swallowed up in a new covenant through which sin would be atoned for, God's Spirit poured out, God's law written on human hearts, and God's purposes finally fulfilled. The kingdom of justice and *shalom* would come in fullness. This was prefigured already in Abraham's encounter with Melchizedek ("King of Righteousness"), who was "king of Salem" (a form of *shalom*) (Gen 14:18–20).

What happens then in the New Testament? God's plan is stated in many ways. Paul says that through Jesus Christ God is reconciling the world (*kosmos*) to himself (2 Cor 5:19). God has a plan or "economy" (*oikonomia*) "to bring all things in heaven and on earth together under one head, even Christ" (Eph 1:10 NIV). The Lord Jesus Christ has been given the power "to bring everything under his control" (Phil 3:21 TNIV). Clearly God's plan of salvation as pictured in the New Testament is continuous with the Old Testament revelation. In the older Testament, we see God's concern for all peoples and the whole earth. So also in the New: God is concerned with all peoples and with the whole earth.

In *The Mission of God: Unlocking the Bible's Grand Narrative,* Christopher Wright shows that this is precisely what the Apostle Paul was announcing in his mission (comparing Acts 13:17–19 and 17:24–26). Using a triangular graphic similar to the one above, Wright shows how the gospel message expands the Old Testament economy of God, Israel, land to include all humanity and the whole earth, just as prophesied. "All that God did in, for, and through *Israel* . . . had as its ultimate goal the blessing of all nations of *humanity* and the final redemption of all *creation.*"[10]

The continuity from Old Testament to New Testament here is crucial. We stress this because Christian theology often over-spiritualizes God's saving plan, as we saw in the first section of this book. The New Testament pictures not a divine rescue from earth but rather the reconciliation of earth and heaven—of "all things, whether on earth or in heaven," things both "visible and invisible." God is "making peace through [Jesus'] blood," shed on the cross (Col 1:16–21). God's plan in both the Old and New

---

10. Wright, *Mission of God,* 395 (emphasis in the original). Although the model presented here was developed independently from Wright's, both make essentially the same points, since both are based on a comprehensive reading of the biblical narrative.

Testaments is to bring *shalom* to the whole creation. In this sense Christians are still "being saved," because ultimately no one experiences *shalom* in its fullness until the whole creation enjoys *shalom*.

Seeing this progression through both Testaments helps prevent a distorted or anemic understanding of salvation, and thus of the *missio Dei* and the church's mission. Moving from the Old Testament to the New we discover this key insight: in the new covenant, God's plan is both *internalized* and *universalized*. The inward thrust is intensified while the outward scope is expanded and made clearer. This internalization and universalization are in fact promised repeatedly in the Old Testament. In the New Testament we see the fuller, deeper meaning of what is promised in the old covenant. More precisely, in the New Testament God's salvation plan is:

1. internalized but not merely spiritualized,

2. universalized but not merely symbolized,

3. partially but not yet fully realized, and

4. clarified as to its final intent.[11]

The climax comes in Revelation 21 and 22 where we see the Holy City descending to earth—not souls ascending to heaven. "God's dwelling place is now among the people, and he will dwell with them. They will be his people, and God himself will be with them and be their God" (Rev 21:3 TNIV). Here is God's plan finally realized, and it is a plan "for the healing of the nations" (Rev 22:2).

We may go a step further, then, in picturing the comprehensive plan of salvation revealed in the Bible. The picture now looks like this:

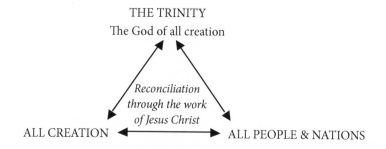

THE TRINITY
The God of all creation

Reconciliation through the work of Jesus Christ

ALL CREATION ←————→ ALL PEOPLE & NATIONS

Scripture thus reveals that the mission of God is to bring comprehensive reconciliation to the whole creation. This is the *missio Dei* which God is accomplishing through Jesus Christ in the power of the Holy Spirit. From this wholistic *missio Dei*, the church derives its mission.

11. Snyder, *Kingdom, Church, and World*, 74–76.

LIVING A TRANSCENDENT MISSION

This is not abstract theology. It is the church's call to mission. As the body of Christ, Jesus' own disciples, *we find our life and vocation within the mission of God.* We live with a transcendent mission that does not belong to us. We are not our own; we "were bought with a price" (1 Cor 6:19–20). This applies equally to God's mission through which each of us personally, all of us together, and the whole church universal find our meaning.

This is wholistic, for it involves not just our private lives or jobs but every area of our lives. Since God's mission touches the land as well as all peoples, it includes how we treat the land and its creatures as well as how we treat people. Simply put, all of this is part of one saving ecology.

To know God's mission is to live under that mission: to live it out. We have been given a comprehensive stewardship of all that we are and all that we "own," control, or influence—personal relationships, time, money, the whole physical creation.

This "surpassing value" (Phil 3:8) of God's mission thus gives direction to every area of life. It helps us discern the best use of one another's gifts. The overarching question becomes: Does this or that decision advance God's mission? Is it *consistent* with our mission as determined by the mission of God?

A FRESH INVITATION TO MISSION

Understanding God's mission biblically is thus an invitation to mission in today's world. God's Spirit calls us to be coworkers with Christ in proclaiming and living out salvation as creation healed.

Faithful Christian mission focuses on the healing of creation for both theological and strategic reasons: theological, because a biblically faithful view of mission necessarily includes what the Bible says about God's intent for the created order; but also strategic, because mission that is as broad as Scripture is much more persuasive in today's world. Do we want people of all nations and cultures to come to faith in Jesus as their Savior and Lord? Then we should proclaim and demonstrate that Jesus is the renewer of the whole creation, the whole face of the earth, and all the dimensions of life. Salvation is that big.

Looking back today over two millennia, we find ourselves somewhere between the beginning and the end of the story. We look back to the beginning in order to understand the journey and perhaps recover what has been lost. And we also look ahead, and look around at where the church is today. We are not yet at the end of the story—mysterious chapters remain. But we do stand at a remarkable time when the church is global and local as never before. We locate ourselves between the ancient church, on the one hand, and tomorrow's global church, on the other.

The church today is in fact at the beginning of a new, challenging, and most promising act in the drama. The stage invites us to act. Can we imagine strategic twenty-first century recoveries that help the church live into its authentic ancient future? Can we imagine being, in dramatically faithful ways and fuller dimensions, the "continuation of God's narrative?"[12]

Early in this book we found some troubling tendencies in the early life of the church—for example the shift from interactive community to hierarchical structure; from charism to institution. We traced the shift in the church's visibility from people and community to buildings and institutions. And we saw the widening divorce between heaven and earth, splitting the wholistic biblical worldview and undermining the biblical promise of restored heaven and earth. Perhaps in God's providence the church is now ready to experience the healing of these distortions. Here are four possible, hugely significant recoveries which together can mean a great new surge in mission:

A Clarified Focus on the Person and Work of Jesus Christ

Over the course of two millennia the grand biblical picture of Jesus Christ has been shrunk to something much smaller than what Scripture promises. Or the picture has been pulled apart into separate pieces, losing the grand mosaic. Today we need a renewed and clarified vision of Jesus, the promised Messiah who rescues his people and brings the kingdom of God in fullness.[13] Jesus, the crucified Savior, risen Lord, and reigning King. This means, in particular:

- A renewed focus on the biblical promises of what Messiah would accomplish.
- A fuller comprehension of the meaning of Christ's life and atoning death.
- A new emphasis on the meaning, power, scope, and hope of Jesus' resurrection and all it means for human beings and the whole creation.
- An emphasis (within a larger Trinitarian framework) on the Holy Spirit's work in bringing the new creation.

Result: Greater honor and glory to Jesus Christ in his *functional role* as Head of the church and bringer of new creation through the Spirit—truly the Great Physician.

A Clarified Vision for the Promise of the Kingdom of God as God's Will Done "on Earth as in Heaven"

Popular Christian piety and much theology see heaven as an ethereal spiritual "place" quite unlike earth, a place of escape at death—a "brighter world above." We have inherited this unbiblical divorce of heaven and earth and think God willed the divorce! Heaven, we think, is where we go, *permanently,* when we die. It is divorced from the biblical promise of the renewed earth and the reconciliation of "all things."

This is not just a question of the nature of life after death. At heart, it is a distorted view of the kingdom of God, both present and future. We need a vision of God's reign that:

---

12. Webber, *Ancient-Future Worship*, 179–83. See also Webber, *Who Gets to Narrate the World?*

13. Frost and Hirsch, *ReJesus* is prophetic in this regard.

1. affirms that Jesus now reigns as King, though in a hidden way;

2. proclaims and expects that God will bring "new heavens and a new earth, where righteousness is at home" (2 Pet 3:13);

3. helps us live now in that certain hope and expectancy, according to the values and virtues of God's reign, becoming "co-workers [*sunergoi*] for the kingdom of God" (Col 4:11) in its visible, if partial, realization in our present time; and

4. knows that this kingdom vision is key in the "continuation of God's narrative." As Robert Webber put it, the biblical promise and mandate "to live in God's will and to make the earth a dwelling for his glory will literally and really be fulfilled in the new heavens and new earth."[14]

Such a clarified vision for God's reign will display these marks:

- A Trinitarian sense of the mission of God (*missio Dei*) which sees the goal of mission as nothing less than God's will done perfectly on earth, a time when "the kingdom of the world has become the kingdom of our Lord and of his Messiah" (Rev 11:15). The promising explorations of the doctrine of the Trinity over the past half-century will be relevant here in multiple ways.[15]

- The Bible primarily, and consensual Christian tradition secondarily, will fulfill their proper role as the church's canonical heritage, guiding, "norming," and—by the Spirit—renewing the church in discipleship and mission.[16]

- The church will live an embodied eschatology that visibly demonstrates *now* the reality and promise of the kingdom of God in its final fullness.

Result: The church lives out its mission in fidelity to the radical hope of resurrection and God's reign, developing a powerful kingdom vision that serves as medicine for our maladies and effectively immunizes against lesser and heretical visions.

A Wholistic, Earthed Discipleship

This is the third recovery we hope for. Evangelicals and others now talk of "holistic mission," "holistic discipleship," "holistic spirituality." But too often mission and spirituality are discussed *as if the earth itself did not even exist*.[17] Our connection with the created order is mostly ignored in Christian writing, except in a few pet areas. Standard works in systematic theology seldom deal in any depth with ecology, culture, the physical earth, creation care, or the practical implications of God's will being done on earth as in heaven. Biblically speaking, this is indefensible; it is a scandal.

14. Webber, *Ancient-Future Worship*, 176.

15. See especially Gunton, *Promise of Trinitarian Theology*; Boff, *Trinity and Society*; Kärkkäinen, *The Trinity*. The doctrine of the Trinity has relevance for mission and for every area of life and culture.

16. See the provocative discussions in Abraham et al., *Canonical Theism*.

17. Because of this misunderstanding of "spirituality," we would do well, as a spiritual discipline, to drop the terms "spirituality," "spiritual life," "spiritual formation," and similar terms for a time until their biblical meaning can be recovered.

The same problem plagues most devotional writing. The *Renovaré Spiritual Formation Bible,* though a marvelous resource, pictures spirituality as largely unrelated to the earth. Key passages in Romans 8 focus on personal piety, not on creation restored.[18] Andy Crouch's excellent book *Culture Making* hints at a more earthed discipleship, but never really explores our stewardship connection with the earth.[19] Yet clearly culture in many senses depends upon the earth.

Faithful mission requires wholistic, earthed discipleship—a discipleship that rejects the divorce of heaven and earth and works for reconciliation. We need a discipleship that is earthed, a lived eschatology—living the kingdom of God *now* in the present, on earth, with all the hope and frustrations that involves, embodying the new creation in the power of the Spirit. This means, for example:

- Spiritual disciplines that include practical creation care, with no split between the material and spiritual dimensions of life. Spiritual disciplines will include recycling and advocacy for sustainable energy as naturally as prayer, meditation, and Bible study. The more traditional disciplines will be enlivened by the intermixing of the material and the spiritual dimensions. We will begin to understand the ecology of spirituality. We will see sacramental life more ecologically.

- Prayer and intercession for the social, cultural, environmental, and economic dimensions of today's world, with sensitivity to God's concerns in all these areas and to our own intercessory opportunity and responsibility.

- Attention, as part of our "reasonable worship" (Rom 12:2), to the physical and ecological dimensions of everyday life. All aspects of life will be woven into our discipleship and our expectancy of the coming kingdom of God.

Result: The church will recover much of the dynamic of the New Testament church, overcoming its one-sided discipleship. Walking in the Spirit, the church will practice an earthed discipleship that makes God's narrative real and dynamic in fresh and comprehensive ways.

A Recovery of Visible Christian Community, Globally and Locally

We may hope for a twenty-first century recovery of visible Christian community. We hope to see the church become authentically but diversely *seeable* in all the world's cultures, nations, and ethnicities.

We purposely list visible Christian community last, rather than first. Real visible demonstration of the body of Christ will not happen unless the church recovers a biblically comprehensive vision of Jesus Christ and his reign. We have reason to hope, however, for a remarkable, visible manifestation of the promise of the kingdom of God through authentic, visible Christian community today. God has in some way been guiding the church. In some sense the church is indeed "the continuation of God's narrative."

18. Foster, *Renovaré Spiritual Formation Bible.*
19. Crouch, *Culture Making.*

Recovering authentic Christian community will mean:

- an awareness that the church's *primary* visibility is through visible local communities of Jesus-like disciples. Jesus said, "By this everyone will know that you are my disciples, if you have love for one another" (John 13:35). The church's sacraments and other canonical traditions are essential for nourishing its life. But it is the church as visible community that is the primary sacramental sign of God's kingdom on earth.
- an affirmation of the church as diverse, charismatic, prophetic, and local as well as one, holy, apostolic, and catholic. The church will celebrate its rich ecclesial DNA which is now more and more visible in the global church. (See chapter 12.)
- "body of Christ" will cease to be an airy metaphor. Instead it will increasingly describe the actual visible presence and functioning of the Christian community.
- The worldwide church of Jesus Christ will experience a new ecumenical unity based on the realization of diversity-in-oneness, the biblical image of body of Christ, the reality of the Trinity, a shared vision for God's reign, and an understanding of the ecological and organic nature of the church and its mission.
- We will celebrate renewed openness to the power and gifts of the Holy Spirit, globally and locally. The church will function and minister with charismatic fullness, not just through its official leadership structures. Church structure will come to be understood more organically and ecologically; less institutionally and hierarchically.

Result: An age of expanded authentic Christian witness worldwide in which the church out-lives, out-loves, out-thinks, and out-serves all other faiths, philosophies, and ideologies. An age in which the church visibly *lives into* the hope and reality of the kingdom of God as it serves the world and participates in the yearning, the "groaning" for the full liberation of the children of God (Rom 8:18–23; cf. 2 Cor 5:2–4). (The larger dimensions of such global, cosmic Christian community are explored in chapter 13, "The Community of Earth and Heaven.")

AN ECCLESIO-MISSIONAL AGENDA

In his significant book *Faith Seeking Action: Mission, Social Movements, and the Church in Motion*, missiologist Greg Leffel calls the church to what he terms a new *missio-ecclesiology*. Reviewing the church's history and theology, the nature of social movements, and the challenges facing today's church, Leffel outlines a theological and sociological vision that sees "the church as a movement bearing and embodying the good news of God's work in the world." Leffel insists, "The point of mission, of course, is to act." The mission of God "becomes our mission in the moment we allow God to inhabit our actions." Missio-ecclesiology thus "describes the church as an unfolding movement of divinely-initiated change."[20]

20. Leffel, *Faith Seeking Action*, 1, 7. Leffel articulates "a missiologically-informed concept of the church" informed by "a sociologically-informed understanding of social action" (ibid., 252).

At its best, the church is a social movement initiated, guided, sometimes judged, and drawn forward into God's promised future by his gracious, sovereign, and extremely clever Spirit. And yet the church is not just born to act. It is also born to be and to contemplate; to live in "quietness and trust" (Isa 30:15; 32:17). The church is to *be* the body of Christ as well as *do* Christ's work in the world. The two are one.

The church often suffers an unbiblical, unecological split just at this point. The church is called and constituted *both* to be and to do, in a mutually reinforcing socio-spiritual ecology. The church does indeed need a biblical (and sociologically-anthropologically informed) ecclesiology, including a fully biblical worldview. The church does indeed have an ecclesio-missional agenda.

Since Christian mission is, first of all, God's mission, this third section of the book has focused on the healing mission of God. The final section focuses on *the Healing Community*—the church and its mission; its ecclesio-missional agenda. We explore the way God uses the healing community as his key instrument for healing all creation. And we ask what kind of worldview, or worldstory, will nourish and sustain the church in its mission.

9

Mission and the Kingdom of God

I must proclaim the good news of the kingdom of God
to the other cities also; for I was sent for this purpose.

Jesus (Luke 4:43)

CHRISTIANS TALK ABOUT THE importance of a biblical worldview. But what is a "biblical worldview"? We certainly don't all agree. For some, a "biblical worldview" means insisting on "absolute truth" in the face of postmodernism and relativism. For others it means affirming "an utterly sovereign and micromanaging deity, sinful and puny humanity, and the combination's logical consequence, predestination."[1] For still others "Christian worldview" is code for an ideology of political conservatism or free-market capitalism. For most of us "biblical worldview" means our particular "take" on Christian doctrine, shaped by our own tradition's interpretation of the faith, whether that tradition is Roman Catholic, Orthodox, Reformed, Pentecostal, or whatever.

But there is a deeper problem with affirming a "Christian worldview." It's not just the issue of differing traditions or of mixing theology and politics. We saw in chapter 4 that much of the church's "view" of the "world" gets distorted by the unquestioned theological divorce of heaven and earth. Christian worldviews have been run through a separator that skims spirit from matter. They have been refracted through a twisted prism that blocks out key hues of the beautiful spectrum of divine light. If our worldview

1. Van Bierma, "New Calvinism," 50. The argument of this book denies theologian Albert Mohler's claim that "The moment someone begins to define God's [being or actions] biblically, that person is drawn to conclusions that are traditionally classified as Calvinist" (quoted by Van Bierma).

rests on an unbiblical split between spirit and matter, between earth and heaven, our theology and our discipleship will be skewed right down the line.

Biblically speaking, a Christian worldview must center in God's self-revelation in Scripture and supremely in Jesus Christ and his reign. But what do we find when we look in Scripture? Not so much a "view of the world" (worldview) as a story and a history—a narrative of the works and mission of God. We might better speak of a Christian world*story* than a Christian or biblical world*view*. The biblical worldstory is a narrative about the Triune God as Creator, Sustainer, and Healer of all creation.[2]

This chapter seeks to heal the malignant hole in Christian worldviews by further elaborating the mission of God through the biblical theme of God's reign. This means also re-examining Jesus' own mission in light of the biblical promise of the kingdom. Here we find wider vistas for comprehending the biblical teaching of salvation as creation healed, and we see what *evangelism* really means when viewed in kingdom perspective.

We begin with the mission of Jesus.

THE MISSION OF JESUS

The mission of God is about the sovereign Lord's relationship with people and the land, as emphasized in previous chapters. But what about Jesus? What was *his* mission?

Discussions of mission often ignore *what Jesus himself said* about his mission and the *missio Dei*. The church tends to explore its own mission more than it does Jesus', which is rather strange, given that the church's mission springs from Jesus' mission and the mission of God.

Some discussions of mission do focus on Jesus' Jubilee proclamation in Luke 4, or the Great Commission, or sayings such as "The Son of Man came to seek out and to save the lost" (Luke 19:10). But Jesus had much more to say about his own mission. He constantly referred to his mission or work, especially in John's account. Some thirty-four times Jesus spoke of being "sent" in phrases like "The Father who sent me," "the will of him who sent me," or "the one who sent me" (John, NRSV). We see one thing immediately: Jesus emphasizes that his mission comes from the Father's mission, the Father's will. He speaks more of the Father's agency than of his own—"I am sent" more than "I have come," for instance—though he does use phrases like "I came" or "have come" about a dozen times. For example, "I came that they may have life, and have it abundantly" (John 10:10) and "I have come as light into the world, so that everyone who believes in me should not remain in darkness" (John 12:46).

What is Jesus' mission, then? Combining Jesus' many statements (excluding, for the moment, his important prayer in John 17) yields this summary:

- My food is to do the will of him who sent me and to finish his work. My Father is always at his work to this very day, and I too am working. The Son can do nothing

2. On the significance and promise of, and criteria for, "worldstory," see Snyder, *EarthCurrents*, 273–90.

by himself; he can do only what he sees his Father doing, because whatever the Father does the Son also does.

- The works that the Father has given me to finish testify that the Father has sent me. I have come down from heaven not to do my own will but to do the will of him who sent me.
- I stand with the Father, who sent me. What I have heard from him I tell the world. I came from God and now am here. I have not come on my own, but he sent me. What I say is just what the Father has told me to say.
- I have come from God and am returning to God. I am the way and the truth and the life. No one comes to the Father except through me. The words I say to you I do not speak on my own authority. Rather, it is the Father, living in me, who is doing his work.
- As the Father has sent me, I am sending you.

This is Jesus' own description of his mission. This is what it means that he was *sent*.

John's Gospel highlights three other terms concerning Jesus' mission: "will," "work," and "works." A dozen or so times Jesus speaks of God's "work" or "works" that he was sent to accomplish. Several times he speaks of doing the Father's "will."

In the other Gospels Jesus, of course, says many other things about his mission. Most importantly, he ties his mission to the kingdom of God—preaching the kingdom, telling his disciples they should seek first God's kingdom, and praying, "Your kingdom come, your will be done, on earth as it is heaven" (Matt 6:10). Key to fulfilling that goal is making disciples among all nations (Matt 28:19–20).

The Apostle Paul and other New Testament writers (as well as Old Testament prophets) elaborate the scope of Jesus' mission, tying it in with God's larger economy or plan "to bring all things in heaven and on earth together under one head, even Christ" (Eph 1:10 NIV), as noted earlier.

In short, the Father sent Jesus into the world to "complete" the work of the Father (John 4:34; cf. 5:36, 17:4). For Jesus, finishing God's work meant his sacrificial death on the cross ("It is finished," John 19:30) and the eventual total triumph of the kingdom of God ("It is done!" Rev 21:6). The church lives now between that first and second "It is finished." We celebrate "the finished work of Christ," but at present we can speak also of the *unfinished work of Christ*—else why pray, "May your kingdom come, may your will be done on earth as in heaven"?

Jesus' mission is, of course, accomplished through the presence and agency of the Holy Spirit. It is Trinitarian. Jesus speaks in John of the role the Spirit will play, and many other Scriptures reveal the Spirit's essential role in bringing Jesus' mission to completion in the church and in all creation (e.g., Acts 1:8 and Rom 8).

Jesus' description of his mission fleshes out, quite literally, the mission of the church, our shared mission. Now we see more vividly the mission of God to reconcile and heal people and the land. Three important things stand out here:

1. *Our mission (the church's mission) is not our own. It is Jesus' mission, and the mission of the Trinity.* Jesus said, "As the Father has sent me, so I send you" (John

20:21). He said his disciples would do "the works" that Jesus did—and even greater, once the Holy Spirit was poured out (John 14:12–17).

Jesus was passionate above all to do the will and works of him who sent him, not his own. So too with us. We live a transcendent mission. Creation healed means knowing and experiencing the visible yet transcendent *connections* between things—because of who the Trinity is.

2. *Our ultimate mission as disciples invited to participate in God's mission is nothing less than the kingdom of God, the reconciliation and restoration of "all things."* It is that grand and comprehensive.

Our task as disciples and Christian communities, of course, is to discern our specific and strategic part in that larger mission of God. So the church must be a discerning, discipling missional community. But we must never lose sight of the big picture, the larger mission within which we find our particular mission.

3. *The power to accomplish our mission comes from God—from Jesus and the power of his resurrection and from the filling, empowering, and guidance of the Spirit.* The power for mission is life in the Trinity through Christian community. Thus Jesus prays in John 17, "Now I am no longer in the world, but they are in the world, and I am coming to you. Holy Father, protect them in your name that you have given me, so that they may be one, as we are one. . . . I am not asking you to take them out of the world, but I ask you to protect them from the evil one. . . . As you have sent me into the world, so I have sent them into the world" (John 17:11–18).

In sum, Jesus' mission was to fulfill the mission of God for which he was sent and of which he was and is the central actor. Jesus' work included forming a community of disciples, nothing less than the body of Christ. The church's mission therefore is to fulfill its role, its "work," in the Trinitarian mission of God for the sake of God's kingdom in the power of the Spirit.

Within this Trinitarian and Christocentric vision of Christian faith and mission we find the key elements of a biblical vision of the world and our place within it—a worldview and a worldstory.

A BIBLICAL EARTH-AND-HEAVEN ECOLOGICAL WORLDVIEW

Sustaining a biblical vision of the kingdom and the radical hope of physical resurrection like Jesus' own requires a big worldview. For many, that means a big *shift* in worldview. In place of sub-biblical or Neo-Platonic views that place spirit above matter and radically split present from future, the global church needs a biblical earth-and-heaven ecological worldview that is in fact the biblical worldstory of the kingdom of God.

James Jones, Anglican Bishop of Liverpool, England, points in the right direction, showing how earth and heaven fit together in the biblical worldstory. He writes:

> It is Jesus the Son of Man who has come down to the earth from heaven who holds together in himself both the earthly things and heavenly things. . . . Here is the reality: Heaven and earth are not to be two separated realms forever, divided by sin and evil, for the ultimate reality is an undivided world where all things

whether on earth or in heaven hold together in Jesus (see Colossians 1). He is central to the earthing of heaven and to the heavening of earth. Earth and heaven belong together.[3]

The biblical worldstory is at heart ecological, as we have seen. It shows how every part of creation is connected with every other. *Ecology and kingdom in fact go together in God's narrative.* God's redemptive plan is his *oikonomia,* his "economy for the fullness of time" (Eph 1:10). God's plan is fundamentally ecological, based on a biblical ecology or ecology-logic (*oikologia*) in which "all things, whether on earth or in heaven," "things visible and invisible," are *in fact* interconnected and participate in the peace Jesus brings "through the blood of his cross" (Col 1:16–20). "Economy of God" and "kingdom of God" are thus mutually reinforcing metaphors for God's creative and restorative plan and work, one based on the extended idea of household (*oikos*), the other on the historic idea of monarchy.[4]

The economy/ecology model is especially timely today. Increasingly the world is thinking ecologically. Science is exploring earth's vast ecology, the complex web of life and matter and its implications for all dimensions of human life and culture. Equally important: today *for the first time in history* we are witnessing the convergence of ecology and economics on a global scale. Economists Herman Daly and Joshua Farley say prophetically that, "the most pressing problems we face today arise from the interaction between two highly complex systems—the human system and the ecological system that sustains it. Such problems are far too complex to be addressed from the perspective of a single discipline [including theology, we might add], and efforts to do so must either ignore those aspects of the problem outside the discipline, or apply inappropriate tools to address them."[5]

Christians, however, have an even broader ecological vision. We understand that our vast ecosystem includes spirit as well as matter. It includes both "things visible and invisible" (Col 1:16), "things present" and "things to come" (Rom 8:38). The Bible shows us that ecology is the true worldview, overflowing with both material and spiritual reality. Ecology shows us the *intricate actual interdependent connections* of all the parts. Whatever touches one part affects all the others, as well.[6] "You can never do just one thing."

Today we need a biblical earth-and-heaven, past-present-future worldview based on what God has done and is doing through Jesus Christ by the Spirit. This worldstory faces squarely sin's alienations but flatly rejects the theological divorce of heaven and earth, affirming instead the biblical "all things" vision. It gives us the basis for engaging today's scientific ecological discoveries while adding the essential spiritual and

3. Jones, *Jesus and the Earth,* 62.

4. Clearly both these metaphors that God uses are culturally rooted and conditioned.

5. Daly and Farley, *Ecological Economics,* xxii (brackets added).

6. God the Trinity is the ultimate personal Ecology through which the universe's vast ecology was created.

theological dimensions that secular, New Age, or other religious ecological visions typically miss.[7]

From the beginning of this book we have pointed out the need to take both history and ecology seriously—to think and act both historically and ecologically. Taking the full range of Scripture seriously and comprehensively requires this.

The important point here—as a worldview issue—is that the biblical story in fact *combines and weaves together* history and ecology. Our discussion of the mission of God and the divine plan for *shalom* in the interrelationships between God, people, and land makes that clear.

Combining *story* or narrative and *ecology* in our understanding and embodying of the mission of God gives us a compelling worldstory that is much more potent, profound, and persuasive over time than contemporary "biblical" or "Christian" world-views.[8] The Bible does in fact give us a compelling historical-ecological vision based in the biblical worldstory and the promise of God's reign. Here is a vision that is better and truer than any so-called "biblical worldview."

This biblical vision offers us an ecological understanding of creation and new creation that is closely tied to the work of Jesus Christ and the biblical narrative of the kingdom of God. Biblically, *ecology and narrative together* form the key elements of God's redemptive plan. This may be pictured quite simply:

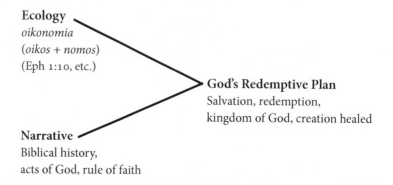

This vision is pregnant with a biblical-ecological theology of culture that sees *all* elements of culture—food, art, technology, music, language, literature, economics, political structures, clothing, soil, minerals, architecture, agriculture, energy, climate, communications, symbols, education, customs, sexuality, entertainment, science, plant and animal life, ethics, and moral values—as all *inextricably* interrelated. Not just in theory, but in fact.

---

7. The implications of this are spelled out briefly in Snyder, *Coherence in Christ*.

8. Biblically and theologically, "story" and "history" may be used interchangeably as long as we are clear that (1) the overall "biblical story" involves actual spacetime history, not non-historical myth or fiction (though, of course, myths and parables also exist in Scripture), and that (2) by "history" we mean the factual existence and progression of the created order, including human history involving real human agency, yet all sovereignly guided by God and his purposes (which so far have been revealed only in part). Thus in this book *story, history,* and *narrative* are sometimes used interchangeably when the sense is clear from the context.

Based on a biblical vision of *creation—incarnation—new creation*—including issues of the fall, depravity, redemption and sanctification—such a theology will learn how to distinguish between the good and the evil in culture. It will emphasize how Rev 21:24–27 describes the New Jerusalem: "The nations will walk by its light, and the kings of the earth will bring their glory into it. Its gates will never be shut by day—and there will be no night there. People will bring into it the glory and the honor of the nations. But nothing unclean will enter it, nor anyone who practices abomination or falsehood, but only those who are written in the Lamb's book of life."

The biblical ecological worldstory thus provides the basis for a dynamic vision of culture. Anthropology and other sciences can be harnessed to make the church more effective in mission and to shape culture and society according to the values and virtues of God's reign.

For Christians, this biblical ecological worldstory nurtures a vision of salvation as creation healed. Exploring biblical and traditional Christian images of salvation as God's way of healing the disease of sin, the church will be able to apply the medicine of God's salvation to *every dimension* of the effects of the fall; every dimension of human, cultural, and ecological damage that results from sin—*provided* that the church walks as God's community, filled with the Spirit. In this way Christians will have the biblical and conceptual resources to engage today's global society effectively and redemptively at every level.

EVANGELISM: ANNOUNCING AND EMBODYING GOD'S REIGN

What then is *evangelism*? How are we to understand evangelism in light of the mission of and kingdom of God? Put differently: What is evangelism, understood within the biblical worldstory of creation healed through the work of Jesus Christ by the Spirit? What does the Bible say?

In the New Testament, the term "evangelism" emphatically refers to the good news of God's kingdom. "To evangelize" literally means to proclaim the good news of God's reign. Jesus came "proclaiming the good news of the kingdom, and curing every disease and every sickness" (Matt 9:35). In Luke 4:43, Jesus says that his central purpose was to "proclaim the good news of [literally, "evangelize concerning"] the kingdom of God." Again in Luke 8:1, Jesus' proclamation of the kingdom is described in the Greek text as "evangelizing." We read in Acts 8:12 that Philip "evangelized about the kingdom of God and the name of Jesus Christ" (literal translation).[9]

In its broadest and deepest sense, evangelism means announcing and embodying the reign of God. It addresses itself particularly to personal faith; to the decision of the heart in response to God's call to follow Jesus Christ, to be born again, and be his disciples. It is concerned with justification and regeneration as well as discipleship and sanctification. Think again of the *circumference* of evangelism as all that is included in the good news of God's kingdom, but the *center* as the appeal to "turn"

---

9. See also Matt 4:23; 24:14; Luke 16:16. A study of the New Testament use of "evangelize" in its various forms shows conclusively that evangelism concerns the full message of God's kingdom.

and be healed and forgiven. (See for example Matt 13:15; Mark 4:12; John 12:40; Acts 14:15, 26:18, etc.)

Consistently in the New Testament, evangelism means proclaiming the kingdom of God and demonstrating the reality of that kingdom. In the Bible, evangelism is not limited to what might be called conversion evangelism—winning converts to Jesus Christ. Evangelism covers much more than this, because it concerns the full message of God's reign.

What then does evangelism really mean, biblically speaking? If evangelism is announcing and embodying God's reign so that God's will truly is done on earth, then evangelism may be pictured like this:

KINGDOM EVANGELISM
Announcing and Embodying the Good News of God's Reign

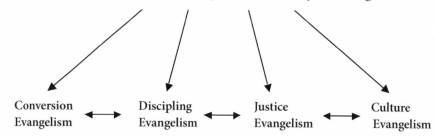

Conversion Evangelism	Discipling Evangelism	Justice Evangelism	Culture Evangelism
We all like sheep have gone astray, each of us has turned to our own way (Isa 53:6).	Observe the commands of the Lord, walking in obedience to him and revering him (Deut 8:6).	This is the fasting I have chosen: to loose the chains of injustice . . . to set the oppressed free (Isa 58:6).	My justice will become a light to the nations (Isa 51:4).
Repent and turn to God, so your sins may be wiped out (Acts 3:19).	. . . teaching them to obey everything I have commanded you (Matt 28:20).	Seek first God's kingdom and its righteousness (justice) (Matt 6:33).	We take captive every thought to make it obedient to Christ (2 Cor 10:5).

Here evangelism is all about the kingdom of God, just as we find in the New Testament. Evangelism means making Jesus and his kingdom known through the church, in the power of the Holy Spirit, throughout culture and in all the earth. Consider these four dimensions of evangelism:

Conversion evangelism is proclaiming and showing by our lives that Jesus Christ is Savior and Lord—the one who came into the world to save sinners. The mission of the church is to lift up Jesus so that people may be convicted of their sins, repent and believe in him, and receive the abundant life and healing he offers.

Conversion evangelism is preeminently the work of *the church*, the Christian community, not of just individuals or specialized organizations—though first and last it is the work of the Spirit. As the body of Christ, a faithful church makes Jesus visible in the world. As it shows forth Christ through word and works, people are won to faith in him and become part of the community of believers.

The church, then, has a central role in evangelism. Its mission is to proclaim Jesus, reveal Jesus in its community life, and be the community that then welcomes and nurtures "those . . . being saved" (Acts 2:47).

Many Christians use the term evangelism *only* in the sense of conversion evangelism. This is too narrow. Evangelism means announcing and embodying the full message of the kingdom.

Discipling evangelism refers to the church making disciples, not just converts or church members. This is Jesus' commission—to "make disciples . . . teaching them to obey everything" that Jesus commanded (Matt 28:19–20).

The true church is a community of disciples, not just believers or "creeders." The church should look like Jesus Christ, visibly representing Jesus and his kingdom in the world. But this will not happen unless churches pay careful attention to disciple-building.

The goal of disciple-making is to form a community that looks and acts like Jesus; that shows forth the character of Christ and the power of the Spirit in its social context. The church does this by being a reconciled and reconciling community. It does this most effectively when it visibly embodies reconciliation between rich and poor, men and women, and people of different racial and ethnic identities.[10] Discipling evangelism thus includes what is sometimes called "lifestyle evangelism"—the persuasive influence of Christians' lives as persons and community. Jesus stressed this: "By this everyone will know that you are my disciples, if you have love one for another" (John 13:35).

Justice evangelism means living out the righteousness and justice of God's reign within the church's social context—locally and globally. Here the church takes seriously the biblical mandate to work for justice in all areas of society, with particular concern for the poor and oppressed. Here the church engages key issues of justice in the world—entrenched poverty, environmental exploitation, ethnic and religious violence, oppression of women and children, sex trafficking, abortion, and the culture of warfare and militarism. Evangelism that does not include this justice dimension is not really evangelism in the full biblical sense.

Justice evangelism includes eco-evangelism—proclaiming and embodying the good news to and for the land, the physical world. People cannot live justly when the land is being unjustly exploited. Eco-evangelism could be viewed as a separate dimension of evangelism, but, in fact, it is interwoven with all the dimensions. Conversion evangelism, discipling evangelism, and culture evangelism all involve reconciliation with the land as well as with God and one another.

Culture evangelism means shaping the world's societies and cultures through the truth and virtues of God's reign. It means engaging society in all sectors—the arts, economics and education, politics and government, science and technology, media and entertainment, philosophy and worldview. This dimension of evangelism calls

---

10. For this reason, Acts 2–5 should not be taken as the primary model for the church, or the full picture of the early church. The multiethnic Antioch church pictured in Acts 11 and 13, for example, gives a fuller picture of the early church than does the Jerusalem church of the first chapters of Acts.

Christians in all sectors of society to give transforming witness to the truth of the gospel. This is the call Andy Crouch issues in his fine book, *Culture Making*.[11]

The Bible tells the truth. It presents a picture of reality—a worldview and world-story—that is distinctly different from all the world's philosophies, religions, and ideologies. Scripture reveals God's truth, demonstrated supremely in Jesus Christ and in his reign. So culture evangelism is essential if societies are to be transformed to reflect the reality of God's kingdom.

These four dimensions of evangelism are all, of course, closely intertwined. They form the ecology of evangelism. Together they compose one picture: the proclamation and living out of God's reign as revealed in Jesus. Wholistic mission means combining these four dimensions of evangelism within each local church, and in the church more broadly.

An important part of this comprehensive picture of evangelism is that it engages *everyone* in the Christian community—every believer and disciple. The priesthood of believers and the diversity of spiritual gifts play a key role here, as we will see later in more detail. Within the church, the Spirit endows believers with gifts to be witnesses and evangelists in different ways. First Corinthians 12 thus takes on added meaning. We learn practically that there are "different kinds of gifts, but the same Spirit distributes them. There are different kinds of service, but the same Lord. There are different kinds of working, but in all of them and in everyone it is the same God at work" (1 Cor 12:4–6 TNIV).

The work of the Holy Spirit is to make Jesus and his kingdom known and visible in the world. Wholistic mission recognizes this broader biblical understanding of evangelism and the essential role of God's particular gifts and callings, so that Jesus may be exalted and his kingdom visibly embodied.

Mission is about the kingdom of God as announced, embodied, effected, and sovereignly guided by Jesus Christ through the Holy Spirit. Christians praise God that he has graciously invited his church, Christ's body, to participate in this godly work of announcing and embodying the kingdom in all its dimensions.

The kingdom of God is another way of speaking of salvation as creation healed. The next chapter explores the meaning of healing in its largest eschatological dimensions.

11. Crouch, *Culture Making*.

10

Mission, Healing, and the End of Eschatology

All the ends of the earth shall remember and turn to the Lord;
and all the families of the nations shall worship before him. For
dominion belongs to the Lord, and he rules over the nations.

(Ps 22:27–28)

"THE END OF ALL things is near," says 1 Peter 4:7. But what "end"? And *to* what end? The Greek word here is *telos*, which in context means neither termination nor expiration of time, but the *goal* toward which things are moving. It means that God is about the business of fulfilling his purposes. It is like saying: "we are in the time of fulfillment."

This chapter begins with the present and ends with the future, "the end." But the whole chapter deals with *telos*, with God's intention and God's way of fulfilling his purposes. So the whole chapter is about eschatology. *The whole thing is eschatology.* This is the biblical sense of "last things."[1]

The end is, in fact, "near" in the biblical sense. This is true not in an evolutionary or dialectical or dispensational or inevitable-progress sense. Nor is it true in an unstoppable-decline sense. Neither the creation nor God's plan comes with a pre-set expiration date. Instead, this chapter is about mission, healing, and eschatology. It

---

1. The word *eschatology* derives from the Greek word *eschatos,* common in the NT, meaning "last" or "furthest." In the gospel it has the sense of ultimate or complete, and is thus related to *telos*—end or goal; fulfillment. Eschatology is the study of last things—not just in terms of finality, but in terms of completion and fulfillment.

explores deeply what creation healed really means, now and in the future, showing how this clarifies the church's mission as a response to, and participation in, God's mission.

We begin with the *telos* or *goal* which God intends.

Telos is a rich biblical word. It is the root of the English word *teleological*, as we noted in chapter 7. *Telos* is best translated as "an end or goal accomplished," or "a purpose fulfilled." Jesus said after his resurrection that everything written about him "is being fulfilled"—literally, "has an end," a *telos* (Luke 22:37).

Telos is a sister word to another common New Testament term, *teleios*, meaning complete, fully mature, or perfect. So Paul writes of Jesus: "It is he whom we proclaim, warning everyone and teaching everyone in all wisdom, so that we may present everyone mature [*teleion*] in Christ" (Col 1:28). This helps us understand what Jesus means in Matt 5:48, "Be perfect [*teleioi*] as your heavenly Father is perfect [*teleios*]." It means to be complete and mature in Jesus Christ, by the Spirit.

If salvation means creation healed, then salvation must be as deep and wide, as high and broad, as creation itself. We don't know—not yet, anyhow—what those saving dimensions might mean for the created order beyond earth, or beyond our solar system. In his science-fiction novels, C. S. Lewis saw the earth as being under divine quarantine because of sin. But we know clearly from Scripture that God has placed God-imaged women and men on earth as the special subjects and objects of his grace, and has given us a special responsibility and opportunity to extend the good news to all creation.

In previous chapters we examined sin as a moral disease, and salvation as the cure. We traced the complex ecology of sin resulting from the fourfold alienation brought into human history by the fall. We saw how the gospel is a complete cure, through the reconciling work of Jesus Christ. This chapter shows *how* the good news of Christ's kingdom heals the God-ward, inward, other-ward, and earthward dimensions of alienation. And it shows what this means for mission and the nature of the church. We will see that—to put it in theological terms—ecclesiology, eschatology, and missiology are all one.

Most Christians understand that Christ's gospel in some way deals with the God-ward, inward, and other-ward dimensions of sin. But due to the longstanding theological divorce between heaven and earth, the whole dimension of earthward reconciliation—the healing of the land—is overlooked. Given this blind spot, this worldview hole, the earthward and creation-care dimensions of the church's healing mission get special focus here.

We will also explain how all this is bound up with the often disputed question of eschatology.

HEALING THE FOURFOLD ALIENATION

Since "new creation" has wonderfully come to us through Jesus Christ, the church seeks to fulfill the "ministry of reconciliation" that is our mission and our joy. "All this is from God, who reconciled us to himself through Christ, and has given us the ministry of reconciliation; that is, in Christ God was reconciling the world [*kosmos*] to himself, not counting their trespasses against them, and entrusting the message of reconciliation to us" (2 Cor 5:17–19).

The good news of Jesus and his kingdom addresses the whole ecology of sin, as this passage suggests—"reconciling the world to himself." All the multiple dimensions of sin and alienation are implied here, as in many other passages. *The ecology of salvation is as full and comprehensive as the ecology of sin.* Anything less is not the whole gospel for the whole world—not wholistic mission.

Reconciling with God

Since all other alienations flow from our separation from God, reconciliation with God through Jesus by the power of the Spirit is the central truth of the gospel. With the Apostle Paul, we celebrate the good news that God "chose us in Christ before the foundation of the world to be holy and blameless before him in love. He destined us for adoption as his children through Jesus Christ, according to the good pleasure of his will, to the praise of his glorious grace that he freely bestowed on us in the Beloved. In him we have redemption through his blood, the forgiveness of our trespasses, according to the riches of his grace that he lavished on us" (Eph 1:4–8). All this is "to the praise of [God's] glory" (Eph 1:14). Our one overriding need—in fact, the greatest need of all creation—is that people be reconciled to God.

The good news of Jesus and his kingdom must be lived out and proclaimed "to the whole creation" (Mark 16:15), "to every creature" (Col 1:13), so that people everywhere may "repent and turn to God and do deeds consistent with repentance" (Acts 26:20).

Since this is the central fact of the gospel, it is the center (though not the circumference) of the church's mission. It is what kingdom evangelism, and particularly conversion evangelism, really achieve, as outlined in the previous chapter.

Reconciliation to God through Jesus Christ involves both church and mission: missio-ecclesiology. Reconciliation implies ecclesiology because in receiving "new birth into a living hope through the resurrection of Jesus Christ" (1 Pet 1:3) we are born into a new family, the church. Being joined to the Head means being joined to the Body. This God-ward reconciliation equally involves mission because, having been reconciled to God, we are now entrusted with the "ministry of reconciliation" (2 Cor 5:19). Here is the full ecology of salvation; God's amazing, gracious *oikonomia*.

Reconciling with Ourselves

Salvation through Jesus Christ reconciles us to ourselves (the inward dimension), bringing a measure of inner healing, countering our self-preoccupation. Regeneration and justification by faith cure us of our rebellion against God, our waywardness, and launch us on a lifelong journey of healing, discipleship, and sanctification. On this journey we follow Jesus in Christian community and learn more and more to live a well-earthed life in the Spirit. God's Spirit in our lives provides the answer to David's prayer in Psalm 86:11, "Give me an undivided heart to revere your name."

When we sing, "I once was lost but now am found," we mean found by God—but also that we have found our true selves. We may well identify with Charlotte Elliott: "tossed about with many a conflict, many a doubt, fightings within, and fears without" ("Just As I Am"). Almost certainly we know what Augustine meant: "Our heart is restless until it finds rest in thee." And we think of the many biblical promises of rest: "Come to me, all you that are weary and carrying heavy burdens, and I will give you rest" (Matt 11:28). "So then, a Sabbath rest still remains for the people of God" (Heb 4:9). "In returning and rest you shall be saved; in quietness and in trust shall be your strength" (Isa 30:15). Such words are directed to the whole people of God, not to persons separately, thus reminding us of the corporate, shared nature of salvation.

Sometimes healing and reconciliation with God are sudden and complete; sometimes the healing is gradual, slow over time; both are usually required. So also with the healing of our inner selves: the development of true *integrity*, "put-togetherness," through the miracle of God's grace. Reconciliation with ourselves begins as we respond in faith and obedience to God's gracious call, and continues and deepens as we walk the life of discipleship in Christian community. Testimonies from around the globe, and throughout history in different places and cultures, suggest that for most people, inward healing is *both* sudden and gradual—both crisis and process. Much of the New Testament aims specifically at growth in grace, through the means of grace, in a community of grace and truth.

Here the church, especially in the West, stumbles across a curious cultural twist. The social sciences since the late 1800s developed mostly like this: psychology, then sociology, then anthropology. Psychology (Freud, Jung, and others) came first, at least in terms of popular awareness and application, then sociology and anthropology followed. This sequence has skewed the church's understanding of salvation, especially in the North Atlantic world where these sciences arose.

The academic sequence is really a cultural sequence, and it explains a lot. The development looks like this:

$$\text{Psychology} \rightarrow \text{Sociology} \rightarrow \text{Anthropology} \rightarrow \text{Ecology}$$

The related cultural sequence is parallel:

$$\text{Self (ego)} \rightarrow \text{Society (group)} \rightarrow \text{Culture} \rightarrow \text{Environment (earth)}^2$$

The direction of this development has been toward increasing comprehensiveness and complexity; in other words, toward a more wholistic picture of the human situation.

This sequential development is pretty obvious in Western Christianity. It helps us understand what the church really needs today. This sequence also explains why the

2. This can be more adequately visualized by imagining circles: First, the free-standing "individual" (actually a myth); then the several interlinked circles, with the self at the center (group, society); then a larger circle, representing culture, within which are the persons and groups that make a culture and its worldview; and finally a much larger circle within which are all the circles that make up the larger ecosystem, including humans and their physical, social, and spiritual environments.

church in its theology and pastoral work throughout the twentieth century focused much more on the psychology of Christian experience than on the sociology and social anthropology of church and mission. Western society was already predisposed to this, of course, because of its deep tradition of individualism. Christian theology and practice naturally paid more attention to *individual* Christian experience than to *shared* Christian experience in the church and in culture. A comprehensive understanding of salvation as truly wholistic requires a correction of this imbalance.

Inward reconciliation naturally involves the same two aspects noted above regarding God-ward reconciliation: church and mission. Inward healing and inhabiting a healing Christian community are reciprocal. True Christians become God's healers, even if wounded healers. The Christian community infectiously carries God's healing throughout society and culture, nurturing cycles of healing and counteracting cycles of death. This also is part of the ecology of salvation.

Reconciling with Others

Which is the greatest commandment, Jesus was asked. He said there are two: "Love the Lord your God with all your heart, and with all your soul, and with all your mind," and "Love your neighbor as yourself"—for "on these two commandments hang all the law and the prophets" (Matt 22:37–40). They are inseparable.

The Apostle Paul insists that the very "mystery" of the gospel is that in the church Jew and Gentile are now "fellow heirs, members of the same body [literally, "bodied together," "co-bodied"], and sharers in the promise in Christ Jesus" (Eph 3:5–6). The vertical and horizontal dimensions—with God and others in one body—are interwoven parts of the mystery of salvation.

So the church proclaims and seeks to embody a healing reconciliation that is other-ward because it is first God-ward, through Christ. The New Testament shows how the Holy Spirit works to build this reconciled and reconciling community so that "speaking the truth in love" the church "grow[s] up in every way into him who is the head, into Christ, from whom the whole body, joined and knit together by every ligament with which it is equipped, as each part is working properly, promotes the body's growth in building itself up in love" (Eph 4:15–16). Here again is missio-ecclesiology, church and mission intertwined, the church a missional community in the healing ecology of salvation.

How foolish, then, to presume that the church can truly be the church or do wholistic mission if it ignores the very earth in which we are planted, on which we depend, where the people we wish to serve get their livelihood, and of which God has made us stewards!

Reconciling with the Earth

A wise farmer once remarked, "Remember the importance of small things done at the right time." Clearly this farmer knew the secret of living peaceably on the land—living *shalom*, practicing reconciliation earthward. This is God's intent—life lived in harmony with the rhythms of nature so that folks may "sit under their own vines and under their own fig trees" in peace, unafraid (Mic 4:4).

Today fewer and fewer people are farmers. Most of us have lost the sense of interdependence with the land. But now come fresh reminders: the groans of creation, as we discussed earlier. More importantly, we have clear biblical teachings about God's "everlasting covenant" with the earth, and we have manifold opportunities to be reconcilers in and with the earth so that God's glory can be seen among the nations (Psalm 8).

The key point—as we have insisted throughout this book—is that the nourishing and flourishing of the earth is not a detached or incidental matter in the gospel and in Christian mission. It is not a separate topic, not a sideline or auxiliary concern. It is an essential part of the textured ecology of creation and redemption. All other dimensions of reconciliation through Jesus Christ are impoverished if we miss the biblical accent on the earth. Even our experience of God is diminished if we miss our—and *God's*—interconnection with the wondrous creation he has crafted. Think again of the magnificent last chapters of Job.

And so, of course, earthward reconciliation is interwoven with mission. The healing of the land inescapably involves these same two linked aspects that we encountered in the other dimensions of reconciliation: church and mission.

CREATION CARE AND WHOLISTIC MISSION

Properly understood, creation healed clarifies all four dimensions of salvation. We see the magnificent interflow of the many-sided reconciliation that the Sovereign Trinity offers his diseased and aching creation. We are reminded again that God seeks to redeem men and women *with* their environment, not *out of* it. We see more deeply the majesty of God's salvific *oikonomia*, the wisdom of his gracious way of restoring a wounded world through Jesus Christ.

Scripture presents a richly textured, comprehensive mandate for honoring God through caring for his handiwork. Biblically, this is part of the good news of salvation in Jesus Christ, not a secondary add-on. The mandate for creation care is richly rooted in Scripture:

- The plan of salvation is one of peace, *shalom*, a deeply ecological concept involving the interdependence of people with their social and physical context.
- The biblical theology of land, from the Old Testament to the New, literally "grounds" salvation in God's plan for the whole earth.
- The theme of the earth as God's habitation implies human respect for and care of nature. The key biblical theme of justice and righteousness—the chief basis for a kingdom of God ethic—rules out harmful exploitation not only of people but of the land.
- The Ten Commandments assume our interdependence with and responsibility for the land.

- The incarnation and servanthood of Jesus show what it means to live righteous and godly lives physically, on earth.
- The biblical doctrine of the Holy Spirit and of the church as a charismatic community underscores the role of the Spirit in both creation and the renewal of creation (e.g., Ps 104:30).
- Finally, the doctrine of the Trinity itself is rich in ecological insights. It implies mutual interdependence and self-giving to the other, rather than self-centered dominance or exploitation. The created order is the way it is because of the way God is. Its unity and diversity reflects in some sense the Triune diversity-within-unity.

In sum, creation stewardship is grounded in God's character, in Scripture from beginning to end, and in the good news we proclaim. Everything in the gospel, in the kingdom of God, comes into clearer focus when viewed through the lens of creation and the promised new creation. Biblically speaking, then, creation care is part of God's creation-healing salvation. It is much more than a question of environmental ethics. The gospel in fact gives us a fivefold rationale for including the earth within our circle of concern:

Creation Care for God's Sake

"The heavens are telling the glory of God; and the firmament proclaims his handiwork" (Ps 19:1). God created the universe, in part, to glorify himself and to enrich humanity's praise of him. We are to praise God through, and because of, his beautiful but complex world. So the primary reason for faithful creation care is simple: caring for God's world is how we glorify God. We glorify him by proper stewardship of the world he has made. We care for creation *for God's sake.*

Scripture affirms that "whether [we] eat or drink, or whatever [we] do," we should "do everything for the glory of God" (1 Cor 10:31). God is glorified when we see his handiwork in the created order, and when we care for the world he has made. Creation care is part of our "spiritual worship"; our basic liturgy (Rom 12:1).

Job had to learn the key lesson that the created order shows God's vast wisdom, and so we humbly praise him. "Hear this, O Job; stop and consider the wondrous works of God" (Job 37:14). We see the hand of God in his works, and lift our eyes from nature to nature's God—but then *look back again* at nature with new eyes, seeing the garden we are to tend. If we only look up, we miss much of the salvation worldstory. By fulfilling God-given stewardship through the God-like powers we have received for good, not for evil, we glorify the Creator.

This is historic Christianity. Alister McGrath and others have documented the long Christian tradition of seeing God's beauty in nature, surely, but also of human responsibility that vision implies. "Something of the torrent of God's beauty can . . . be known in the rivulets of the beauty of creation. This has long been recognised as one of the most basic religious motivations for scientific research," McGrath notes, and should stir our passion for creation care, as well. Thomas Aquinas wrote, "Meditation on God's works enables us, at least to some extent, to admire and reflect on God's wisdom."[3] Jesus-followers should take the next logical step: The God who is reflected and glorified in the created order is honored and served through creation care.

John Wesley is a good representative of what might be called the great tradition of Christian appreciation of the created order and the responsibility that implies. "How small a part of this great work of God [in creation are we] able to understand!" Wesley wrote. "But it is our duty to contemplate what he has wrought, and to understand as much of it as we are able."[4] Wesley argued that such contemplation is a theological, not just a devotional, exercise. He affirmed,

> God is in all things, and . . . we are to see the Creator in the [mirror] of every creature; . . . we should use and look upon nothing as separate from God, which indeed is a kind of practical atheism; but with a true magnificence of thought survey heaven and earth and all that is therein as contained by God in the hollow of his hand, who by his intimate presence holds them all in being, who pervades and actuates the whole created frame, and is in a true sense the soul of the universe.[5]

The created order shows us God's wisdom, glory, and beauty, Wesley said, leading us to praise him and live responsibly before him in the world. Creation is the God-given "book of nature." In its light we interpret the Scriptures, and vice versa.

We learn of our own stewardship from God's care for his creatures. Caring for and protecting God's world is part of our worship and service. We care for creation for God's sake.

Creation Care for Our Own Sake

Creation care is essential to our own well-being. We should care for creation as if our life depends on it, because it does.

We forget how much we rely upon the physical environment—"a few hundred yards of air and a few inches of soil." Most of the time, we are oblivious to our dependence upon the earth. But then hurricanes, tornadoes, earthquakes, volcanoes, or other "natural events" show our vulnerability. "Mother Nature has gone on a rampage," people say. But we are no less vulnerable when the sun shines, flowers bloom, and birds sing—we're just less conscious of it. Here environmental science helps us, and we need to pay attention to what it teaches.

If we are passionate about people, we will be passionate about their world. Christians often help feed the hungry and shelter the homeless. This Christ-like concern should widen to include the environmental conditions that affect food production and the well-being of our planet-home. In many places, people lack food and shelter because forests have been destroyed or the water supply has disappeared.

---

3. McGrath, *Re-enchantment of Nature*, 16.

4. Wesley, Sermon 56, "God's Approbation of His Works." Wesley, *Works*, 2:387.

5. Wesley, Sermon 23, "Upon our Lord's Sermon on the Mount, Discourse III." Wesley, *Works*, 1:516–17.

These ecological issues cannot be solved simply by relief efforts. They require careful, informed, sustained creation care.

In North America, and increasingly in other technologically-advanced nations, most people have enough food, but not much *healthy* food. Industrial food, increasingly concocted from chemical compounds, high-fructose corn syrup, and artificial or so-called "natural" flavors, contributes to obesity and the illusion of being well fed. Most North Americans live in a state of food ignorance due to the industrialization and globalization of food since World War II.

Every person should be able to answer the four most basic food questions: What is it? Where did it come from? How did it get here? Is it good for me? But most Americans today, and millions of other people in the increasingly globalized food market, simply cannot answer these most basic questions. If they look at the list of ingredients, they are quickly mystified by unknown chemical compounds and unfamiliar technical terms. We simply have no idea how much of our food comes from factory farms, laboratories, and fossil fuels, rather than from healthy farms that nurture and preserve the earth. Often we simply do not know what we are eating.

In *The Omnivore's Dilemma: A Natural History of Four Meals*, Michael Pollan shows how this situation developed over the past half-century. Today, "foods of astounding novelty fill the shelves of our supermarket," Pollan notes, "and the line between a food and a 'nutritional supplement' has fogged to the point where people make meals of protein bars and shakes." Yet this "suits the food industry just fine. . . . The more anxious we are about eating, the more vulnerable we are to the seductions of the marketer and the expert's advice."[6]

Look at your dinner plate. If you're a typical North American, most of your meal traveled some 1,500 miles to get there, and ninety percent of what you paid for it went to processing, retailing, advertising, and transportation (mostly fossil fuels). The food itself cost only about eight cents of every dollar you spent.[7]

This sad situation is ripe for reform. The whole system, not just the food, is unhealthy. Caring for creation means knowing the connection between the earth and our stomachs. Restoring food production to more healthy and sustainable forms of agriculture is part of the agenda of creation care. Healing creation means reforming the system. Scott Sabin puts it this way: "The more closely agriculture mimics natural ecosystems, the more sustainable it is"—and thus the closer to God's intent. "God's ability to work things together for good is obvious in the intricate ways that ecosystems fit together. Nothing is wasted; everything has its niche. Everywhere, life springs forth from death, and resurrection is foreshadowed."[8]

Scripture is the story of God's people serving God in God's land. If God's people are faithful, the land prospers. Conversely, if the land suffers, we suffer. This theme echoes throughout the Old Testament, as we saw in chapter 8. It permeates the law, the

6. Pollan, *Omnivore's Dilemma*, 301.

7. Ibid., 239, 242.

8. Sabin, "Whole Earth Evangelism," 29.

prophets, and the wisdom literature, coming to special focus in the Jubilee legislation of Leviticus 25–26.

The key fact is ecological interdependence. If we care about people, we will care for the land and air and many species on which our well-being depends.

Creation Care for Creation's Sake

We also care about the created order because it has its own God-given right to flourish, independently of us. The world after all is *God's* handiwork, not ours. "Everything under heaven belongs to me" (Job 41:11 TNIV). God created the universe for his good purposes, *not all of which are known to us*. We need a certain eschatological humility and reserve. We should honor God's creative work and fulfill our responsibilities as stewards of what he has made.

God's other creatures depend heavily upon us for *their* well-being and survival. Increasingly, we see that the whole biosphere is more dependent on human nurture and care than we had imagined. We need to recover the biblical sense of why creation exists, how it proclaims God's glory, and how all nature will participate in God's salvation.

John Wesley had a profound sense of this. One of his favorite phrases was "the restitution of all things," the King James Version of Acts 3:21. In that passage Peter says the time is coming when God will "restore everything, as he promised long ago through his holy prophets" (TNIV). Wesley wrote:

> While "the whole creation groans together" (whether [we notice it] or not) their groans are not dispersed in idle air, but enter into the ears of him that made them. While his creatures "travail together in pain," he knoweth all their pain, and is bringing them nearer and nearer to the birth which shall be accomplished in its season. He seeth "the earnest expectation" wherewith the whole animated creation "waiteth for" that final "manifestation of the sons of God": in which "they themselves also shall be delivered" (not by annihilation: annihilation is not deliverance) "from the" present "bondage of corruption, into" a measure of "the glorious liberty of the children of God."

Referring then to Revelation 21, Wesley notes that the promised destruction of death, evil, and pain is not limited to humans. Rather, we may expect that the "whole brute creation will then undoubtedly be restored, not only to the vigour, strength, and swiftness which they had at their creation, but to a far higher degree of each than they ever enjoyed"—each creature "according to its capacity." Then will be fulfilled the great promise of Isa 11:6–9, the *peaceable kingdom*.[9]

Since all God's creatures reflect God's glory and have a place in his plan, they are part of legitimate Christian concern. If God cares about the creatures, so should we. So it is with all creation, not just animals—for all living things meet in one vast ecosystem. This is why matters of the earth, of food and agriculture, are not just human concerns. They are creation concerns. Creation care and sustainability are good for the earth and good for us, for all are connected.

9. Wesley, Sermon 60, "General Deliverance." Wesley, *Works*, 2:449.

From this perspective, some recent earth-care developments are good news. Growing and buying food locally or regionally, instead of from half a world away, is an expanding movement in the U.S. Organic agriculture is no longer a marginal enterprise. And now The Land Institute in Kansas, after decades of research, is starting to market perennial grains that combine the hardiness of native grasses with the productivity of wheat. In addition to reducing erosion and soil deterioration by eliminating annual planting, these perennial grain crops make chemicals and constant irrigation largely a thing of the past.[10]

Creation Care for the Sake of Mission

Here is another key reason Jesus-followers should be passionate about creation care. It is essential for effective mission today.

The biblical doctrine of creation means wholistic mission must include mission to and on behalf of the earth. The biblical vision has not changed: God's people serving God's purposes in God's land.

The reasons for this are both theological and strategic: theological, because fully biblical mission will necessarily include the dimension of creation care; but also strategic and pragmatic. Mission that incorporates creation care is simply more persuasive. Do we want people of all nations and cultures to come to faith in Jesus as Savior of the world? Then we should proclaim and show that Jesus is the renewer of all creation, the whole face of the earth. Salvation is that big. This is a grander portrayal of Christ than we sometimes present. It both honors our Savior and makes the gospel more persuasive when we present a gospel of total healing—the healing of creation; the restoration of all things. This is truly the whole gospel for the whole world.

Creation Care for the Sake of Our Children and Grandchildren

Here is a final persuasive motive for creation care today: our children and grandchildren, our descendants yet unborn. As Scripture teaches, we have a responsibility—a stewardship—on behalf of generations yet to come.[11]

Today we look back at the Protestants of the 1500s and ask: Why did they not have a vision for global missions? Or we look back at Christian slaveholders in the 1700s and 1800s and ask: How could they not see that slavery distorts the gospel? What did they think they were doing?

The arguments of the nineteenth-century abolitionists can teach us. Antislavery activists used four arguments that echo today's creation-care debate: (1) The Bible does not justify the practice of slavery today; (2) the issue is moral and spiritual, not

10. The Land Institute. The Institute's mission statement is consistent with Scripture: "When people, land and community are as one, all three members prosper; when they relate not as members but as competing interests, all three are exploited. By consulting nature as the source and measure of that membership, The Land Institute seeks to develop an agriculture that will save soil from being lost or poisoned, while promoting a community life at once prosperous and enduring."

11. Recall the discussion of generations in chapter 5.

just political or economic; (3) the only proper response therefore is repentance and the ending of slavery; and (4) the key theological issue is *creation*. Slaves are our fellow humans, created in God's image. Abolitionists were a minority in the 1830s, yet today most Christians accept these arguments.

Now we are in a similar place with regard to the stewardship of God's good creation, and similar arguments apply. Creation is now in bondage (Rom 8:21). Clearly this is a biblical concern. Yet today advocacy of creation care is as controversial to some as was early abolitionism.

Our grandchildren, as they wrestle with a damaged and rampaging environment, will look back on this generation and ask: How could they not see our Christian responsibility for the earth? Why did they wait so long? What did they think they were doing when they failed to defend the forests and the seas and to protect earth's endangered species? Did they not understand what they were doing to their own children and grandchildren?

We are the generation that must rediscover and proclaim creation care as part of the gospel, part of the mission of God. Saleemul Huq, a Bangladeshi biologist and internationally recognized climate scientist, says, "Climate change is the greatest weapon of mass destruction of our times. Unless we . . . recognize this fact and do something about it, we are guilty of crimes against humanity."[12] Here certainly is a call to Christian mission in behalf of people everywhere.

We hope our children and grandchildren will know and serve Jesus Christ. We also hope that they will inherit a world that is not choked and poisoned by pollution or made uninhabitable by environmental disasters and a changing climate. If that is our hope, the time for action is now. We should treat future generations the way we would want to be treated.

THE END OF ESCHATOLOGY

It should be clear by now that this entire book is about eschatology, for it focuses on God's overall plan for the total healing of creation.

"Salvation means creation healed" is an eschatological claim in three ways. First, it means that the end or *telos* of history foresees complete healing, restoration, and reconciliation—complete *shalom*. Second, it means that the church's present being and mission are defined by this end. Finally, it means that, ultimately, God's economy or *oikonomia* and eschatology are one.

Eschatology has troubled the church from the beginning. Since the future is largely unknown to us, we naturally wonder and speculate. What will happen? The Bible pictures the end of the story in various ways. Some appear more positive and optimistic; others, more negative and pessimistic.

Especially in times of stress and controversy, the church has pondered the future. It has tried to figure out how and when God would accomplish his purposes, and

12. Quoted in Hertsgaard, *Hot*, 218.

what that meant for the present. Often in trying times the church has cried out with the psalmist, "How long, O God, is the foe to scoff? Is the enemy to revile your name forever?" (Ps 74:10). "O Lord, how long shall the wicked, how long shall the wicked exult?" (Ps 94:3).

Times of stress and times of renewal give rise to conflicting interpretations of eschatology. This in turn produces differing visions and theories of the kingdom of God.[13] How much of the hope of the kingdom may we expect to see realized now? How much awaits the distant, or perhaps not-so-distant, future?

The Dispensation Delusion

One way to answer this question is through some theory of *dispensations*—different ages of history in which God works differently.

The New Testament speaks of "this age" and "the age to come" (Matt 12:32; Luke 18:30; Eph 1:21). Our Bibles are divided into "Old" and "New" Testaments. However, dispensational theories, like those of Joachim of Fiore or John Nelson Darby, typically propose not just two, but three or six or seven "dispensations" or "ages."

Dispensational theories divide God's redemptive activity into separate periods or "dispensations," often according to some biblical schema—the six days of creation, the biblical covenants, the seven churches of Revelation 2–3, or whatever. The Bible is full of numbers which can be pressed into speculative eschatological service.

Dispensationalism resolves the basic present/future tension in biblical teaching about the kingdom of God through a process of historical segmentation. Once the church had developed the doctrine of the Trinity, three-part theories of history like that of Joachim of Fiore emerged: the age of the Father, the age of the Son, and the new age of the Spirit. In most of such theories the last age is seen as just about to dawn.[14]

Dispensationalism then, and most millennial theories, divide up God's plan or economy into different ages or dispensations. The New Testament speaks simply of "this age" and "the age to come," whereas dispensational theories subdivide the "age to come" into a whole succession of stages.

For our purposes, three points are important here. First, all dispensational theories go way beyond Scripture, using some external theory as the key to understanding the Bible. This is dangerous, whatever the theory. It distorts the dynamic biblical story by wrapping a non-biblical straitjacket around the Bible.

---

13. Snyder, *Models*.

14. For a fuller exposition of dispensational logic, see Snyder, *Models*, 123–26. The name Dispensationalism traces back to the word "dispensation," found four times in the King James Version of the Bible. A key verse is Ephesians 1:10, which in the KJV reads, "That in the dispensation of the fulness of times he might gather together in one all things in Christ, both which are in heaven, and which are on earth." (The word occurs also in 1 Cor 9:17; Eph 3:2; and Col 1:25.) Interestingly, in the KJV "dispensation" translates the Greek *oikonomia*, which as we have seen means God's overall "economy" or "plan" of salvation. In the KJV *oikonomia* is also translated "stewardship," as in Luke 16:2 ("give an account of thy stewardship"). Most contemporary biblical versions translate *oikonomia* (which occurs repeatedly in the New Testament) as "plan," "commission," "trust," "administration," or "management." See the discussion in chapter 1 of this book.

Second, because of this, dispensational theories are usually more pessimistic or more optimistic than the Bible itself. Here dispensationalists divide into two main camps: premillennialists and postmillennialists. Premillennialists hold that Jesus will return *before* (pre) a thousand-year millennium. Postmillennialists say Jesus will return *after* (post) a millennial age, either a literal thousand years or a less defined period of gospel success.[15] Generally premillennialists tend to be pessimistic about society, for their theory requires that things get progressively worse, so Jesus can return. Postmillennialists tend to be socially optimistic, for their theory holds that God's Word will prosper more and more, and then Jesus will return in triumph. Both views are problematic and biblically one-sided.

Third, dispensational theories are often hugely important because *eschatology shapes ethics*. What we believe about the future determines how we act in the present. Hope shapes expectations, and expectations move actions. We behave in certain ways because of what we think the future holds. The same is true with regard to creation care: if we believe "it's all going to burn up anyway," we will be less likely to care about the earth's welfare. If we believe that God will somehow redeem the earth, we are more likely to care what happens to it now. Or more generally with regard to the kingdom of God: if we believe God really intends to answer Jesus' prayer that God's "will be done, on earth as it is in heaven" (Matt 6:10), we will work now to show the truth of God's reign in all areas on earth.

Both premillennialism and postmillennialism can, in fact, function as self-fulfilling prophecies. If Christians believe society can only get worse, they will not work to redeem it, so society will, in fact, get worse. If Christians believe society can be transformed, they will work to redeem it, and society will get better, possibly both locally and globally.[16]

Of course, people can be better or worse than their theories. Some premillennialists practice creation care, and many postmillennialists don't. The larger point however is this: though we are shaped by our eschatological expectations, no theory can capture the full dynamic of the biblical story.

There are other eschatological views and theories besides premillennialism and postmillennialism, and there are many variations of each of these.[17] Many Christians are amillennialists, holding that since the numbers in Revelation are highly symbolic, we should not anticipate a literal one-thousand-year period in salvation history. Many

---

15. The whole idea of a "millennium" (literally, one thousand years) is based on a sole biblical passage, Rev 20:2–8. Given the symbolic nature of numbers in Revelation and the absence of any teaching about a millennium elsewhere in Scripture, we should be wary of theories that espouse a literal thousand-year period in salvation history. Three other biblical passages mention a thousand years (Ps 90:4; Eccl 6:6; 2 Pet 3:8), but all are rhetorical. The comment in 2 Pet 3:8 should caution us against eschatological mathematics: "With the Lord one day is like a thousand years, and a thousand years like one day."

16. "To dream the impossible dream" is actually a Christian sentiment if properly tied to the resurrection of Jesus Christ and the whole *oikonomia* of the Triune God—not based on humanistic optimism or mere pop psychology or "positive thinking" or some form of New-Age pantheism.

17. "Progressive dispensationalists" hold a less rigid form of premillennialism that is more compatible with Scripture.

premillennialists and postmillennialists also take the thousand-year number to mean an indefinite period of peace and righteousness, not necessarily a literal thousand years.

It is not necessary here to sort out the different theories. The key underlying issue remains: is the future predetermined, or not? Much eschatology, and most millennial theories, assume that the future *is* largely predetermined. A correct theory can map it out pretty clearly. But this does violence to Scripture. Such theories can be sustained only by a selective hermeneutic—that is, by emphasizing some passages and ignoring or misusing others.

Eschatological Openness: The Two Ways

Does God know the future? Yes, in ways known only to God. Does God *predetermine* the future? The Bible shows that God, who is sovereign and not confined to spacetime history, has determined or "guaranteed" (to speak humanly) the final victory, the final healing of all creation—but this still leaves a lot of space for creaturely action and initiative. In other words, there is genuine *contingency* in history. God, like an infinitely clever chess player, superintends and guides history toward final healing. But he gives freedom to other "players" genuinely to act.

This historical contingency is grounded, first of all, in creation itself, as established by God. The early church father Athanasius saw this clearly. As Thomas Torrance summarizes, "the independence given by God to the creation is itself dependent upon God. God made nature in such a way that it operates with a certain measure of autonomy. . . . And yet the very reality of this independence of nature is itself dependent, or contingent, upon God." God has given the creation "an authentic reality and lawfulness of its own which he unceasingly sustains through the presence of his Creator Word and Spirit." For "in Jesus Christ God has established and secured a new relation between the creation and himself in which the creation is given a freedom grounded in the transcendent and unlimited freedom of God."[18] Historical contingency is thus grounded in the nature of the Trinity and derivatively in the nature of the creation where God still acts by his Word and Spirit.

To say that history within God's economy is *contingent* means that many things may or may not happen, depending on multiplied factors. To view history *contingently* and to view it *ecologically* are thus two sides of the same coin, given a sociocultural and physical ecosystem with billions of actors.

This view of God's economy is deeper and richer than dispensational theories. It makes good sense of Scripture. As noted above, the Bible is both "optimistic" and "pessimistic" about the future. Is it inconsistent? No. It makes perfect sense when we realize the degree of freedom God gives his creatures (humans, angels, demons, even animals and plants in a limited degree) to act in a variety of ways.[19]

18. Torrance, *Trinitarian Faith*, 101, 102, 106. Torrance shows how "the contingence of the creation" and therefore its freedom is a necessary implication of the biblical doctrine of creation *ex nihilo* and foundational for biblical teachings on the restoration of creation (ibid., 98–109).

19. Anyone who has observed animal behavior closely can't help being impressed with the way animals make what appear to humans as choices, and how some birds and animals occasionally veer

Here we find, in fact, a key theme of Scripture. God sets before us two ways, two paths, and states the consequences of choosing one or the other. Over and over God says in various ways what Joshua said to the Israelites after the conquest of Canaan: "Choose this day whom you will serve" (Josh 24:15). This is especially clear in Deuteronomy 27–30, where God dramatically sets out blessings and curses—blessings for following God's way, curses for following the idolatrous ways of the nations. These sobering chapters are well worth the church's reading and rereading, for they show clearly the options, the contingencies, always facing God's people.

The stunning conclusion comes in Deut 30:19–20: "I call heaven and earth to witness against you today that I have set before you life and death, blessings and curses. Choose life so that you and your descendants may live, loving the Lord your God, obeying him, and holding fast to him; for that means life to you and length of days, so that you may live in the land that the Lord swore to give to your ancestors, to Abraham, to Isaac, and to Jacob." Here are the two ways—and with an accent on *the land*. The relationship between God, Israel, and the land will be healthy, nurturing, "shalomistic," if Israel follows God's way and keeps the covenant. Going the other way spells disasters thrice over.

The language is truly dramatic. If you follow my way, God says, I will "bless you in the land" I am giving you. "You will be blessed in the city and blessed in the country. The fruit of your womb will be blessed, and the crops of your land and the young of your livestock" (Deut 28:3–4 TNIV). But if you take the wrong track? "The fruit of your womb will be cursed, and the crops of your land, and the calves of your herds and the lambs of your flock" (Deut 28:18 TNIV). "The Lord will plague you with diseases until he has destroyed you from the land you are entering to possess" (Deut 28:21 TNIV). "The whole land will be a burning waste of salt and sulfur—nothing planted, nothing sprouting, no vegetation growing on it" (Deut 29:23 TNIV). What a vivid picture of the ecology of sin and righteousness, the interplay between God, people, and land, and eschatological contingency![20] We are offered two ways. The right way is commanded, but the people must choose. Their response is not coerced or predetermined.

This theme of two ways—which requires choice and contingency—runs throughout the Old Testament. God says, "See, I am setting before you the way of life and the way of death" (Jer 21:8). In the book of Proverbs, wisdom and folly both cry out for people to follow their ways: "Therefore walk in the way of the good, and keep the path of the just" (Prov 2:20). "Do not enter the path of the wicked, and do not walk in the way of evildoers" (Prov 4:14). "The Lord watches over the way of the righteous, but the way of the wicked will perish" (Ps 1:6).

So also in the New Testament: Jesus in his teaching and his person sets up a *crucis,* a crucial decision point between two ways. His teachings imply choice and

from the group norm, seemingly acting independently. While plants may not make choices, they do respond to various stimuli in a variety of (unpredictable?) ways. In God's creation, little if anything is truly inert.

20. These passages also look ahead to the new covenant, for Moses promises, "the Lord your God will circumcise your heart and the heart of your descendants, so that you will love the Lord your God with all your heart and with all your soul, in order that you may live" (Deut 30:6).

contingency. Build your house on rock or on sand (Matt 7:24–26). A man invites guests to a wedding feast, but many refuse to come (Matt 22:3). Jesus says to Jerusalem, "How often have I desired to gather your children together as a hen gathers her brood under her wings, and you were not willing!" (Matt 23:37; Luke 13:34) The outcome of choice is stark: the unrighteous "will go away into eternal punishment, but the righteous into eternal life" (Matt 25:46). So Paul writes, echoing Moses and Joshua and Jesus: "The wages of sin is death, but the free gift of God is eternal life in Christ Jesus our Lord" (Rom 6:23).

The entire New Testament teaching on the church and discipleship assumes the two ways, with related blessings and curses. Paul says, "Just as you used to offer yourselves as slaves to impurity and to ever-increasing wickedness, so now offer yourselves as slaves to righteousness leading to holiness" (Rom 6:19 TNIV). Paul and other New Testament writers say in various ways, "lead a life worthy of the calling to which you have been called" (Eph 4:1); "lead a life worthy of God, who calls you into his own kingdom and glory" (1 Thess 2:12). Paul insists, "You must no longer live as the Gentiles live, in the futility of their minds. . . . You were taught to put away your former way of life, . . . and to be renewed in the spirit of your minds" (Eph 4:17–23). These teachings make sense only if people have real freedom to choose one way or the other—to make real choices with genuinely positive or negative outcomes.

The whole Bible teaches eschatological openness under God's sovereignty. The real mystery of eschatology is the mystery of contingency—of historical indeterminacy under God's sure reign. This is in fact *the nature of narrative.* It is what makes stories interesting and mystery novels fascinating. This is the way the sovereign God, the great Author and Playwright, works in history.

THE MISSIONAL-ESCHATOLOGICAL CHALLENGE

God says to the church today, as always: I set before you two ways—two eschatological choices. Choose life! Seek first God's kingdom and his justice. Seek the way of creation healed through Jesus by the Spirit.

The Bible's eschatological openness thus charges the church with eschatological responsibility. It spells *hope,* because God's Spirit is at work to renew the face of the earth. The Triune God is on the side of those who seek now his will on earth as in heaven. Richard Foster is right: "ours is an open universe, not a closed universe. God has sovereignly chosen to invite us into this process of bringing about his will on the earth. . . . We are, as the apostle Paul puts it, colaborers with God, working together to determine the outcome of events."[21]

This truth is key to the church's mission, to creation healed. What happens in the future—positively or negatively, "optimistically" or "pessimistically," healing or disease—depends in large measure on the church's missional fidelity or infidelity.

So the church is entrusted with eschatological responsibility and present hope as it cooperates with God's *oikonomia,* his salvation plan. As Thomas Oden phrases it,

21. Foster and Beebe, *Longing for God,* 99.

"We are now called to understand our present ecological accountability within creation as a final accountability to which we will be called on the last day."[22] The whole eschatological project, reduced to its most basic, is this: God's will done on earth as in heaven—the earth full of the knowledge of the Lord. And mission at its most basic is this: "Your kingdom come, your will be done"—loving God with all we are and our neighbor and neighborhood as ourselves.

We saw earlier (see n. 14) that the biblical term behind the English word "dispensation" (in the KJV) is *oikonomia*, God's overall economy or plan—a "mystery" (Eph 3:3–9) known fully only to God. To map out God's grand economy as a sequence of predetermined time segments or dispensations belittles the wonder, the majesty, and openness of God's plan. In fact, it compromises God's sovereignty. God is bigger than all our dispensationalism. Salvation surpasses all our theories.

We are left not with a closed theory of dispensations, but with the openness and grandeur of God's *oikonomia*. We are left, in other words, with *stewardship*—a key meaning of the word *oikonomia*. Not discreet dispensations, but dynamic stewardship. The church has been given an eschatological stewardship—the "management" or "administration [*oikonomia*] of God's grace" (Eph 3:2 TNIV); "the administration" or "stewardship [*oikonomia*] of this mystery" (Eph 3:9 TNIV). This was Paul's apostolic commission, and it is part of the church's apostolic witness. As the Apostle Peter declares, Christians are called to be "stewards [*oikonomoi*] of God's grace in its various forms" (1 Pet 4:10 TNIV) so that God's kingdom may come and his will be done on earth as in heaven.

The church's commission, then, is the stewardship of the mission that God has given it. The church is called to the stewardship of God's redemptive plan, not to the elaboration of dispensational theories. Although much of God's plan still remains a mystery, the central secret "has now been revealed by the Spirit to God's holy apostles and prophets"—namely, salvation for all, Jew and Gentile alike, through faith in Jesus Christ, all "according to his eternal purpose that he accomplished in Christ Jesus our Lord" (Eph 3:5–11).

THE BIG MEANING OF STEWARDSHIP

Not dispensational speculation, but faithful stewardship of God's grace—this is the church's eschatological challenge. Living now in "the powers of the age to come" (Heb 6:5 TNIV), filled with the Spirit, the body of Christ has a stewardship not only for this age but also for the coming age of *shalom* (see Eph 1:21).

Given the biblical meaning of "economy" (*oikonomia*) and the related dynamic of ecology, the rich meaning of stewardship becomes clear. Biblically, stewardship is *oikonomia*—the proper way of running a household (*oikos*).

Scripture teaches two basic kinds of stewardship—stewardship of the earth or land, and stewardship of God's grace (1 Pet 4:10). They go together in wonderful

22. Oden, *Wesley's Scriptural Christianity*, 130.

balance. Here is the church's stewardly mission: care of the earth, now diseased by sin, and proper use of God's grace, which provides the cure. All other kinds of stewardship flow from our stewardship of God's many-colored grace (as the words can also be translated—1 Pet 4:10) and our covenant care of the created order—including land, time, money, and all other resources.

The Bible says, "The Lord God took the man and put him in the Garden of Eden to work it and to take care of it" (Gen 2:15 TNIV). Humans were commissioned to care for the garden. We know from Genesis 1 that "the man" here means "humankind," man and woman jointly, since the creation account explicitly says that Adam and Eve are jointly to "rule over" the created order (Gen 1:26–28) as his God-imaged stewards. Genesis 2:15 makes it clear that "rule" means "care for"—the kind of rule that implies protection and nurture, not relentless exploitation. That's how God rules. That's the example Jesus gives.

This is the meaning of stewardship at the creation level. But then the New Testament teaches, "Each of you should use whatever gift you have received to serve others, as faithful stewards of God's grace in its various forms" (1 Pet 4:10 TNIV). We are to be "faithful stewards of God's grace." This is our biggest and broadest steward-ship responsibility—conscientious care in using "God's many-colored grace" for his kingdom purposes.

After the fall and the flood, God reinforced the stewardship mandate spelled out in the first covenant he made—the covenant "between me and you and all living creatures of every kind" (Gen 9:15 TNIV)—that is, "the covenant I have established between me and all life on the earth" (Gen 9:17 TNIV), as discussed in chapter 8. The new covenant in the blood of Jesus Christ by the Spirit provides the power, the essential gracious resource, by which the church can fulfill humanity's long-neglected commission to properly care for and "manage" all God's good gifts.

Stewardship, of course, is a relationship—a relationship in two directions. A steward is responsible *to* someone *for* something. Stewardship thus implies a three-dimensional covenant. In Genesis 1, 2, and 9, the three dimensions of this covenant are God, humankind, and the earth, as we saw earlier.

Both the Greek New Testament and the Greek translation of the Old Testament, the Septuagint, use the term *oikonomia* (economy) to express this meaning of steward-ship. Since English Bibles use a variety of terms to translate *oikonomia* (as well as the related terms *oikos,* "house" or "household," and *oikonomos,* "steward" or "manager"), the importance of the term and concept is often obscured.

Another word for stewardship of the earth, particularly as a form of witness, is eco-evangelism. This means living out the good news in relation to the earth and all its inhabitants. As Elaine Heath puts it, eco-evangelism is "being good news to creation in the name of Jesus." As we learn the real meaning of ecology and of God's economy or *oikonomia,* we come to see that "ecological commitments are not limited to animals, plants, water, and air. Eco-evangelism requires the church to engage the interlocking systems of exploitation that poison rivers, force children to slave in cigarette factories, give blood diamonds their name, and pump toxins into the air. Eco-evangelism is about redeeming the earth that God made."[23]

Scott Sabin, who directs the organization Plant with Purpose, calls this "whole earth evangelism." Sabin shows how working to heal the creation God loves is integral to the Great Commission and the Great Commandment. "We have little choice as to whether we will interact with creation," Sabin notes. "But we can choose whether our interactions will be life-giving or death-dealing."[24]

The point is this: God has a grand plan for the fullness of time to heal all creation through Jesus Christ by the Spirit—and the church is called, commissioned, and empowered by the Spirit to fulfill this eschatological stewardship. In this biblical sense stewardship is mission, and mission is stewardship.

CONCLUSION

We have a great commission and a wonderful opportunity to make Jesus Christ known today, to proclaim the gospel of the kingdom, to declare God's glory among the nations. We have a stewardship to fulfill—a stewardship of God's "manifold works" and his "manifold grace" (Ps 104:24, 1 Pet 4:10). Creation is our garden and grace is our resource.

The same God who is concerned with the renewal of the church is concerned with the renewal of creation. The same Spirit who hovers over the church hovers over the waters, seeking to bring both into reconciliation under the headship of Christ. If we are concerned about mission in its truest sense, we will be concerned about every good thing God has made. Conversely, if we are really concerned with God's world, we will want to see the Holy Spirit renew God's people, sending a revival of such depth that it not only stirs our hearts but also heals our land.

We want to see creation healed. We are hopeful because God has promised it will be so. We especially want to see our sisters and brothers throughout the earth healed of the disease of sin, brought into new-creation life through Jesus and the Spirit. We want to live and proclaim the good news of the kingdom so that more and more people globally keep covenant with God and with his good earth, assured that "the creation itself will be set free from its bondage to decay" and "the earth will be full of the knowledge of the Lord as the waters cover the sea."

How will this happen? The church has a key role to play. God intends and empowers the church to be his healing community. The final section of this book shows what it means for the church to be this healing force, how the church plays a key role in creation healed.

---

23. Heath, *Mystic Way*, 111.
24. Sabin, "Whole Earth Evangelism," 27–29.

PART FOUR

The Healing Community

11

Rediscovering the Church

Christ loved the church and gave himself up for her.

(Eph 5:25)

WHAT DOES JESUS PRAY for the church? "I am not asking you to take them out of the world" (John 17:15). Is that not still Jesus' prayer for the church—present and future; historically and eschatologically? Not removal, but fidelity; not escape, but leavening witness. This is God's intent: The church *in* but *not of* the world, a faithful witness to God's salvation and reign.

God's intent has never been to take his people out of the world, but to take evil out of the world. John says, "For this purpose the Son of God was manifested, to destroy the works of the devil" (1 John 3:8). The world is not the work of the devil; it is the good work of God. It is evil, not the world, that will be destroyed, or perhaps will self-destruct. The earth, we read, God "has founded forever" (Ps 78:69).

And so the church has a mission on earth. Since salvation means creation healed, the church is called to be God's healing community here and now and for eternity. The whole matter of the church (ecclesiology) is that simple and that profound.

Scripture nowhere gives a neat definition of the church, but pictures it through a broad array of images and metaphors. Four of the most basic are the church as the people of God, the body of Christ, the community of the Spirit, and the community of Jesus' disciples. Historians and theologians use dozens of other images—for example, the church as sacrament, as servant, as liberator, as exiles, as a complex organism, or as an echo or image of the Trinity.[1]

---

1. For an overview, see Snyder, *Community of the King*, especially chapters 2, 3, and 5; Snyder, *Liberating*, especially chapters 4–7; Snyder and Runyon, *Decoding the Church*; Minear, *Images of the Church*; Dulles,

Two reasons, at least, explain this profusion of images. First, as the New Testament itself shows, the church is a mystery because it participates in the mystery of salvation itself, of Jesus' incarnation and work of redemption, and the mystery of the kingdom of God. Second, the church in history is ambiguous. It has been different things at different times, with vastly different degrees of faithfulness or unfaithfulness to her Lord.

Given the vastness of salvation and the complex ecology of God's plan, no one image of the church is rich enough. In this book we emphasize the church as God's healing community on earth, including all the dimensions of healing discussed in earlier chapters. The reasons for this are, first, to clarify what the theme of creation healed means for the church, and second, to show how this emphasis enriches other images of the church.

Salvation means creation healed through Jesus Christ by the work of the Spirit. Jesus established a community, a people of growing numbers and multicultural complexity, to serve as his agent of healing in the world throughout history and to all the earth. At its best, the church has always been God's healing community on earth. Through the church God has applied the medicine of salvation, reconciling people to himself through Jesus Christ and healing broken relationships. However, because of the theological divorce of heaven and earth the medicine of salvation has often been applied only partially. The cure is much less than it could and should have been. Rediscovering the church means recognizing and applying the *full* healing of the gospel to the *whole* disease of sin. It means being God's agent of reconciliation to overcome the fourfold alienation that resulted from the fall.

The question is, how can the church truly be God's healing community on and with the earth today? If salvation means creation healed, how does the church—and how *could* the church—serve faithfully as God's healing community on earth until Jesus returns in glory? This final section of the book answers that question, exploring the church as God's healing community. Previous chapters (especially chapter 4) have shown how popular Christianity understands, or misunderstands, salvation—how it often shortchanges the gospel's full healing power. This chapter identifies popular views of the church that often reinforce this too-limited gospel. We will see here and in the next two chapters how the true church of Jesus Christ can be rediscovered.

We look first at the church as it actually appears today—the visible face it shows the world, especially in its worship patterns. We then picture the church as God's healing community on earth, starting with an emphasis on the Trinity. Key marks and traits of the church are elaborated more fully in the final two chapters, leading to a final vision of the Community of Earth and Heaven.

THE POPULAR FACE OF TODAY'S CHURCH

The remarkable Protestant global missionary enterprise of the 1800s spread a concept and form of the church that by the 1900s had become the trademark of much

---

Models of the Church; Driver, *Images of the Church*; Frost, *Exiles*; Volf, *After Our Likeness*; Tillard, *Flesh of the Church*; Prusak, *Church Unfinished*.

of Protestantism worldwide. Kenneth Scott Latourette, mission historian, notes, "Especially through its share in shaping the United States of America Christianity gained in the total world scene" during the nineteenth century.[2]

Due largely to the Evangelical Awakenings in Europe and North America in the 1700s, the global expansion of Christianity in the 1800s was notably evangelical in tone and theology. An evangelical understanding of ecclesiology thus became dominant in much of Protestantism worldwide, and this continues to be true today. In the United States, as denominational labels have lost much of their meaning, "a generic form of evangelicalism is emerging as the normative form of non-Catholic Christianity," reports *Christianity Today*, citing a 2009 survey by the Trinity College Public Values Program. Since 1990 the number of U.S. Christians who consider themselves "nondenominational" or "evangelical" has shot up from only about 200,000 to eight million—suggesting a shift to a sort of generic, soft evangelicalism of vague and undefined boundaries. The very use of the term "evangelical" here shows the parentage of such believers and their congregations.

What church face has evangelical Protestantism presented to the world? In chapter 3 we traced the streams of renewal that enlivened much of Christianity during this period. What was the ecclesiology—the concept and form of the church—which resulted?[3]

The ripple effect of the Great Century of Christian missions is obvious if you visit an evangelical church almost anywhere in the world today, especially in the great urban centers. Despite differences in denominational traditions and the worldwide spread of Pentecostalism since 1906, a dominant ecclesiology is generally evident—or rather, one dominant pattern with four variations. Drop in of a Sunday morning or evening and you will likely find one of four quite distinct liturgical patterns, or perhaps some blend of them. These public worship patterns are tell-tale signs of the varied history of evangelicalism and its global missionary outreach. We will describe these four patterns briefly, then ask what they say about the church as God's healing community on earth.

The popular face of Christianity today has four expressions, but they all show a family resemblance. They are recognizable in different worship patterns that we may label *Traditional-Liturgical, Revivalist, Pentecostal-Charismatic,* and *Rock Concert.*

Most evangelical worship exhibits one more of these four patterns. These patterns in turn suggest different ideas of what the church is. The face of public worship reveals how salvation itself is understood, what the church believes about the healing power of the gospel. Each pattern has its own general time frame, though, of course, times can vary. We suggest average time frames based on our experience of visiting churches in the United States and in other countries.

---

2. Latourette, *History of Christianity*, xxv. As noted in chapter 3, Latourette called the period from 1815 to 1914 the "Great Century" of global Christian, and particularly Protestant, missions.

3. Some of what follows is adapted Snyder, "Marks of Evangelical Ecclesiology," 77–103.

The Traditional-Liturgical Pattern

The Traditional-Liturgical pattern generally runs about an hour. Worship employs a traditional liturgy tracing back many centuries. It includes readings from both the Old and New Testaments, often based on a lectionary, read prayers, and hymns in predictable meter, often based on the Psalms and biblical imagery.

The singing is accompanied, and in some cases overwhelmed, by organ music. The hymns will be more doctrinal than experiential in tone. Often the hymns are Trinitarian in form. There will be no hand-clapping. A fairly brief sermon or homily will be given, and quite possibly Holy Communion will be served, seen as the central act in worship.

In most cases the architecture, like the liturgy, traces back to medieval Europe. The congregation will mostly be quite well educated and economically rather secure. This Traditional-Liturgical pattern is familiar to everyone in the Christian liturgical tradition. Its roots are found in medieval and earlier Roman Catholicism, reformed or modified by the English or Continental Protestant Reformation. Lutheran worship often represents a Germano-Catholic variation of the same form.

The Revivalist Pattern

The Revivalist pattern is distinctly different. It often takes a little longer, averaging from about sixty to seventy-five minutes. Anyone who knows the history of revivalism recognizes that the worship service has roots in the old-time revival meeting. Much of the music will be gospel songs from nineteenth- and early twentieth-century America or England, or maybe translations from the Continental revivals of the 1700s. The songs will have several verses, plus a chorus with repeated phrases.

I found this pattern, surprisingly, in Shenzhen, China, when I visited a church there several years ago. The church used a hymnal published before the 1949 Communist revolution. Although I didn't understand the language, I recognized the gospel songs, such as "Savior, Like a Shepherd Lead Us."

In the Revivalist pattern, worship is informal. Hymns and songs are experiential, much of the language focusing on "my" experience of God and on "my" conversion and Christ's atonement, with very little emphasis on the Trinity. Emotive biblical imagery is used effectively. The biblical promised land is symbolic of salvation or the Christian life or heaven, often quite individualized and spiritualized. Singing is usually accompanied by piano or electric organ, unless this happens to be a church in the non-instrumental tradition. Possibly a guitar or digital keyboard or other instruments will be added.

Usually just one Scripture will be read, and will provide the sermon text. No lectionary will be followed. Though singing is very important, the sermon will be the high point and will probably end with some type of appeal for commitment. Generally the accepted response will be for people to raise their hands or to come to the altar or the front of the sanctuary for prayer.

In the Revivalist pattern, architecture is usually a hybrid—an adaptation of the plain meeting-house style with elements from older traditional styles. There probably will not be stained-glass windows, except perhaps at the front; however windows may have the pointed arch that originated in the Gothic cathedrals of the 1100s and 1200s. The most visible religious symbols will be a cross, a pulpit, an altar rail, and an open Bible.

A profile of the congregation would likely find that overall the people rank somewhat lower than the Traditional-Liturgical folks in education, income, and jobs. Average age may be somewhat lower. If this is the United States, a significant proportion of the congregation will be school teachers, nurses, small entrepreneurs, and office workers.

In my own experience, growing up in the Free Methodist Church, I found that these first two patterns usually were blended. Generally the morning service was more recognizably Traditional-Liturgical, but with some revivalist elements. The regular Sunday evening service, often called the "evangelistic service," was almost pure revival-meeting style. Holy Communion was celebrated quarterly on Sunday mornings and was even more Traditional-Liturgical, with a liturgy tracing back a thousand years before the Reformation.

Most traditional African American worship follows the Revivalist pattern, though with distinctive cultural elements. Generally there is more use of choirs and longer, more interactive preaching. The service typically will last two hours or more, with some people coming and going throughout the service, unlike in predominantly Anglo-American congregations. Depending on the locale and history of the congregation, some elements of the Pentecostal-Charismatic pattern may also be included in an African American congregation in the revivalist tradition. If the congregation has a Methodist heritage, some Traditional-Liturgical elements may be present.

The Pentecostal-Charismatic Pattern

This pattern (say, seventy-five to 105 minutes) also has identifiable elements, though it covers a broad range from classical Pentecostalism to more recent Charismatic styles. Overall this pattern resembles the Revivalist more than the Traditional-Liturgical genre. The service however will be more emotive and energetic, with an accent on the Holy Spirit and the present experience of the Spirit more than on Jesus Christ and conversion.

Music consists largely of praise songs coming from the twentieth-century Charismatic renewal and the Jesus Movement, with some folk elements mixed in. The singing will be accompanied by guitars and possibly other instruments, including a piano or electronic keyboard, and several onstage singers or a praise choir. During many of the songs people will clap rhythmically and enthusiastically. A traditional hymn may be sung with an upbeat tempo. The service will have quite long periods of singing and praise, interspersed with brief prayers and possibly "singing in the Spirit." Probably there will be some speaking in tongues within the congregation, and perhaps from the platform.

In the Pentecostal-Charismatic pattern, the worship space will be a large auditorium, possibly a converted theater or warehouse. Few or no liturgical symbols will be present, unless banners have been added. The sermon will focus on daily Christian living and practical life problems; how to live in the Spirit in the everyday world. Many in the congregation will be young professionals, though this can vary, and a considerable socioeconomic range may be evident. If the congregation is more classically Pentecostal, other Pentecostal elements such as words of prophecy (perhaps spoken in tongues), healings, and earlier Pentecostal songs may be present, and the architecture may possibly reflect some older Protestant traditions.

The Rock Concert Pattern

The Rock Concert pattern has emerged since the birth of rock 'n' roll music in the 1950s. It may blend in elements of the Revivalist and Charismatic patterns, but still it is distinctive. The time frame generally runs ninety to 120 minutes.

In this pattern the underlying rock-concert structure is dominant, even if the service at first appears to be Pentecostal or Charismatic. The important point is not just that the music has been influenced by rock music, but that the *structure* of the rock concert has become a liturgical form. The whole service will be high-energy and electronically juiced, with an ensemble of electric guitars, keyboards, and drums, and a noticeably higher sound volume. There will be extended "sets" of music in which most of the people remain standing, possibly with hands raised, but more likely with fingers pointing upward or other gestures derived from rock concerts rather than the typical receptive open-palm gesture of Charismatic worship.

The music consists of short phrases repeated many times. The content may be biblical expressions or phrases relating to feeling God's presence, often with a focus on commitment or recommitment and on the present and future coming of the Spirit. There will be a syncopated or irregular rhythm underscored by a strong pulsing beat. The congregation will often applaud after each song, or set of songs.

In the Rock Concert pattern, often no Scripture is read. There will be little prayer, except perhaps briefly toward the beginning or between songs, or a few moments of quiet meditation before or after the teaching. The sermon may be a Bible teaching relating to personal experience and perhaps delivered in the form of a personal testimony, perhaps reinforced by a brief dramatic presentation. The congregation will tend to be quite young—or aging a bit, if the congregation has been around for a decade or two.

Here, then, we have four worship patterns: Traditional-Liturgical, Revivalist, Pentecostal-Charismatic, and Rock Concert—the four most common public faces of popular Christianity. Even if not complete, this fourfold typology does capture the main flavors of evangelical worship today. Like all typologies, it is an oversimplification. However, we have, in fact, often encountered these patterns just as described here. Sometimes we experience blendings and mutations of them, though the distinctive elements are still recognizable. So the four patterns are, so to speak, partly overlapping circles.

In the United States and increasingly globally, an influential blending of these styles is the Willow Creek model, developed by Willow Creek Community Church in affluent Barrington, Illinois, northwest of Chicago. The Willow Creek model is a "soft" blend of the Charismatic and Rock Concert patterns with some elements of a nightclub (comfortable; non-threatening). Yet it is carefully time-limited and high-tech, with an emphasis on planned excellence. It can also be seen as an adaptation of the Revivalist pattern in that the primary focus is evangelism and the communication of the core gospel message, as understood in this tradition.

The point in identifying these four patterns is not to make a sociological or generational analysis. Nor is it to evaluate or criticize these patterns. Our point, rather, is to ask: What does this range of worship patterns say about popular conceptions of the church today? Do these patterns represent distinctly different ecclesiologies, or variations of an identifiable (largely Western) evangelical ecclesiology? Or do they suggest an absence of ecclesiology, as some allege?

THE ROOTS OF POPULAR CHRISTIANITY

History is important. The early chapters of this book showed how the theological divorce between heaven and earth developed over centuries, making it difficult for the church to fully grasp or embody the full salvation of creation healed. Streams of renewal following the Protestant Reformation and later the Great Century of missions brought new life to the church and spread the gospel around the world as never before. The great Protestant missionary enterprise of the 1800s was in fact a key fruit of the evangelical awakenings of the 1600s and 1700s.[4]

This history was a main source of today's popular Christianity. Along the way other influences and streams got mixed in, producing the popular face of Christianity profiled above.

Ecclesiologically speaking, today's popular evangelicalism is a hybrid. This is so because conceptions of the church involve not only doctrine but also social practices, manner of life, various structures—in short, the whole spectrum of the social embodiment of the church. Popular ecclesiology springs from a complex range of sources which shape not only its form but also its theology. The four patterns sketched above hint at this.

Where did these dominant popular forms of the church come from? Some hints were given above, but it will help to identify five key sources in more detail. These are the roots of the ways evangelical churches *actually function*, regardless of how they explain themselves theologically.

Traditional-Liturgical and Reformed/Lutheran-Catholic Heritage

Whenever a church or movement gives birth to another movement, the new group carries a lot of its parent's DNA. This is true even when the new movement wants

4. Snyder, *Signs of the Spirit*. Throughout church history, and not just Protestant history, renewal movements have often given rise to impulses of mission and social reform, and sometimes vice versa; the two dynamics are interlinked. With regard to the North American scene, see for example Stafford, *Shaking the System*.

radically to reform the old. The Protestant Reformation, after all, was a *reformation*, not a re-creation or reconstitution of the church.

The Reformation in its main branches was mainly a change in the way personal salvation was understood (soteriology). Much less was it a reformation of the way the church was understood (ecclesiology). A lot of medieval Roman Catholicism was carried over into Protestantism. The main reforms in church life and practice concerned the sacraments, the centrality of Scripture and therefore of preaching, and perhaps some increased emphasis on congregational life. But three big ecclesiological carry-overs from medieval Christianity remained: (1) acceptance of the clergy/laity division, despite the Reformation emphasis on the priesthood of believers; (2) the established-church arrangement, whereby only one church was recognized by the government; and (3) the centrality, in practice and theology, of church buildings, with the marginalization or prohibition of house churches or "conventicles." And very importantly—as noted in chapter 3—the divorce between heaven and earth was not really challenged.

So the earliest root of today's popular ecclesiology is the Roman Catholic heritage carried over into Protestantism at the time of the Reformation.

The Radical Reformation and Free Church Tradition

Many of today's churches have roots in the Anabaptist, Believers' Church, and Free Church traditions. Although Anabaptist and Free Church ecclesiologies may differ in some ways, they really represent one tradition.[5]

This radical Protestant stream still owes something to Roman Catholicism, but much of the Free Church or Anabaptist view of church life and discipleship has more in common with pre-Reformation sectarian or "schismatic" groups like the Waldensians than it does with Catholicism. Roman Catholics, and later some Protestant churches, persecuted or excommunicated such groups and tried hard to stamp them out.[6]

As the terms "*Free* Church" and "*Believers'* Church" imply, ecclesiology is the key issue here. What does it mean to live as faithful people of God in the world? What social form is the faithful church called to? This is a major concern in the Anabaptist and Free Church tradition. Anabaptist writers have always said that the Reformation was incomplete. The reformers failed to really remake the very life and social form of the church. Faithfulness to Jesus Christ requires that the church return to the pattern and dynamic of the early or "primitive" church.[7]

Here is a key and curious point with regard to today's popular Christianity: consciously or unconsciously, most churches now accept the Free Church argument that church and state should be separate. Few churches, however, have fundamentally cri-

---

5. See Durnbaugh, "Free Church Tradition in America"; Littell, *Free Church*; Durnbaugh, *Believers' Church*; Callen, *Radical Christianity*. Parallels can be drawn between Anabaptist groups and Roman Catholic orders; see, e.g., Snyder, *Signs of the Spirit*, 54–61.

6. "Free Church Movements as Heresies," chapter 2 in Westin, *Free Church*.

7. *Primitivism*, *restorationism*, and *restitutionism* are thus key ecclesiological themes. See Hughes, *American Quest for the Primitive Church*.

tiqued the traditional clergy/laity division. They have not adopted the doctrine of the priesthood of believers as a fundamental *ecclesiological* principle that defines ministry in the church, even though most have accepted it soteriologically (Jesus is our great High Priest; direct access to God comes through him by faith, not through a human priest). Also, most Christians center their church life and discipleship primarily in church buildings, rather than in homes or in the public square or the marketplace.

Most popular Christianity thus has a double heritage, springing both from the "mainline" Reformation and the Radical Reformation. Yet these traditions are in conflict with each other at basic points. Evangelical ecclesiology is in some ways schizophrenic. Today most evangelical bodies have essentially a Lutheran, Reformed, or Wesleyan official theology mixed with a mostly Anabaptist view of the church. So the Anabaptist or Free Church tradition is an important source of much popular ecclesiology. Add to this the fact that, whatever their official theology, most evangelical churches have also been heavily influenced by dispensational premillennialism, as noted in earlier chapters.

The Influence of Revivalism

Revivalism is a third important source influencing popular Christianity. In the American experience, especially, revivalism has shaped the contours and concepts of church life.

Although revivalist influence traces back to eighteenth- and nineteenth-century Evangelical Awakenings in Europe and North America, as noted earlier, its most potent form was the American revivals beginning with Charles Finney in the 1820s and continuing in different ways with D. L. Moody, Billy Sunday, and others on into the early twentieth century.

Revivalism tends to reinforce Free Church ecclesiology through its emphasis on voluntarism, adult individual decision, and the importance of vital congregational life. Revivalism can, of course, flourish in a variety of Protestant and even Roman Catholic settings.[8] As a tradition, however, revivalism tends to reinforce a kind of Free Church ecclesiology, but with some key twists. Revivalism is more individualistic than historical Free Church ecclesiology. It tends to foster the boom-and-bust or up-and-down "revival model" of church life—periodic dramatic renewals with, implicitly, intervening low points. Revivalism also accents the emotional experience or appropriation of faith. It consequently tends to de-emphasize steady, ongoing discipleship in simple obedience to Christ—a key accent of Anabaptism. Revivalist influence was strongly reinforced by the popularity of revivalist gospel-song hymnody. In short: revivalism once worked dramatically as a form of awakening and evangelism but is problematic as an ecclesiology.

Nineteenth-century American Methodism provides an instructive case study here. In the United States, Methodist patterns of evangelism, nurture, discipleship, and—to some degree—worship underwent a transition from about the 1820s to the

---

8. See for example Dolan, *Catholic Revivalism*.

1850s. This was due in large measure to the influence of revivalism, though other currents were also at work. The class meeting, a key Methodist structure for evangelism, discipleship, and socialization, declined as churches adopted revivalistic prayer meetings. The decline of the weekly class meeting and rise of the revivalistic camp meeting were interrelated developments. Long-term, life-long discipleship and sanctification tended to be replaced by the revivalist model. To some degree the Holiness Movement, sparked largely by Phoebe Palmer and her associates, followed more the psychology of Charles Finney than of John Wesley.[9] Revivalism thus played a key role in pushing popular American Christianity into a more emotional, individualistic, and cyclical pattern of church life.

American Democracy

American democracy has also influenced the shape of popular Christianity. Though "democratization" can be understood in various ways and affected church traditions unevenly, virtually all North American churches in one way or another embraced the spirit of democracy and the democratic ideal.[10]

American democracy (more accurately, democratic republicanism) reinforced some aspects of Free Church ecclesiology while undermining others. Voluntarism tended to replace or reshape hierarchy, but individualism undercut community and covenant solidarity. The result was the American denominational system; denominationalism became "the shape of Protestantism in America."[11] The American experience thus added another accent and dynamic to the mix that today manifests itself in popular church life.

In the first half of the nineteenth century, a number of American churches adopted more democratic forms of polity and decision making. Also, most of the numerous new church movements that arose in this period were more democratic than the traditions to which they traced their roots.

Methodism is perhaps the most instructive example. By 1850, Methodism in its several branches was the largest denominational family in the nation. But it had split into several groups, largely over demands for more democratic government and more "lay" involvement in decision-making.[12]

9. A significant study is Hardt, "A Prudential Means of Grace." Based on New York City Methodist class records, Hardt documents several divergences from "the original Wesleyan model" of the class meeting. For a variety of reasons, however, the Methodist Episcopal Church from the 1850s on did not for the most part follow Palmer's lead but in its ecclesiological practice and self-understanding moved more toward the Traditional-Liturgical side of the spectrum.

10. The "democratization" of American Christianity has been widely documented and debated. See especially Hatch, *Democratization of American Christianity*; Noll, *America's God*.

11. Richey, *Denominationalism*. Sidney Mead entitled his contribution to this book, "Denominationalism: The Shape of Protestantism in America."

12. Debates over slavery, slaveholding, and abolitionism within Methodism were closely intertwined with issues of polity, particularly episcopal authority. Thus the abolitionist Wesleyan Methodism Church, founded in 1843, did away with episcopacy.

Thus emerged the American denominational system, with inbuilt assumptions about democratic processes and decision-making. On the one hand, this development enhanced a sense of ownership and personal involvement on the part of church members. On the other, it reinforced within the church the individualist character of American society. The result is what sociologists Roger Finke and Rodney Stark call America's "free-market religious economy."[13]

The story was somewhat different in Canada. Due to its different history and the fact that thousands of Christians migrated to Canada after the American Revolution in order to remain loyal British citizens, popular Canadian Christianity tends to be a bit less individualistic and a bit more global in perspective. Over time, however, revivalism and popular U.S. Christianity also worked their influence in Canada.[14]

American Entrepreneurship

Finally, American entrepreneurship has left its mark on popular Christianity, especially among evangelicals.

Entrepreneurship was a key dynamic in nineteenth-century American society. The rise of the railroads as America's first big business, the growth of financial capitalism, and the American industrial revolution introduced dynamics that were only latent at the time of the Revolution. From the 1860s on, the United States became a dynamically entrepreneurial nation.[15]

Not surprisingly, American denominations and local churches are often entrepreneurial enterprises. The same is true of many evangelistic, missionary, and service agencies. American society provides both the culture and the models for dynamic entrepreneurial ventures. Entrepreneurship influences ecclesiology by providing the opportunity, the mindset, the models, the methods, and the media for building a certain type of church enterprise. The dynamism is often matched by an absence of theological reflection, making the church liable to being shaped by the world's mold.

In sum: most popular church life in America is a varied blend of five elements: Protestant tradition tracing back into Roman Catholicism, the Free Church tradition, revivalism, and American democracy and entrepreneurship.

Question: Where is the Bible, and where is the earth, in all this? Strikingly, Scripture is a pretty faint source in much popular ecclesiology. These five sources seem

13. Finke and Stark, *Churching of America 1776–2005*. See also H. Richard Niebuhr's classic study, *Social Sources of Denominationalism*.

14. Guder, *Missional Church*, 31–36, 55–60; Wolffe, *Expansion of Evangelicalism*; Stackhouse, *Canadian Evangelicalism*, 177–204.

15. See Phillips, *Wealth and Democracy*, 35–37. Phillips notes that a "surprising number of the commercial and financial giants of the late nineteenth century" at the time of the Civil War were "young northerners" who "used the war to take major steps up future fortune's ladder." Here one might ponder also the significance the nineteenth-century "benevolence empire" of mission, social reform, and philanthropic societies funded largely by evangelical businessmen and entrepreneurs; see Rosell, "Charles Grandison Finney and the Rise of the Benevolence Empire." Here again the Canadian experience was somewhat different.

to dominate. To the degree that Scripture is a factor, it is mediated mainly through the Protestant/Catholic and Free Church traditions.[16] In neither case does the Bible really determine *ecclesiology* (the basic concept or model of the church) though it may be front-and-center with regard to other doctrines, especially *theology* (in the narrow sense), Christology, and soteriology—and thus evangelism and missions.

So also with regard to the earth. God's good creation plays a tiny part in contemporary popular Christianity, compared with the place it has in the Bible. For most Christians the actual physical earth has become at the same time secularized and spiritualized—cutting the nerve of both creation care and hope for the marriage of heaven and earth and the fulfillment of the biblical promise of the kingdom of God.

REDISCOVERING TRINITARIAN COMMUNITY

If salvation means creation healed, faithful Jesus followers will live and proclaim that reality. They will hold out that hope. Their churches will look like signs, way stations on the road to the new heaven and new earth. This is possible only as the Holy Spirit works within churches to make them actually, visibly the body of Christ. God works through his Spirit to heal our relationship with him, and thus with one another and with the earth, if we let him. The church thus becomes part of God's agency in the world to heal all creation.

We noted in chapter 9 that Christian mission is Trinitarian; that the power for mission is life in the Trinity through Christian community, as Jesus prays in John 17. We showed that the church's mission is to fulfill its role, its "work," in the Trinitarian mission of God for the sake of God's kingdom in the power of the Holy Spirit. We have noted also (chapter 10) that the Trinity is, in its tri-personal selfhood, a deeply ecological reality and mystery.

What does it mean to be the Trinitarian community for the sake of creation healed? God has chosen to work through the church to manifest his kingdom and healing redemption on earth. Rediscovering the church as Trinitarian community is key.[17]

---

16. The largest impact that the Bible has had on evangelical ecclesiology probably comes in the form of primitivism and restorationism, which are key themes in the Anabaptist and Free Church traditions. These themes emphasize that the true church should be like the early church of the New Testament or the first centuries. This is a key dynamic within the Free Church tradition, but at some level the primitivist and restorationist impulse has always been at work in the church, and it seems always to be present in church renewal movements. See Snyder, *Signs of the Spirit*, especially 40–42; Hughes, *American Quest*.

17. As with "mission of God," the doctrine of the Trinity and its implications for church and mission have received much fruitful reflection over the past half-century or so (Snyder, *Community of the King*, 54–60). Two cautions should be raised, however. First, the important point is not to emphasize the doctrine of the Trinity *per se*, but to actually *be* Trinitarian in our whole theology, worldview, and understanding of the church. Second, it is crucial that Trinitarian reflection remain carefully grounded in Scripture as a safeguard against mere speculation. This is true of all doctrines, of course, but especially here. Since the Bible does not use the term "Trinity" or teach the doctrine explicitly, we are duty-bound to keep our Trinitarian reflections closely connected with what Scripture does reveal about the Father, the Son, and the Holy Spirit. We do well also to remember that we are speaking of a multidimensional ecological mystery that far exceeds our grasp.

So we close this chapter with a reflection on the church as Trinitarian community, and in the last two chapters rethink the "marks" of the church and the larger dimensions of community in light of the Trinitarian project to heal all creation.

The key point here is that the church is, and is called to be, a *Trinitarian community*. This affirmation can be sustained from many angles, but we find its most profound basis in Jesus' words in John 17:

> My prayer is not for [these disciples] alone. I pray also for those who will believe in me through their message, that all of them may be one, Father, just as you are in me and I am in you. May they also be in us so that the world may believe that you have sent me. I have given them the glory that you gave me, that they may be one as we are one—I in them and you in me—so that they may be brought to complete unity. Then the world will know that you sent me and have loved them even as you have loved me. (John 17:20–23 TNIV)

The church is the "I in them and you in me" community, the community of the Father, the Son, and the Holy Spirit. The Trinitarian existence of the church grounds the Christian community in Reality—the most fundamental of realities: God as source of life and being, creator, providential sustainer, and new-creation-bringer.

Because the church is Trinitarian—based on what God the Father has done and will do through Christ by the power of the Spirit—the church is at the same time *incarnational* and *eschatological*. It is incarnational, because "the Word became flesh and lived among us" and so revealed God's glory (John 1:14), and the church is to be the visible body of Christ. It is eschatological because it now lives out—and so becomes an agent of—the hope of creation finally healed.

Four Dimensions of Trinitarian Community

Reflection on God as Trinity hints that the church is Trinitarian community in four ways.[18] First, *the church is fundamentally the community gathered around Jesus.* Given the reality of the Trinity, the church is essentially social and relational, bound together by mutual love and self-giving interdependence because of Jesus.

Granted, the church is not often perceived in this way and frequently does not visibly embody this truth. That does not undercut the fact that it is so, for the Bible constantly emphasizes that we are to *live into* and *live out* this reality. As Paul puts it, we are "to lead a life worthy of the calling to which [we] have been called" (Eph 4:1).

The church is fundamentally a community of disciples, a missional community whose life, being, and mission are grounded in the Trinity and thus in the mission of God.

Second, *the church is a Trinitarian worshipping community.* The church in its worship, and often most explicitly in its hymns and liturgies, worships the Trinity: Father, Son, and Holy Spirit. Further, the Trinity forms the basis of the church's healing mission as the community responds to the call of the Trinity to participate in the *missio Dei*,

---

18. A somewhat similar discussion of the church as Trinitarian community is found in Snyder and Runyon, *Decoding the Church,* 54–56.

the mission of God. In worship the community draws near to God and comes to understand the Father's creative love and care for all God has made, the Son's self-giving in becoming a servant for our salvation, and the Spirit's call and push to go into the world "as the Father" has sent the Son (John 5:26; 15:9; 20:21). Genuine worship impels into mission.

The theological richness of the church's great Trinitarian hymns is one reason vital churches need the church's historic hymnody as well as contemporary praise songs—and why contemporary songwriters should reflect more on the Trinity and the mission of God. For those in the Traditional-Liturgical and Reformed/Lutheran-Catholic traditions, the traditional liturgies and prayers also convey this rich Trinitarian legacy.

The call to worship God the Trinity means that the church has a mission *to* God as well as a mission *from* God to the world. There is a reciprocal back-and-forth action here that is grounded in the classic doctrine of *perichoresis* (literally, "dancing together" or "dancing around"—mutual inter-sharing of characteristics). "Dancing together" is of course a mere human analogy; historically *perichoresis* has been understood to mean the *mutual indwelling* of the Trinitarian persons. That indwelling in love overflows through Christ by the Spirit into the church, and the church responds in worship and service. We give ourselves to God (our mission to God) and he gives himself back to us with an overflow of love that impels us out of ourselves and into mission. This seems, in part, to be the point of John 17: "As you have sent me into the world, I have sent them into the world. . . . I in them and you in me, that they become completely one, so that the world may know that you have sent me and have loved them even as you have loved me" (John 17:18, 23).

Worship and mission, then, are interrelated in one ecology. Mission in Trinitarian perspective is never one-way. We do not simply go out in mission because the Trinity sends us; rather, mission is reciprocal. In response to God's grace, we carry out our mission to God and thus are "carried" into mission in the world by the Holy Spirit who in fact goes ahead of us. This happens not in a way that overwhelms us and turns us into zombies or robo-evangelists. Rather, the Spirit empowers us to will to do God's will (John 7:17; Phil 2:13; Gal 5:23).[19]

The church is Trinitarian. Its worship and its mission are grounded in the Trinity. And in Trinitarian perspective, the church's mission includes its mission to God, to one another, and to the world, the whole earth. Here is the church's mission to the whole of creation, for God is the Lord of and actor in all creation, bringing the healing medicine of salvation (Rom 8:19–21).

Third, *the Trinitarian community is sent especially to the poor.*[20] Though "being in very nature God," Christ "made himself nothing by taking the very nature of a servant"

19. The divine *perichoresis* of the Trinity thus is reflected in, and carried over into, the life of the church. See especially Gunton, *Promise*, chapter 4, "The Community: The Trinity and the Being of the Church."

20. Karl Barth wrote, "The Church is witness of the fact that the Son of man came to seek and to save the lost. And this implies that—casting all false impartiality aside—the Church must concentrate first on the lower and lowest levels of human society. The poor, the socially and economically weak and threatened, will always be the object of its primary and particular concern, and it will always insist on

(Phil 2:6–7 TNIV) in carrying out his mission. This is literally a demonstration of the "wisdom of God." For God "chose the foolish things of the world to shame the wise; God chose the weak things of the world to shame the strong. God chose the lowly things of this world and the despised things—and the things that are not—to nullify the things that are, so that no one may boast before him. It is because of him that you are in Christ Jesus, who has become for us wisdom from God—that is, our righteousness, holiness, and redemption" (1 Cor 1:27–30).

God's special concern for the poor, and Jesus' explicit mission to the poor, are grounded in the Trinity, not in sociology or politics. That is why the theme of the poor, the widow, the orphan, and the alien crops up so often in Scripture.

The Trinity is unbounded self-giving love each to the other, always seeking the best for the other and receiving back love in return. Since the church's mission grows out of the overflow of this love, it is a mission to all people and the whole creation.

Amazingly, however, in his incarnation Jesus Christ becomes the suffering Trinity, and thus the Father and the Spirit have particular compassion for him in his sufferings. This is mirrored in God's concern then for the poor and the oppressed generally and for the "groaning" of creation. Thus this concern is mirrored also in the mission of the church—as it often has been when the church is at its best.

God loves everyone, but especially those who suffer. It is as simple as that—and as profound. The mutual love of the Trinity impels God, and therefore the church, to incarnate the gospel among the poor. Thus Jesus can say, in words that echo the mystery of the Trinity, "The Spirit of the Lord is on me, because he has anointed me to proclaim good news to the poor" (Luke 4:18). Because of this, John Wesley said, the poor have a "peculiar right to have the gospel preached unto them."[21] The church's preference for ministry to the poor is grounded in the Trinity, especially as demonstrated by Jesus Christ.

Fourth and finally, *the church's whole ministry is grounded in the Trinity.* Ministry of all stripes—ordained or unordained, paid or unpaid, local or global—is rooted in the Trinitarian mystery. The roots of authentic ministry are found in Spirit-empowered community, not in organizational hierarchy.

The Trinity is in fact the opposite of hierarchy.[22] The church's ministry, including its leadership, is non-hierarchical. The deep theological grounding of this is the Trinity itself, not some philosophical egalitarianism. The Trinity, and the very nature of the material creation God has made, show us that we should conceive of the church and its ministry in organic, relational terms, not primarily in institutional or hierarchical ones. The church is not so much a rational organization or religious machine as it is a complex organism. The Trinitarian nature of the church is built into the church's very DNA.

---

the State's special responsibility for these weaker members of society." Barth, "Christian Community and Civil Community," 36.

21. Wesley, Sermon 1, "Salvation by Faith," Wesley, *Works,* 1:128.

22. Theologians have at times tried to reconcile the Trinity and hierarchy, especially in the Western tradition. This confuses categories, however, and tends to compromise the very meaning of the Trinitarian comm–unity of Father, Son, and Spirit.

This is not an argument against institutional or administrative structures. It does, however, provide some guidance for structuring an organization. For most of human (not just Western) culture, hierarchy is the assumed, unevaluated, default model for organizations. This assumption needs to be questioned, however, in light of the Trinity—to say nothing of Jesus' example and explicit teaching.

The nature of the church is determined by the nature of God as revealed in Jesus Christ and in Scripture. The church is essentially a community in mission and in movement. It *is* because of who God is as Trinity and how he is manifesting himself in the world.

Here the mission of God (*missio Dei*) and the reality of the Trinity converge and point in the same direction. The mission of God reflects the Trinity in Godself (to the degree that has been revealed to us) and as we learn about God's nature through the life and ministry of Jesus Christ.[23]

Living in Trinitarian Community

How can Christians actually structure their life together so that it reflects the ways the Trinitarian God has revealed himself? How can the church incarnate organic, mutually relational and mutually submissive modes of being as it determines structures, roles, responsibilities, and accountability?

The major implication of God-as-Trinity is that we are called to live in *interdependent community*. The key principle: "Submit to one another out of reverence for Christ" (Eph 5:21 TNIV). This captures what Jesus taught and modeled.

Every sphere of Christian living is to be marked by interdependent community—family, church, and also Christian organizations and institutions (colleges, mission societies, or whatever). This is a principle that lies behind and transcends the structures and role differentiation that are necessary within an organization. A certain tension exists here, and a key test of our discipleship is whether we actually practice this mutual interdependence—or allow it to be compromised by our institutional structures and relationships.[24]

Practically, this means working hard to see things from others' points of view. It means respecting, honoring, and learning from the diversities of cultures and gifts of the whole body of Christ, and of each person in their various roles. This practice and sensitivity actually builds and nurtures community.

Because the Father sent the Son into the world in the power of the Holy Spirit, Trinitarian community means missional community. Jesus made this clear, as we saw

23. Behind this affirmation is the discussion regarding the "immanent" and "economic" Trinity. I agree with Karl Rahner's formulation, "The economic Trinity *is* the immanent Trinity"—i.e., that the Triune God is in essence what the Trinity is revealed to be in Jesus Christ—though that affirmation is as much a logical deduction and statement of faith as of revealed truth (See Kärkkäinen, *Trinity*, 76–87). Rahner's formulation may be seen, analogically, as the $E=MC^2$ of Trinitarian theology, the Higher Theory of Relativity.

24. For the conceptual and theological background here, see Snyder, *Community of the King*, chapter 9, "Form of the Church," especially 184–92, "Church and Institutional Structures"; Snyder, *Problem of Wineskins*, 159–68.

earlier in examining Jesus' own sense of mission (chapter 9). "God so loved the world that he gave his only Son, so that everyone who believes in him may not perish but may have eternal life" (John 3:16). "As the Father has sent me, so I send you" (John 20:21). Because of Jesus' mission and the work of the Holy Spirit, the church is most fundamentally community-in-mission. It exists not for itself but for the one who forms and sends the church into the world to do Jesus' works and to fulfill its role in God's larger economy for the healing of all creation.

The church is genetically missional because it is the community of Jesus Christ, God's great missionary. It is the Body of Christ, sharing its Head's DNA. The church is the community called into existence by the mission of God. All ecclesiology should be viewed from this angle—rather than primarily from the perspective of the traditional structures of cultural Christianity inherited from two millennia of Christendom.

However, living in Trinitarian missional community is not so much a duty as it is hope-inspired joy because of God's promises, the presence of the Holy Spirit with us, and supremely the resurrection of Jesus Christ. Missional kingdom living is all about "righteousness and peace and joy in the Holy Spirit" (Rom 14:17). For "the fruit of the Spirit," the one who makes Jesus' resurrection and the promise of creation healed real in us, "is love, joy, peace, patience, kindness, generosity, faithfulness, gentleness, and self-control"—matters of character and community, not a set of legal requirements (Gal 5:22–23).

In his book *Surprised by Hope,* N. T. Wright captures this sense of missional hope. Wright invites Christians to:

> think through the hope that is ours in the gospel; recognize the renewal of creation as both the goal of all things in Christ and the achievement that has already been accomplished in the resurrection; and go to the work of justice, beauty, evangelism, the renewal of space, time, and matter as the anticipation of the eventual goal and the implementation of what Jesus achieved in his death and resurrection. That is the way both to the genuine mission of God and to the shaping of the church by and for that mission.
>
> All of this means, of course, that the people who work at and for this mission in the wider world must themselves be living, modeling, and experiencing the same thing in their own lives. There is ultimately no justification for a private piety that doesn't work out in actual mission, just as there is ultimately no justification for people who use their activism in the social, cultural, or political sphere as a screen to prevent them from facing the same challenges within their own lives—the challenge, that is, of God's kingdom, of Jesus's lordship, and of the Spirit's empowering. If the gospel isn't transforming you, how do you know that it will transform anything else?[25]

Wright is speaking here of Trinitarian community—of what it means to rediscover the church and live as Christ's body today. Wright notes that "all sorts of positive and practical results" come from living *now* the resurrection life, from really setting our minds "on the world that is now Jesus's primary home, the world that is designed

25. Wright, *Surprised by Hope*, 270.

to heal and restore our present one." And this involves *"actual current physical reality, shot through now with the life of heaven"* because of Jesus' resurrection.[26]

As we have insisted throughout the book, this is not a matter of abstract or other-worldly spirituality. It is not just a matter of attitude and devotional life. It also involves worldview, or worldstory and missional living. As Wright puts it:

> Part of getting used to living in the post-Easter world—part of getting used to letting Easter change your life, your attitudes, your thinking, your behavior—is getting used to the cosmology that is now unveiled. Heaven and earth . . . are made for each other, and at certain points they intersect and lock. Jesus is the ultimate such point. *We as Christians are meant to be such points, derived from him.* The Spirit, the sacraments, and the Scriptures are given so that the double life of Jesus, both heavenly and earthly, can become ours as well, already in the present.[27]

Wright is right. But we would go even further. Looking at the world biblically and ecologically, we can affirm that heaven and earth are intimately interconnected across the whole story of creation healed, as we have argued throughout the book.

Rediscovering the church means first understanding how today's popular forms of Christianity developed, then what our calling really is as God's healing, missional, Trinitarian community on earth.

In the next chapter we examine the visible marks of God's missional community.

26. Ibid., 251 (emphasis in the original).
27. Ibid., 251–52 (emphasis in the original).

12

The Marks of
Healing Community

By this everyone will know that you are my
disciples, if you have love for one another.

(John 13:35)

Hㅤow can Jesus' body on earth be recognized? What are the marks of God's
faithful healing community today, and through history?

The Bible answers this question. Down through history theologians and church
councils have offered their own answers, though not always fully biblical ones. In his
letters the Apostle Paul mentions three key marks of the church: Faith, hope, and love.
He tells the Colossians, "We have heard of your *faith* in Christ Jesus and of the *love* that
you have for all the saints, because of the *hope* laid up for you in heaven" (Col 1:4–5).
He thankfully commends the Thessalonian believers for their "work of *faith* and labor
of *love* and steadfastness of *hope* in our Lord Jesus Christ" (1 Thess 1:3). Paul famously
wrote, "And now *faith, hope,* and *love* abide, these three; and the greatest of these is
love" (1 Cor 13:13). This reflects Jesus' key words: "By this everyone will know that you
are my disciples, if you have love for one another" (John 13:35). Faith, hope, love—
marks of the true body of Christ. In the New Testament these are not vague ideals or
philosophical virtues. They are tied directly to the good news of Jesus Christ, as we will
see. They are interwoven with the ecology of God's plan for creation healed.

This chapter explores the identifying marks of the church as God's healing community. It reopens the historic question of the church's marks through the lens of salvation as creation healed. We look first at Scripture, then review the centuries-long

debate about the church's key marks. The chapter ends with the question: What are the marks, the *stigmata,* of the faithful global and local church of Jesus Christ today, and how can they be seen?

THE NEW TESTAMENT MARKS OF THE CHURCH

God intends the church as body of Christ to be his healing, missional, Trinitarian community on earth, and the New Testament shows how. Jesus' words in John 13:35—"everyone will know that you are my disciples, if you have *love* for one another"—make clear that the supreme distinguishing mark of the church is love. This is the love of the Trinity expressed in Jesus Christ and thus in his body by the Holy Spirit. For Jesus said, "As the Father has loved me, so I have loved you; abide in my love" and so "bear much fruit," truly being "my disciples" (John 15:8–9). This is the background of Jesus' commission in John 20:21, "As the Father has sent me, so I send you."

The Apostle Paul, as we have seen above, commonly uses the triad: faith-hope-love. All the New Testament writers speak of faith and love when describing God's action in Jesus and the human response by which we become "members of [his] body" (1 Cor 12:12) and "participants of the divine nature" (2 Pet 1:4).

The accent on hope is often tied to God's historic promises. Paul speaks of his "*hope* in the promise made by God to our ancestors" (Acts 26:6). Peter writes, "By his great mercy [God] has given us a new birth into a living *hope* through the resurrection of Jesus Christ from the dead" (1 Pet 1:3). Christians should "set all [their] *hope* on the grace that Jesus Christ will bring [them] when he is revealed" (1 Pet 1:13), for their "*faith* and *hope* are set on God" (1 Pet 1:21). The letter to the Hebrews says Christians should show "diligence so as to realize the full assurance of *hope* to the very end" (Heb 6:11). "We have this *hope,* a sure and steadfast anchor of the soul, a hope that enters the inner shrine behind the curtain, where Jesus, a forerunner on our behalf, has entered" (Heb 6:19–20).

Finally, Paul speaks of hope for all creation healed, "for the creation was subjected to futility . . . by the one who subjected it, in *hope* that the creation itself will be set free from its bondage to decay and will obtain the freedom of the glory of the children of God" (Rom 8:20–21, a passage that actually is clearer if the comma after "it" is removed).

Faith, hope and, supremely, love—these are the key marks of the church of Jesus Christ. This triad is not a formula or prescription or surefire litmus test. Faith, hope, and love can mean different things to different people. In the New Testament, faith, hope, and love are overlapping marks of the one body of Christ, for the church is a complex organism, a mystery of the Spirit, the body of Christ with its own profound ecology.

Faith, hope, and love are not mere private virtues. They're not so much about a Christian's personal salvation as they are about life in *community.* In the biblical narrative, faith, hope, and love are woven into the whole fabric of God's *oikonomia* for creation healed.

We are saved by grace through faith in Jesus Christ. But Jesus is not just our "personal Savior"; he is the one in whom "all things hold together." The risen Jesus Christ is "the head of the body, the church" (Col 1:18); he is also the one through whom God is bringing "all things in heaven and earth together under one head" (Eph 1:10 NIV).

When we speak of Christian *faith*, we express our confidence in what God has done and will do through the sacrifice, resurrection, and ongoing reign of Jesus Christ. This is the faith of the church as participant in God's great plan for creation healed.

Hope is a key sign of the true church. This is more than hope for eternity in heaven or prosperity on earth. Rather it is the hope of creation healed, the marriage of earth and heaven. Paul prays that the church may have "a spirit of wisdom and revelation" so that it "may know what is the hope to which he has called" the church and "the riches of his glorious inheritance among the saints" (Eph 1:17–19). It is the sure hope (not optimism or wishful thinking) that "the creation itself will be set free from its bondage to decay and will obtain the freedom of the glory of the children of God" (Rom 8:21); that God's will really will be done on earth as in heaven. This is the larger meaning of "Christ in you, the hope of glory" (Col 1:27).

So, when we speak of Christian hope, we express our certainty that God in Christ by the Spirit is fulfilling his mission to heal all creation. This is the hope of the church as an actor in God's great mystery of redemption and healing.

In a similar way, *love* is a key sign of the church—love for God, for one another, for neighbors near and far—seen and unseen, local and global. And love for the whole garden God has made, loving it even in its semi-spoiled state.

By the Spirit, through the church, the "God so loved the world" of John 3:16 becomes the demonstrated love of the church. We understand that the words "Do not love the world or the things in the world" (1 John 2:15) refer not to the physical creation but to the distorted, sinful "desire of the flesh, the desire of the eyes, [and] the pride in riches" (1 John 2:16). So when we speak of Christian love, we mean the love of God for the world—for all God has made and is determined to redeem. This becomes the demonstrated love of the church as co-workers in the marvelous economy for creation healed.

In the economy of God, faith, hope, and love thus become key signs of the faithful church-in-mission. *Faith* is the assurance given those who are justified by faith that God will heal all creation, fulfilling his promises. *Hope* is the certainty that God "in accordance with his promise" will bring "new heavens and a new earth, where righteousness is at home" (2 Pet 3:13). "For in this hope we were saved" (Rom 8:24 TNIV). *Love* is sharing in the divine nature (2 Pet 1:4), filled with the love of Christ, so that we love God, one another and all God's creation—loving all that is included in God's "everlasting covenant" with the earth (Gen 9:15–16).

Within the full biblical narrative and ecology, faith, hope, and love in these larger dimensions are marks of Jesus' true church. Because of God's promises, we know that "hope does not disappoint us," for "God's love has been poured into our hearts through the Holy Spirit that has been given to us" (Rom 5:5).

RETHINKING THE TRADITIONAL MARKS

It is strange then that faith, hope, and love—so prominent in the New Testament—have not often been seen in church history as the church's primary marks. As the church developed its structures, gradually diversifying in differing cultural contexts and struggling with doctrinal issues, a different set of distinguishing marks emerged.

By the late fourth century the church had developed a theory of the "marks" or "notes" of the church—ways of identifying the true church.

One Holy Catholic Apostolic Church

As noted in chapter 1, the first Council of Constantinople in 381 AD described the church as *one, holy, catholic,* and *apostolic.* This formulation has shaped much of the church's self-understanding throughout history, finding its way into many creeds.

But what of the biblical basis for these "marks" or "notes"? Is it possible that the Nicene-Constantinopolitan formula has actually kept the church from seeing the body of Christ biblically? For surely the Bible has priority over church creeds; all creeds, from whatever time or source, must be tested biblically.[1]

Consider the four classic marks or "notes" (*notae*) of the church: *Unity, holiness, catholicity,* and *apostolicity* (*ecclesia una, sancta, catholica, et apostolica,* according to the creed of 381 AD). Jaroslav Pelikan writes, we speak of "the one holy catholic and apostolic church" based upon "the four classic notes of the church defined in the Nicene Creed."[2] These four attributes are understood to be essential marks or characteristics of the church. That is, whatever else may be claimed about the church, it is essentially one, holy, catholic, and apostolic, or it is not the true church of Jesus Christ.

Since these "marks" or "notes" are enshrined in the earliest great creeds, they have been almost universally accepted through the centuries. Other marks have sometimes also been lifted up—for instance, that the church is constituted by the Word and the Spirit—but these four have remained unquestioned. G. C. Berkouwer observed that although "there was much difference of opinion about the number of *notae*" during the Reformation, still "the four words themselves were never disputed, since the Reformers did not opt for other 'attributes.' There is a common attachment everywhere to the description of the Church in the Nicene Creed: one, holy, catholic, and apostolic. Even after the Reformation, in spite of all the differences in interpretation which appeared with respect to the four words, this usage remained the same." Berkouwer added, "The striking thing here is that the general question about whether the Church is truly one and catholic, apostolic and holy, is not asked; rather, a number of [additional] marks are mentioned, [such as] the pure preaching of the gospel, the pure administration of the sacraments, and the exercise of church discipline."[3]

---

1. The following discussion parallels but is somewhat different from the discussion of the church's marks in Snyder and Runyon, *Decoding the Church,* 17–31, and Snyder, "Marks of Evangelical Ecclesiology," 81–92.

2. Pelikan, *Emergence,* 156.

3. Berkouwer, *The Church,* 14–15. Berkouwer is speaking here specifically of the Belgic Confession, but the point applies more generally.

The so-called Apostles' Creed, older than the Nicene Creed, describes the church as "the communion of saints." Craig Van Gelder points out that "communion of saints" describes "the social reality of the church" and may be seen as a fifth classic mark. Thus these "five attributes came to be the common way of describing the church over the next centuries."[4] The four classic marks have had an especially strong influence, however, and need rethinking.

Two things become clear when we examine the four marks in the light of history. First, this formulation of the essential, defining character of the church arose in a particular context and was in fact used as a test to exclude Christians who saw the church differently. Second, at various points in history earnest, fully orthodox Christians have argued that other, different marks more truly define the essence of the church's being and faithfulness.

From the standpoint of Scripture and creation healed, the four marks do raise some questions. Times of church renewal and reformation often spark new thinking about the church. Generally the classic marks themselves have not been questioned, but the example of Jesus Christ and of the church in Acts has often been raised up in criticism of contemporary church practice and theory, thus implicitly challenging the traditional marks.

Consider the example of early Methodism in England and the United States. John Wesley put a lot of emphasis on preaching the gospel to the poor. Some early Methodists argued that the gospel for the poor was an essential mark of the church. In the United States, the influential Methodist leader Stephen Olin (1797–1851), president of Wesleyan University, said that the church is not really apostolic if it does not preach the gospel to the poor as Jesus did. In his sermon on "The Adaptation of the Gospel to the Poor," Olin said:

> There are hot controversies about the true Church. What constitutes it—what is essential to it—what vitiates it? These may be important questions, but there are more important ones. It may be that there can not be a Church without a bishop, or that there can. There can be none without a Gospel, and a Gospel for the poor. Does a Church preach the Gospel to the poor—preach it effectively? Does it convert and sanctify the people? Are its preaching, its forms, its doctrines adapted *specially* to these results? If not, we need not take the trouble of asking any more questions about it. It has missed the main matter. It does not do what Jesus did—what the apostles did. Is there a Church—a ministry—that converts, reforms, sanctifies the people? Do the poor really learn to love Christ? Do they live purely and die happy? I hope that Church conforms to the New Testament in its government and forms as far as may be. . . . I wish its ministers may be men of the best training, and eloquent. I hope they worship in goodly temples, and all that; but I can not think or talk gravely about these matters on the Sabbath. They preach a saving Gospel to the poor, and that is enough. It is an apostolic Church. Christ is the corner-stone. The main thing is secured, thank God.[5]

4. Van Gelder, *Essence of the Church*, 50.

5. Olin, "Adaptation of the Gospel to the Poor," in Olin, *Works of Stephen Olin*, 1:345 (italics in the original). This had been a common Wesleyan emphasis since the days of early British and American Methodism, but by the 1850s it was fading or even under attack within Methodism.

Two key claims about the true church are made here: First, that preaching the gospel to the poor is an essential identifying mark. Second, that this mark is a test of whether the church is genuinely *apostolic*—is the church walking in the steps of Jesus? The church that preaches the gospel to the poor "is an apostolic Church," Olin said. True apostolicity means the church following in the steps of Jesus. Note that Olin appeals to Scripture, particularly to the teaching and example of Jesus Christ, not to particular creeds.

So, what about the marks of the church as God's healing community on earth? How does the New Testament accent on faith, hope, and love relate to the church as one, holy, catholic (universal), and apostolic? What about Jesus' own focus on the gospel to the poor?

A Broader View of the Church's Ecology

We have already seen the prominence the Apostle Paul gives to faith, hope, and love. If we examine the Gospels and Acts, we find that preaching the gospel to the poor has more obvious biblical support than do the four classic marks. Scripture stresses ministry to and among the poor more than universality or catholicity, for example, as a key sign of the church's faithfulness.

How biblical, then, are the four classic marks? How do they relate to the church's mission in the healing of creation? The four marks themselves are highly ambiguous. Theologians have long debated just what they mean. Frequently the marks have been interpreted so as to harmonize with some other schema.

Why should we accept these marks as true or authoritative? Are they really biblical? Ephesians 4:3–6 may be cited as the key text for the classic marks: "maintain the unity of the Spirit in the bond of peace. There is one body and one Spirit, just as you were called to one hope of your calling, one Lord, one faith, one baptism, one God and Father of all, who is above all and through all and in all." This important passage highlights the *unity* (and by implication *catholicity*) of the church—"one Lord, one faith, one baptism." Other passages in Ephesians accent the church's holiness (especially 5:26–27) and apostolicity (especially 2:20, "built upon the foundation of the apostles and prophets," and 3:5, "revealed to his holy apostles and prophets by the Spirit"; cf. 4:11). A number of other New Testament passages may be cited—especially John 17 on the unity of the church. In other words, texts can be found in support of unity, holiness, catholicity, and apostolicity as key marks. But other accents are at least equally prominent in Scripture, if not more so.

Certainly we should affirm the traditional marks—unity, holiness, catholicity, and apostolicity—as essential marks of the church, especially as they distinguish the church from the rest of society. But, in fact, the classic fourfold formulation tells only part of the story. This is obvious even in Eph 4:3–6, for the very next verse says, "But each of us was given grace according to the measure of Christ's gift," thus introducing the accent of charismatic diversity.

The four traditional marks highlight just one side of the church's ecology. The church of Jesus Christ is more complex, diverse, and glorious than the classic marks suggest. It is biblically more accurate, in fact, to say that the church is:

DIVERSE as well as ONE

CHARISMATIC as well as HOLY

LOCAL as well as CATHOLIC (or Universal)

PROPHETIC as well as APOSTOLIC

Classic orthodox theology speaks of *one holy catholic* and *apostolic* church. It generally has failed to speak of the church as also *diverse, charismatic, local* and *prophetic*. This second set of qualities is just as visible in the New Testament as the traditional marks. In Acts, for example, the *diversity* of the church is clear when we look at the early Christian communities—Jerusalem, Antioch, Philippi, Corinth, for example. The *charismatic* nature of the early church is obvious in the "signs and wonders" accent in Acts (4:30; 5:12; 14:3; 15:12). The *locality* or contextual rootedness of the church is evident precisely in the fact that the church was planted in specific local social environments. The *prophetic* character of the early church is seen in its formation of a contrast society whose values and worldview clashed with those of the dominant society.

A key function of the traditional marks historically has been to identify characteristics that distinguish the church from the rest of human society. This we affirm today, as well. But in today's highly complex world, and with concern for reflecting today the full dynamic of the early church as we see it in the New Testament, it is also necessary—both theologically and missionally—to note the significance of the church's diversity and contextuality; its charismatic and prophetic dimensions.

Diverse, Charismatic, Local, Prophetic

The diversity, contextual locality, prophetic witness, and charismatic life of the church become obvious when we delve into the New Testament. Here we find a healing, reconciling community of faith, hope, and love that incarnates good news among the poor and begins to reach the nations, extending its witness "to the ends of the earth" (Acts 1:8). So we see:

1. The church is not only *one*; it is also *many*. Manifold and diverse. Look at the diversity of the first Christian congregations from Antioch to Colossae to Rome. Note how Paul's letters celebrate the ethnic, socioeconomic, and class diversity of the church (Gal 3:23–29; 1 Cor 12:13; Col 3:11). Surely the point here is not only the unity we have in Christ but also the diversity that is reconciled and yet celebrated in the church. This diversity is partly what makes the unity so impressive.[6]

6. Unity in diversity is a theme throughout Scripture. Israel, though one, was twelve tribes; she was to have particular concern for aliens and sojourners who acknowledged God and became part of God's people. God repeatedly reminded Israel that his people would eventually incorporate people from many nations. OT passages that link sojourners and aliens with "the fatherless and widows" suggest a relationship between the diversity of God's people and his particular concern for the poor and oppressed (e.g., Deut 14:29, 16:11, 16:14).

The "one body, many members" teaching of 1 Corinthians 12 and Romans 12 can be extended to the universal as well as the local church. The point is that the church, local and global, is *both* one and many.

2. The church is *charismatic* as well as *holy*. The same Holy Spirit who sanctifies the church blesses it with diverse gifts (Eph 4:7–16; 1 Corinthians 12; Heb 2:4). It is the *Holy* Spirit who gives gifts. The church functions best with both the fruit and the gifts of the Spirit, incarnating both the character and the charisma of Jesus.[7]

At first glance holiness and charism might not seem connected. But two things stand out in the biblical teachings. First, Scripture directly links the holy (sacred, set-apart) character of the church with its being a gift-endowed community of the Spirit (e.g., Acts 1:8; 2:4–38; Heb 2:4; 1 Pet 2:9). Second, the church is repeatedly described in Scripture as both holy and charismatic, though in different passages.

The church has often found it hard to hold these two sides together. History offers many examples of tensions at this point, including the early twentieth-century split in the Holiness Movement that produced modern-day Pentecostalism.[8] But in fact holiness and charism need each other.

3. The church is both *local* and *universal*. It exists both as the worldwide body of Christ (in this world and beyond), and as very diverse, particular local communities, each with its own special flavor, style, and culture. The church both transcends culture and is incarnate in particular cultures.

Here also the church has struggled to hold two key things together, for a whole range of historical, theological, and sociological reasons. In its mainline forms the church tends to value uniformity over particularity; universality over locality; transcultural transcendence over cultural incarnation; predictability over innovation. Or at times the church swings to the opposite extreme, losing itself in adaptation and innovation.

Clearly, in the New Testament the church is both local and universal. The New Testament use of the word "church" itself shows this.[9] Further evidence is the actual history of the early Christian communities (pictured especially in Acts) and apostolic teaching about adapting to local customs regarding food and dress (e.g., Rom 14:21; 1 Cor 8:13). The New Testament puts at least as much stress on the local character of the church as it does on its universality. In fact, it is the local character of the church that makes its universality all the more profound, and vice-versa.

4. The church is as truly *prophetic* as it is *apostolic*. The church is built, after all, "upon the foundation of the apostles and prophets, with Christ Jesus himself as the cornerstone" (Eph 2:20; cf. Eph 3:5; Rev 18:20). Jesus is both the Apostle and the Prophet

---

7. Snyder, "Church as Holy and Charismatic"; Snyder, "Spiritual Gifts and Church Vitality," chapter 10 in Snyder, *Yes in Christ* (201-20).

8. See Synan, *Holiness-Pentecostal Tradition*.

9. Consider Matt 16:18, 18:17; Acts 8:1; 9:31; 11:22–26; 13:1; 15:22; 20:17; 1 Cor 12:28; Eph 1:22; 3:10; 5:29–32; Revelation 2–3.

who establishes the church (Acts 3:22; Heb 3:1). The biblical pairing of "apostles and prophets" is a sign that these two emphases go together.[10]

The church is apostolic: it is *sent* into the world as the Father sent Jesus; sent to continue the works Jesus began (John 14:12; 20:21).[11] Jesus first sent out his twelve apostles, then Paul and an expanding corps of apostolic witnesses (Rom 16:7; Eph 4:11). Faithfulness to both the *words* and the *works* of Jesus Christ—both his life and his teaching—constitutes true apostolicity. But apostolicity also involves faithful witness to who Jesus really is in truth—fidelity to both the gospel *of* Jesus and the gospel *about* Jesus.[12] Faithfulness to the words, works, and life of Jesus Christ together define the real meaning of apostolicity and thus of "apostolic succession."

But the church is also prophetic. If its apostolicity is really empowered by the Holy Spirit, it *will* be prophetic. The church is prophetic in two ways: First, in being an actual community that visibly incarnates the prophetic message of creation healed found in the Old Testament prophetic books as well as in the life of Jesus. In other words, the church is prophetic, first of all, in *what it is* as God's healing community on earth. Second, it is prophetic in proclaiming the good news of the reign of God within the present world. This may mean different accents in different historical contexts, but it always means being salt and light right now (Matt 5:14; John 8:12; Phil 2:15).[13]

"Built upon the foundation of the apostles and prophets" means the church is an apostolic people, not just a church with apostles. It is to be a prophetic people, not just a church with prophets. There is the apostleship and prophethood of all believers as surely as there is the priesthood of believers. This becomes actual, visible reality when all the gifts in the church, functioning together, make the church a prophetic people (1 Corinthians 12; Eph 4:7–16; Rom 12:8–10). This is how the Spirit builds and works through the church as his healing community on earth.

Maintaining Ecological Balance

In sum, if we consider the full range of Scripture we see that the church is *both* one and diverse; *both* holy and charismatic; *both* universal and local; *both* apostolic and prophetic. The church becomes powerfully dynamic on any turf when these truths are incarnated in its actual experience. So if we are biblical, we will see the church as *diverse, charismatic, contextual,* and *prophetic* as well as *one, holy, catholic,* and *apostolic.* Here

---

10. Theologically there is a certain priority of apostles over prophets, as suggested in 1 Cor 12:28 and Eph 4:11. Apostles (down through history) establish the church on the basis of and under the authority of Jesus Christ and have initial supervisory or oversight responsibility. Apostles are followed by prophets who stir up, inspire, invigorate, and when necessary pronounce judgment on the church. Both the New Testament and church history provide many examples. Yet in the NT apostles and prophets are seen not as offices but as gifted persons (Eph 4:11) who, in all ages, provide the functional "foundation" upon which Jesus Christ builds his church.

11. See the discussion in chapter 9 on the mission of Jesus.

12. Arias, *Announcing the Reign of God,* 8–10.

13. Snyder, *Community of the King,* 123–37.

is a much fuller—more ecological, more dynamic, more healing and missional—profile of the church than is captured by the four traditional marks.

These differing marks are not in conflict. Given the mystery of the church as multifaceted emblem of God's reign, we can view these contrasting accents as correlatives—complementary truths about the one mystery that is Christ's Body.

We do, however, find a healthy creative tension between these two sets of marks. This is simply part of the church's ecology as a living organism. The four complementary marks—diversity, charismatic endowment, locality, and prophethood—function in creative tension with the traditional marks. In fact, these four marks balance out the traditional four marks, sort of like genetic pairing.

- The church's *unity* is paired with its *diversity*;
- Its *holiness* is linked with its *charismatic fullness.*
- Being *catholic* or universal is ecologically paired with being *contextualized,* or locally incarnated.
- Being *apostolic* is paired with being *prophetic,* focused on justice as well as truth; on being a healing contrast society as well as a winsome evangelistic community.

What would happen if we took these complementary qualities with equal seriousness in the church as God's healing community on earth? That is what this book tries to do. In history, these two sets of marks have often been pulled apart. Diversity, for example, becomes the enemy of unity, or local adaptation threatens catholic uniformity. This is contrary to the church's true ecology.

Setting unity *against* diversity, or sanctity *against* charismatic fullness, or apostolic fidelity *against* prophetic witness, fractures the church's ecology. It wounds the church and undercuts its healing mission. Pitting these marks against each other, in fact, leads to two very different kinds of church. If we focus solely on the four traditional marks, or conversely just on the four contrasting ones, quite different—and anemic—churches result. Church history can actually be read as a battle between two sets of marks that should be held together.

Movement versus Institution?

This becomes clear especially when we examine the church as a movement. Church history often reveals a tension between the church as a *movement* and as an *institution.* Generally the four classic marks have been used to define and defend the church more as institution than as a movement. In contrast, the church is more likely to be diverse, locally incarnated, charismatic, and prophetic when it is a movement.

The four classic marks tend to predominate during times of emphasis on institution and organization; the other four marks are more evident during times of movement and revival. When the church is a dynamic movement it tends to be prophetic, charismatically empowered, diverse (perhaps in contrast with the larger church), and more contextualized to its immediate social environment. But when the church shifts to a more settled institution it begins to celebrate (and perhaps enforce) its oneness, holiness (that is, sacredness as institution), universality, and apostolic authority.

But this very tension—sometimes leading to schism—actually testifies to a deep theological truth about the church. To be an agent of creation healed, the church needs both the classic marks and the corresponding balancing marks. Faithful churches live in dynamic tension with these pairs of character traits. That simply goes along with the church's Spirit-endowed ecology.

The Full Ecology of God's Healing Community

The four traditional marks package ecclesiology too neatly, too tightly, setting the stage for splits and new movements that know intuitively that something is missing. But if we see the four contrasting marks as the missing half of the church's DNA, a dynamic picture emerges. We see that the true church is always, at one and the same time:

ONE ⟷ MANY / DIVERSE

HOLY ⟷ CHARISMATIC

APOSTOLIC ⟷ PROPHETIC

CATHOLIC ⟷ PARTICULAR /LOCAL-CONTEXTUAL

This is much closer to the view of the people of God pictured in both Testaments. It fits well with the biblical narrative of God—People—Land. Living faithfully on and with the land requires overarching truths and also local adaptation—being both faithful to God and rooted in the earth.

If we ground ecclesiology in the fullness of biblical revelation, we have a more potent and truer image of the mystery that is the body of Christ than we do if we accept uncritically the four classic marks. We see that in God's economy there is not simply "one holy catholic apostolic church" but at the same time many, particular, charismatic, prophetic churches called to live in the faith, hope, and love that the gospel gives.

The traditional formula offers useful insights. But due to the theological divorce between heaven and earth traced in this book, the traditional theory of the marks is inadequate in three ways. First, it fails to fully incarnate the central mark of love. Second, it fails to incarnate the dynamic of the church's full ecology. Third, it misses the full scope of creation healed. Without a comprehensive biblical foundation, the four traditional marks can actually reinforce the earth-heaven split rather than helping to heal it. But woven into the biblical vision of creation healed, the four marks and their four complements help us see the mystery of the church in God's healing plan.

THE STIGMATA TODAY

What are the distinguishing marks of Christ's body, the church, today? Does it have any *stigmata*, any signs that point to Jesus?

We have lifted up the marks of faith, hope, and love—not as vague ideas or ideals, but as real *behaviors* that rise from the risen Jesus Christ and the active presence of the Holy Spirit in Christians' lives. Faith, hope, and love—not as private virtues but as qualities nourished by the full biblical promise of creation healed.

We see also that as God's healing community on earth, the global-local church is at once one and many, holy and charismatic, universal and local, apostolic and pro-phetic. How beautiful is the body of Christ—not *without,* but *with* its *stigmata*! How broad and wise is God's redemptive plan. "O the depth of the riches both of the wis-dom and knowledge of God! How unsearchable are his judgments, and his ways past finding out!" (Rom 11:33 KJV).

Jesus said, "As the Father has sent me, so I send you" (John 20:21). He said the church would "do the works that I do" (John 14:12). "By this everyone will know that you are my disciples, if you have love for one another" (John 13:35). The church is not Jesus. But as his body it can have the mind of Christ (Phil 2:5), and so fulfill its healing mission within God's economy of salvation.

Two final words remain to be said: One about the gospel for the poor; one about the everyday practice of the church's marks.

The Mark of the Poor

Earlier we highlighted the gospel to and for the poor. Is this another essential mark of the church? If so, how does it link with the other marks?

The answer is found in Luke 4:16–30.[14] The issue is the mark of apostolicity, as Stephen Olin pointed out. The truly apostolic church continues in the world the works Jesus began. This is why Jesus sent word to John the Baptist, "Go and tell John what you hear and see" (Matt 11:4). The key point: "the poor have good news brought to them" (Matt 11:5). "This was the crowning proof that He was the *One that should come.* . . . He that thus cared for the poor must be from God."[15] The New Testament shows that the gospel for the poor is a test of the church's apostolicity, its authentic sent-ness.

The gospel for the poor is powerful precisely because it weds the apostolic and prophetic notes. This perhaps is what John Wesley meant when he said preaching the gospel to the poor is "the greatest miracle of all"[16]—miracle, for the church will never do this unless moved by the Spirit and captured by the character of Christ.[17] The church is uniquely, divinely both apostolic and prophetic when it ministers the gospel to and

14. See Jones, *Christ's Alternative to Communism.*

15. Roberts, "Free Churches" (emphasis in the original).

16. Wesley, *Explanatory Notes New Testament,* comment on Luke 7:22. Cf. Wesley's comment on Heb 9:11, "for they shall all know me, from the least even to the greatest": "In this order the saving knowledge of God ever did and ever will proceed; not first to the greatest, and then to the least."

17. This point merits some extended reflection. Wesley is claiming, it seems, that for a church to preach the gospel to the poor is more of a miracle than are physical healings. Of all "signs and wonders" in the church, this is the greatest. It is more miraculous for the church in this way to transcend the "laws" of sociological dynamics than for the "laws" of physics or physiology to be transcended in a healing or physical miracle.

among the poor, in fidelity to the words, work, and life of Jesus. Clearly this requires being empowered by the Holy Spirit, the one through whom the Son "made himself nothing, taking the very nature of a servant," humbling himself, becoming "obedient to death" (Phil 2:7–8 TNIV). This is the Christological model for ecclesiology.

The gospel visibly working among the poor is thus a key sign of the church's faithfulness—a test of apostleship. "Apostolicity" can be vague. It easily loses its grounding in the actual ministry of Jesus and turns into a question of authority or institutional "apostolic succession." Apostolicity needs the proof of practice, following the footsteps of Jesus, who sent apostles into the world to proclaim him and build his body.

Whatever else apostolicity means, it means the gospel to and with the poor. Ministering among the poor is concrete action, not abstract concept. It is done or not done. Claims of apostolicity ring hollow if the church is not visibly being good news for the poor. "The poor, the socially and economically weak and threatened, will always be the object of [the church's] primary and particular concern," Karl Barth said.[18]

In faithfully sharing the gospel with and among the poor, the church is both apostolic and prophetic. It is both holy and charismatic, because it demonstrates God's holy love empowered by the Spirit.[19] It is both catholic and local because ministry to and among the poor is always a matter of flesh-and-blood people in specific local contexts, even as it is a universal, global passion. Similarly, preaching the gospel to the poor involves both the unity and diversity of the church, joining Christians in a common gospel mission while also affirming the world's cultural mosaic as the church incarnates Jesus' love among diverse pockets of the world's poor.

The growth of the gospel among the poor puts flesh and blood on faith, hope, and love. These virtues find deeper meaning in churches of the poor—and also in affluent churches with a missional passion for the poor. "Has not God chosen the poor in the world to be rich in faith and to be heirs of the kingdom that he has promised to those who love him?" (Jas 2:5). "God chose what is weak in the world to shame the strong; God chose what is despised in the world, things that are not, to reduce to nothing things that are, so that no one might boast in the presence of God" (1 Cor 1:27–29). Knowing their need, the poor often gladly open their hearts in faith to Jesus and his healing. Living without hope, they find transforming hope in Jesus that changes their lives and gives them audacious confidence that God will bring his healing kingdom in fulness. Love for one another encourages community and builds solidarity, enlivening the church as a true sign of God's reign and of creation healed.

Faithful global and local churches today demonstrate the mind of Christ in their ministry to all nations, with particular concern for the poor.

---

18. Barth, "Christian Community and Civil Community," 36.

19. The essence of God's holiness is love (as John Wesley emphasized), which disinterestedly does good to all, and especially the poor. Further, the biblical truth of the *charismata* has particular relevance for and among the poor. The doctrine of spiritual gifts is especially good news for the poor, because it teaches (and demonstrates!) that divine empowering doesn't depend on status, wealth, education, or credentialing, but on mere openness to the direct operation of the Holy Spirit. This is why "charismatic" movements (sociologically speaking) generally have, in the first instance, been movements of the poor.

Practicing the Marks Today

As Jesus' healing community on earth, the church worldwide has the opportunity to live out principles of healing and to engage in healing practices that show and spread salvation in the world around us, local and global.

Four Key Principles

As God's healing community, the church is nourished by the disciplines of prayer, Bible reading, worship, and Christian counsel. These traditional practices expand in scope and effectiveness as they are seen within the biblical narrative and economy of creation healed.

Because of the divorce of heaven and earth, spirituality has become too spiritual.[20] Spirituality has come to mean the opposite of physicality and materiality. This always happens when spirit and matter are made opposites, as in pagan religions. In God's economy, spirit and matter are interlinked dimensions of God's good creation, yet both are liable to distortion and the disease of sin.

The Christian life—the spiritual life, spirituality—needs to be refounded on a more biblical basis—more material basis, so to speak. This means paying close attention to the created order and the key principles God the architect built into it, and by which it functions. These are basic to the creation as an ecosystem and thus to the ecology of the church's witness.

The Bible is rich in its teachings about the creation. It gives us not only the big picture of transformation and healing but also practical principles by which our Christian mission and stewardship can be actually lived. Christian biologist Calvin DeWitt helpfully identifies four principles rooted in Scripture that should be woven into the church's self-understanding and practice. Although DeWitt applies these primarily to practices of creation care, clearly they relate to all dimensions of what we commonly call spirituality and discipleship.[21] All four dovetail nicely with the central argument of this book. Practicing these principles enriches the church's spirituality and enlivens its witness.

1. *The Earthkeeping Principle*: Just as the Creator keeps and sustains humanity, so humanity must keep and sustain the creation. This succinctly states a key element of the biblical God—People—Land nexus we explored in chapter 8. The point here is that spirituality and mission (which, at heart, are one) must attend to the earthward relationship as well as to the God-ward relationship. Once this principle sinks into our worldview and worldstory, it enriches all our discipleship and Christian community.

2. *The Sabbath Principle*: The creation must be allowed to recover from human use of its resources. Grounded already in creation (Gen 2:1–4), the Sabbath principle is a key part of the Mosaic covenant. It resonates as well with God's everlasting covenant

---

20. See chapters 1, 2, and 8.

21. DeWitt, "Ecology and Ethics," 838–48. DeWitt suggests some other principles, as well—what he calls the buffer principle (related to limits), the contentment principle, the priority principle, and the praxis principle.

with the earth (Genesis 9) and is the foundation for the sabbath year, the Jubilee year, and the biblical promise of ultimate Jubilee, healing, and *shalom* (e.g., Isa 61:1–4; Luke 4:16–21).[22]

The Sabbath principle guides us in the care of the earth. It guides us, too, in the care of our bodies, each other, and God's abundant resources of grace and of matter which together form our Christian stewardship. The church is healthier and more helpful in its healing ministry as it lives by the principle and the rhythms of Sabbath.

3. *The Fruitfulness Principle*: The fecundity of the creation is to be enjoyed and guarded, not destroyed. The Genesis commission to "be fruitful and multiply" expands in meaning and depth as the Bible unfolds. God promises Israel that if she remains faithful, "I will look with favor upon you and make you fruitful and multiply you; and I will maintain my covenant with you" (Lev 26:9). Jesus tells the Twelve, "My Father is glorified by this, that you bear much fruit and become my disciples. . . . I appointed you to go and bear fruit, fruit that will last" (John 15:8, 16). Christians belong to Christ "in order that we may bear fruit for God" (Rom 7:4). And so Christians are to flourish with "the fruit of the Spirit . . . love, joy, peace, patience, kindness, generosity, faithfulness, gentleness, self-control" (Gal 5:22–23). Finally, in the new creation, the tree of life produces different kinds of fruit each month, "and the leaves of the tree are for the healing of the nations" (Rev 22:2).

In the economy of God and the ecology of the church's life, fruitfulness has many dimensions. It joins together what we commonly think of as the fruit of the Spirit and "the fruit of the ground" or earth (Gen 5:3; Deut 26:2; Isa 4:2; Jas 5:7). The fruitfulness principle thus touches all dimensions of life and witness, from evangelism to creation care.

4. *The Fulfillment and Limits Principle*: God has set limits to humanity's role within creation, and these boundaries must be respected. Genesis 1 and 2 picture the ordering of all creation. God has set boundaries—physical, social, economic, moral—and it is precisely within these limits that humans and all creation find fulfillment. Earth is to be filled and flourish with diverse and abundant life.[23]

This could also be called the *sustainability principle*. Sustainability means recognizing the bounds within which systems thrive, and that violating these leads to disease or death. We sustain healthy bodies, for example, by food, rest, exercise, work, and social interaction within healthy bounds. The same applies to the body of Christ—in fact, to the whole created order. It applies to earth's climate, as we noted in chapter 6.

Since principles of sustainability run through and connect all dimensions of creation, we find guidance here for sound economics and creative cultural life, as well as for the church's internal health and healing mission.

---

22. For a succinct summary of the meaning of Sabbath and Jubilee see Snyder, *Kingdom, Church, and World*, 59–76.

23. Fulfillment and limits may in some sense be a reflection of the life of the Trinity, for while God may be in some senses unlimited, the logic of the Trinitarian relations perhaps suggests some form both of self-limitation and of mutual fulfillment.

These key dimensions of creation thus apply to the visible life of the church. In honoring, not disregarding, these principles the church is more visibly the redemptive, healing community that God intends. As such principles are integrated into global mission practice we will see the healing power of the gospel as never before in history. Spirituality will be much richer with multiple dimensions that touch and engage "all things in heaven and on earth, . . . visible and invisible" (Col 1:16). Spirituality becomes physical, earthy, and global as well as spiritual, heavenly, and internal.

Practical Steps

How shall we live then, honoring God in God's world? How can the church embody faith, hope, and love, and the varied dimensions of the church's marks? How do we put principles of simplicity, creation-sensitivity, and biblical stewardship into daily practice?

The church as people of God and community of Jesus' disciples is both a charismatic organism and a historical reality within God's narrative and economy. In the previous chapter we showed how the church can live and witness as Trinitarian community. Elsewhere the church has been pictured as an organism of three key interacting dimensions: worship, community, and witness, with practical implications for leadership, spiritual gifts, and the structure and witness of the church. These are central themes especially in the book *Community of the King*.

All that is relevant here. Many good books in fact give guidance on the practical functioning of the body of Christ, especially at the local level. But there is a missing dimension in most such resources. The missing piece is the mission of creation care. Yet fulfilling the biblical mandate of eco-evangelism is basic to the faithful witness of the church. We are coming to understand creation care as a thread that knits together the whole fabric of the church's faithful witness and increases the church's visible marks.

Practicing Creation Care

Stewardship of creation begins with three key facts:

1. Creation care is a covenant commission from God, given first to all humanity.

2. Through the resources of God's grace and the stewardship of "the manifold grace of God" that has been given us (1 Pet 4:10), creation care is now integral to the church's local and global mission.

3. Creation care touches every dimension of life on earth, from time and finances to our interactions with all this delightful yet diseased creation.

Each church, like each person and family, will decide how to make eco-evangelism visible in its own local place and also in its global connections, since in today's world every church is globally connected.

Each congregation is an organism with its own internal ecology—and is also part of the larger community ecology where it lives and functions. Increasingly, it is also part of the global ecology and economy. So each church needs to ask how the earth and the passion for creation healed touch all aspects of its life—how this mission shapes its teaching, discipleship practices, community formation, and larger world witness.

The hope of creation healed should be a natural central theme in sermons—in all Bible teaching, in fact. Creation care should mark all the church's community life, becoming visible in the care of each other and the care of the earth. Creation care will figure largely in the design of buildings, the use of church property, and the practices of community. Any real estate owned by the church should be a demonstration plot of creation healed. Eco-evangelism will mean recycling *nearly everything*, ending the throwaway practices so unthinkingly woven into consumer society. When a church bans the use of Styrofoam cups and plates, for example, it shows that it understands how seemingly small things feed either cycles of life or cycles of death. U.S. congregations might take a cue from a church in Tanzania that makes tree planting part of each confirmation class. Through its classes and tree nurseries, over 500,000 new trees are growing, restoring a key water source that was failing.[24]

On a more personal level, simple creation-care practices show the marks of the church as healing community. Adapted to varying contexts, these practices can stimulate further creativity. Practices like these can be woven into our Christian discipleship, showing the physicality of true spirituality:

1. *Bible study.* Study the Bible (personally and in groups) with creation-care eyes. Learn what the Bible teaches about the creation, earth, God's covenant with the earth (Gen 9), and God's plan for creation healed. Key biblical themes worth studying are *earth, justice, land, shalom, the poor, the nations, Sabbath/Jubilee,* and *reconciliation.*

2. *Prayer* (privately and in groups) for the healing of the land and the nations. We can pray for reforestation in Haiti and devastated areas of Africa; peace in places where war ravages the environment; God's sustenance for frontline missionaries and earth healers—and for discernment: "Lord, what would you have me to do?"

3. *Recycle* rather than throwing things "away," realizing that waste products never really "go away." Support community-wide recycling efforts. Remember that manufacturing recycled beverage cans is about 90 percent cheaper and more ecologically responsible than making new ones. Recycling helps economically as well as ecologically. Recycling slows rather than speeds up the entropy of the created order. Many cities are beginning to discover they can save millions of dollars in city services by encouraging recycling.

4. *Support local, state, and federal legislation and international agreements that protect the environment and promote creation care.* Whether it is strengthening endangered species laws, supporting international accords to limit greenhouse gases, or teaching tomorrow's leaders (our students and children) to live ecologically, the church can help nudge the world toward effective stewardship and real sustainability. Locally we might work for bike lanes on city streets, more parks and footpaths, community gardens, energy-saving building codes, and expanded recycling. This is all part of eco-evangelism.

24. Sabin, "Whole Earth Evangelism," 29.

5. *Make Sundays (or another day) real Sabbaths* by spending at least an hour reading good books and articles on creation and wholistic mission and discipleship. Combine this with walks (alone or with friends) in fields and woods or city streets, paying attention to God's other creatures.

6. *Join or start a group* that focuses on the creation-care dimensions of mission and discipleship—prayer, study, conversation, action.

7. *Write a poem, hymn, song, or meditation* celebrating the wisdom of God in creation. Psalms and Job provide wonderful models. Or figure out the creation-care implications of your job, your hobbies, or your teaching or preaching.

8. *Form creation-affirming habits*—moderate eating, regular exercise, walking (if possible) instead of riding or using elevators, bird-watching, nature photography, gardening—whatever fits your situation. Use personal disciplines and exercise for the benefit of creation and others, not just for your own health. Leave the iPod and cellphone behind when going for walks. Make multi-tasking into multi-attending to creation.

9. Relatedly, *eat locally, as much as possible.* Support the local economy by enjoying food that is locally produced. This is a push-back against the kind of "industrial food" that Michael Pollan writes about in *The Omnivore's Dilemma*. Industrial food is "Any food whose provenance is so complex or obscure that it requires expert help to ascertain."[25] Buying locally, we know where the food comes from and what it contains.

Buying and eating locally helps heal the land while improving our own health. Consider the benefits: 1) fresher, more nutritious, and better tasting food; 2) less ingestion of unknown and unneeded chemicals, artificial flavors and coloring, and obesity-inducing high fructose corn syrup; 3) reduction in the fossil fuels and pollution involved in shipping food around the world; 4) encouragement of the local economy. Supporting the local economy is an act of social justice; a revolutionary act of resistance against the unhealthy industrialization of our food supply. It reinforces the growing movement toward healthier, more sustainable local and global economies.

There are also great family discipleship lessons here. Our children delightedly discover what a real tomato or strawberry or healthily-produced egg is actually supposed to taste like! They taste the difference between a tomato picked green thousands of miles away, perhaps artificially reddened, then shipped to our local big-box supermarket, and a plump red vine-ripened tomato grown naturally in one's own town or yard.

10. *Practice energy conservation*—for the sake of the planet and the poor, not just to save money—in home-building or renovation, transportation, entertainment, and daily habits.

11. *Join an organization or network* that promotes the healing of creation from a biblical standpoint. The Evangelical Environmental Network and the organization Blessed Earth are good places to start and sources of information on various other networks, resources, and programs.[26]

---

25. Pollan, *Omnivore's Dilemma*, 17.

26. Many excellent resources are now available. See for example Ball, *Global Warming and the Risen Lord*; Brown, *Our Father's World*; J. Matthew Sleeth, *Serve God, Save the Planet*; Nancy Sleeth, *Go Green, Save Green*. These books list a range of additional resources as well, including numerous Internet sites.

Global and local churches today face a great opportunity to channel the healing, transforming grace of God into multiple dimensions of creation stewardship, giving witness to the healing good news of Jesus Christ.

JESUS THE HEAD—WE THE BODY

Ultimately the marks, the visible identity of the true church, bring us back to Jesus Christ—his person and mission. What "body of Christ" means depends on who Jesus is. Ecclesiology in this sense depends totally on Christology.

Biblically, we can summarize this truth in terms of *the great confession* ("You are the Christ," the anointed Messiah, Matt 16:16) and *the great identification* ("As the Father has sent me, so send I you"). The *great confession* is that Jesus Christ is Lord, Savior, Healer, and Liberator of the world. The *great identification* is that we are his Body, called to walk in his steps (1 Pet 2:21). We, the church, are his disciples, servants and priests, wounded healers. We think of the many "as" passages ("Love one another *as* I have loved you"—e.g., John 15:12). Or in the words of the Apostle John, "Whoever claims to live in him must live as Jesus did" (1 John 2:6 TNIV).

The church is born in this great confession and great identification. So Jesus said, "Where two or three are gathered in my name, there am I among them" (Matt 18:20). Jesus spoke of his disciples "abiding" or "remaining" in him; of finding their life in him (John 15:4–7). This is the great identification. If the Spirit of the Lord is upon us, this will lead us to live out the mind of Christ, fulfilling the healing mission God has given.

This is biblical ecclesiology; the meaning of "body of Christ." The church is born out of this *koinonia* of the Spirit; this identification with Jesus. Thus the identification with Jesus through the Spirit issues in the *great communion,* the church (*koinonia;* the communion of saints) and the *great commission,* the disciple-making mission of Christ as given in such passages as Luke 4:18–19, Matt 28:19–20, and 1 Pet 2:9.

This chapter's overview of the church's marks does not of course exhaust the meaning of the marks or the mystery of the church. But it does show us three things:

1. *The four classic marks of the church by themselves don't give a full enough picture of the church.* The traditional model, being one-sided, is more useful when woven into a larger biblical understanding of the church as God's healing community on earth, and when combined with the notes of faith, hope, and love.

2. *A fuller understanding of the marks of the church* stresses the balancing complements to unity, holiness, catholicity, and apostolicity, yielding a vision of the church that is theologically richer, missiologically more powerful, and functionally more potent for the church's healing mission. Seeing the church as also many, charismatic, locally rooted, and prophetic is a richer and more biblical picture of the church's ecology.

3. *Biblical ecclesiology takes seriously that the church is the body of which Jesus alone is Head.* Faithful churches radically identify with the life, works, and words of Jesus Christ, and with his mission. One key sign of faithfulness is incarnating the gospel with

and among the poor through the power of the Holy Spirit. This yields an ecclesiology born in mission, not in theological abstraction or institutional self-preservation.[27]

The church is a mystery because by grace it participates in the mystery of the Incarnation, the mystery of the Trinity, and the mystery of God's kingdom (Matt 13:11; Mark 4:11; John 17:23; Eph 1:9–10; 3:6–10; 5:32; Col 1:26–27). But God has revealed to us "the plan [*oikonomia*] of the mystery" centering in Jesus Christ, Head and Body (Eph 3:9)—in Jesus' life and work, reflected in the church. The church has the high calling—and the high possibility and potential, through the Spirit—to embody the good news within contemporary society so that we increasingly see signs that God is answering our incessant prayer that his kingdom may come and his will be done on earth as in heaven.

The church always tends over time to drift away from the more radical "movemental" marks of the church to the more stable, manageable ones. The penchant remains to over-objectify the marks, making them abstract attributes of the church as institution, or invisible claims rather than visible witnesses. So the church must always be alert to the biblical marks of the church (especially the more "radical" ones), staying close to Scripture and to the radical experience of Christian community.

An analysis of the church's marks does not yield a full ecclesiology, but it does help us identify some essential aspects of the church as body of Christ in mission. It gives a broader picture of the church's mystery and complexity, which is very useful in the church's actual life and healing mission.

Hear now the story of a young Christian named Amber Medin. Her experience highlights key themes of this book. Amber discovered that seeing salvation as creation healed does not mean reducing all mission to creation care; it means seeing the *connections* between all aspects of creation and all the dimensions of redemption and healing.

Amber had been a Christian a long time. But then she had what she calls her "eco-conversion." As a middle-class American, Amber lived "in utter ignorance of what my daily choices meant for the Earth, the animals, and the poor." She saw creation as existing "for *my* benefit, *my* pleasure, and *my* comfort—and I, in turn, had no responsibilities. I viewed God's creation as a collection of objects rather than a communion of subjects."

Amber became alarmed when she discovered her "complete lack of awareness" that she had unconsciously assumed an "it's-all-about-me lifestyle." Though a faithful member of the Salvation Army, she began to see that "'disconnects' were everywhere" in her life. "Water didn't come from evaporating reservoirs; it came from the faucet. Electricity didn't come from mercury- and arsenic-producing coal-fired plants; it came from the light switch."

Gradually God led Amber on a "journey of connection," as she puts it. "I came face to face with the fact that I was actively contributing to the degradation of the Earth, the extinction of species, and the oppression of the poor."

27. This is a main theme of several recent books on the church and the renewal of mission, such as Hirsch, *Forgotten Ways*, and Frost, *Exiles*.

Amber adopted new habits that cooperate with, rather than exploit, God's good creation—healthier eating, a more fuel-efficient car, and other changes. "With each step, I realized that I was engaging in the spiritual discipline of simplicity—and that this simplicity is an untapped part of practical holiness. Less became more."

Amber concludes, "After my eco-conversion, I found I had added an entirely new dimension to my sacramental living. . . . I am beginning to view myself as part of the created order rather than the pinnacle of it, as a member of a worshipful orchestra rather than the principal soloist. I am learning to worship the Creator, rather than myself, just one of His creations."[28]

Creation healed means seeing the *connections*—because of who the Trinity is. The best mark of the church is a community of disciples that discovers and lives the interconnected strands which together weave the intricate tapestry of creation healed.

28. Medin, "My Eco-Conversion," 40–41.

13

The Community of
Earth and Heaven

Therefore, since we are surrounded by so great a cloud of witnesses,
let us also lay aside every weight and the sin that clings so closely,
and let us run with perseverance the race that is set before us, looking to Jesus the pioneer and perfecter of our faith, who for the sake
of the joy that was set before him endured the cross, disregarding its
shame, and has taken his seat at the right hand of the throne of God.

(Heb 12:1–2)

SALVATION AS CREATION HEALED puts Christian community in a whole new light.
God the Trinity is, in a profound sense, community. Human beings are made for
communion with God and nurturing relationship with one another. Creation healed
therefore means the restoration of healthy community in multiple dimensions.

Since in Christ God is "reconciling the world to himself" and is "entrusting the
message of reconciliation to us" (2 Cor 5:18–19), we all are involved in reconciliation,
in the restoration of community, and in the healing of creation. Through Jesus Christ
God "was pleased to reconcile to himself all things [not just some things], whether on
earth or in heaven [not just one or the other], by making peace through the blood of
his cross" (Col 1:20). And so Christian community in some sense involves "all things
. . . things in heaven and things on earth" (Eph 1:10).

What then is Christian community, in light of creation healed? What is the nature
of the community, the "shared life," that Christians talk so much about? Confusion
often reigns here. We can talk very superficially about community and forget that we

are dealing with profoundest realities. Over the years I have pondered this question. Gradually I've come to see the depth of the meaning of community in Jesus Christ.

COMMUNITY IN SIX DIMENSIONS

Christian community does, in fact, have many levels. It is multidimensional. Viewed biblically and theologically and in light of the church's history and mission, genuine Christian community appears in six different forms. This final chapter explores these six dimensions and their meaning for the church as healing community today.

Some of these dimensions are obvious. Others are perhaps new or strange. Yet no one form of community stands alone. The wonder of the body of Christ lies in the fullness of Christian community.

1. *Community with God through Jesus Christ by the Holy Spirit*

This is the communion we have with God based upon repentance and faith in Christ; in new birth. When by faith we give ourselves to God and receive justification and regeneration we experience a new and living communion with God. This is God's gift to us, and the way we enter this first dimension of Christian community—community with God through Jesus Christ. We receive new life, the beginning of life in abundance (John 10:10). This is a central New Testament theme. We come into fellowship or communion with God through reconciliation in the blood of Jesus. "Our fellowship is with the Father and with his Son Jesus Christ" (1 John 1:3).

This and the other dimensions of community discussed here can be illustrated by two biblical images: the rising sun with its rays and colors, and the rainbow (see Gen 9:13–16). As the rising sun gives energy and light, so this first dimension is the central source of all the other dimensions. And as the rainbow is born of the sun's light interacting with the atmosphere's moisture, so the other dimensions of community follow. (See the illustration at the end of this chapter.) Thus, church renewal and vitality begins here: community or fellowship with God through the salvation provided in Jesus Christ.

Julia Foote's experience of God in the early 1800s provides a remarkable example of such community with God by the Spirit. Born in Schenectady, New York, in 1823, the child of slaves, Julia initially rebelled against God. As a teenager, however, she came to know God personally. Later she would become an effective African American evangelist.

Both Julia's parents had suffered under slavery. Her mother, especially, endured violence and abuse before her father was able to buy freedom for himself and then for his family.

Julia was decisively converted at a quarterly conference of the African Methodist Episcopal Zion Church when she was fifteen. A few years later, after her marriage to George Foote and now living in Boston, Julia felt a clear call to preach the gospel.

Neither her husband nor her pastor supported her. How could she—a black woman from a poor family—be a preacher and evangelist?

But God reassured Julia through a remarkable Trinitarian vision that sealed her call forever. Elaine Heath tells the story:

> The vision was multisensory, including sight, sound, touch, taste, and smell. It lasted for many hours, beginning during a time of fervent prayer on a Sabbath evening. An angel came and led Foote to the Father, Son, and Holy Spirit beneath a massive tree. Many others were there as well, but she could not tell whether they were angels or people. God the Father told her she must make her choice about answering her call, warning her of eternal suffering if she refused. When she remained silent, God took her hand. Foote thought she was going to be led to hell, so she cried out that she would obey God and go anywhere God led her. God then pointed in many directions, each time asking if she would go there. To each question she answered, "Yes."
>
> After that God led her to the edge of a great sea, where he brought her to Christ. There she experienced an extraordinary cleansing, healing, and commissioning that was nuanced with baptismal and marital overtones: "My hand was given to Christ, who led me into the water and stripped me of my clothing, which at once vanished from sight. Christ then appeared to wash me, the water feeling quite warm." She goes on to say that during this time there was a "profound silence" from the shore. When she emerged from the water an angel provided a clean, white robe that the Father put on her. Then she heard incredible music and shouting. As they all went back to the tree where she had first encountered the Trinity, the Holy Spirit plucked some fruit from the tree and gave it to Foote. After she had eaten it, God the Father told her she was now ready to be sent into the world to go where he would command.[1]

Julia Foote's vision has overtones of community and of creation healed. Images of the Holy Trinity combine with the physical senses and with symbols of nature—water, a tree, fruit—themselves biblical images of God's salvation and healing. The symbolic combining of heaven and earth points to creation healed—and also to mission, and to the interplay of the multiple dimensions of community and reconciliation.[2]

Julia Foote's encounter with God was more mystical than what most Christians experience—though dreams and visions of God's presence may be more common than we sometimes think. In this case, perhaps God graciously appeared visually to Julia because of the oppression and prejudice she had suffered and would continue to face as she lived out her calling. But her story illustrates a truth common to all Christians: through Jesus Christ by the Holy Spirit we come to know God deeply. This community with the Triune God is the root and source of the expanding dimensions of community that we experience as we continue to follow Jesus.

1. Heath, *Mystic Way,* 87, citing Julia Foote, "A Brand Plucked from the Fire," in Andrews, *Sisters in the Spirit.*

2. Some striking similarities are found here with the way Father, Son, and Spirit appear to the main character in William Young's novel *The Shack.*

2. *Community with One Another in the Local Body of Christ*

This is the community we have together in the church within a local congregation. It is Christian fellowship or *koinonia* in local space and time. We participate in a community that visibly transcends and reconciles differences of gender, socioeconomic status, education, and ethnicity. As we see in the New Testament, here is a community that unites rich and poor, master and slave, educated and uneducated. Even though our churches may embody this only imperfectly, it is an essential dimension of the gospel. Through the power of the Spirit this dimension does exist and can exist more perfectly, more visibly.

Scripture is clear that this kind of community is inseparable from the first. Community with one another is grounded in our communion with God. This is a major New Testament focus. In fact, the New Testament (particularly the epistles) devotes more space to this dimension of community than to any other. Key Scriptures are 1 Corinthians 12–14, Romans 12, and Ephesians 2–5. But most New Testament passages either teach or clearly assume this kind of community.[3] "If we walk in the light as he himself is in the light, we have fellowship with one another, and the blood of Jesus his Son cleanses us from all sin" (1 John 1:7).

When we are converted or make a genuine profession of faith in Christ, we begin to participate in and enjoy a new community, a new social reality—the church, body of Christ. We enter into a *new kind* of human community. We experience Christian *koinonia*, "shared life" or "life in common" (Acts 2:42 and related passages). This is the essential horizontal dimension of the vertical reconciliation we experience with God through Jesus by the Spirit. Such community exists and expresses itself in local space and time, within a particular history and culture.

Scripture makes it very clear that this dimension of Christian community is inseparable from the first—communion with God. Community with God through Jesus Christ already implies community with other brothers and sisters in local Christian community. Biblically and theologically speaking, it is impossible to separate or divorce the vertical and the horizontal. To use a different image, they are two aspects of the same reality.

3. *Community with the Broader Church within One's Region or Nation*

This obviously is a wider dimension of Christian community, yet it also is clearly present in the New Testament. The first-century church throughout the Roman Empire was built up and networked by Paul and the other apostles and by a host of informal connections and relationships. In the first century this wider community grew and flourished throughout much of the Roman Empire. The way Peter, Paul, John, and others of the apostles and prophets maintained contact with the growing network of local Christian communities is impressive and teaches us a lot both theologically and sociologically.

3. This is a major theme in Snyder, *Problem of Wineskins*; Snyder, *Community of the King*; Snyder, *Liberating the Church*; and Snyder, *Decoding the Church*.

The New Testament church practiced effective *translocal networking*. It nourished a vital interconnection among its hundreds of local churches, using the comings and goings of apostles, prophets, and others as well as many hand-carried letters and oral messages. This networking was not a denominational structure or formal organiza- tion. On the other hand, neither did it mean that each local body of believers was isolated or totally independent. The model of the early church was *interdependence* and vital interconnection. Early Christians maintained a sense of community beyond the local congregation—a sense of the catholic or universal body of Christ.

We get many hints of this in the New Testament. Consider the many references to people who traveled with, or were sent back and forth by, Paul and other apostles and leaders.[4] After the meeting of the apostles and elders recorded in Acts 15, the decisions reached were carried to all the churches through two leaders, Judas and Silas. Acts 15:30–33 records, "So they were sent off and went down to Antioch. When they gathered the congregation together, they delivered the letter. When its members read it, they rejoiced at the exhortation. Judas and Silas, who were themselves prophets, said much to encourage and strengthen the believers. After they had been there for some time, they were sent off in peace by the believers to those who had sent them."

Consider also the community and networking implications of Acts 20:2–4 and the seven "networkers" in addition to Paul who are identified: "[Paul] traveled through that area, speaking many words of encouragement to the people, and finally arrived in Greece, where he stayed three months. Because some Jews had plotted against him just as he was about to sail for Syria, he decided to go back through Macedonia. He was accompanied by Sopater son of Pyrrhus from Berea, Aristarchus and Secundus from Thessalonica, Gaius from Derbe, Timothy also, and Tychicus and Trophimus from the province of Asia" (TNIV).

In addition to such face-to-face contacts, which no doubt were numerous, the many letters to the churches that form so rich a part of the New Testament are them- selves evidence and examples of such networking. These were the ways the early church maintained a sense of community and ongoing vitality.

The assumption in Acts (as elsewhere in the New Testament) is that the many local congregations composed in a larger sense *one* church which *in practical ways* was connected through a lively variety of contacts. This appears to be a normal and basic part of biblical ecclesiology.

We should note, though, that this broader translocal reach does not take the place of local community. We all need both these forms of Christian community. This third dimension is different, however, simply because of the realities of space and time. Obviously, we can enjoy more intimate and constant community with our local sisters and brothers than we can with the church regionally or nationally. But both are neces- sary and normative. We will see later why both are important.

Today, denominational networks and associations of various kinds can be helpful in maintaining this sense of the more-than-local body of Christ. Even though they

---

4. Note for example Acts 8:14; 9:32, 38; 10:23; 11:1, 12, 25–30; 13:3–6; 12:25; 13:49; 14:21–27; 15:1–4; 15:22—16:5; 18:22–28; 20:1–6, 17; 21:8–10; 27:1–2; 1 Cor 16:3–12, 17–18; Eph 6:21; Col 4:7; Tit 3:12.

may not include all Christians within a region or nation, denominations and associations do give Christians some sense of the reality and interdependence of the larger church.

4. Community with the Global Church—All Christian Sisters and Brothers throughout the Earth

Is it really possible to have community with the entire body of Christ throughout the whole wide world? Yes! Of course, we can never sit down with all our Christian brothers and sisters worldwide and talk or worship with them face-to-face. Such *koinonia* normally is found only in the local church. Still, it does make sense to speak of *koinonia* also in the global sense. Our Christian brothers and sisters throughout the earth *really are* our family in Christ. We are all related and responsible for one another. "So then you are no longer strangers and aliens, but you are citizens with the saints and also members of the household of God" (Eph 2:19)—both locally and globally.

Even though global Christian community cannot be face-to-face, it can be *genuine* community in terms of mutual affection and concern, of "disinterested love" and "beneficence" (Wesley) toward all Christians worldwide. Practical expressions include prayer, economic sharing (mutual dependence), various forms of communication (today including the Internet) and information sharing in other ways.

Global Christian community (the church worldwide) should be defined as genuine community—a form of *koinonia*. But focus on this global dimension does not mean we should depreciate or devalue, or fail to embody, the local dimension. The fact is that the church's life flows from dimensions one and two (community with God and with one another locally). Some Christians emphasize these larger, global dimensions of the church but neglect the local church. This is a big mistake. *Every believer* needs to experience the church in the first two dimensions—that is, community with God and in and through the local church. Here is the source of the life than enlivens the whole church.

Note that dimensions 2, 3, and 4 (local, regional and global Christian community) are not only spiritual but also physical. Each is material, economic, and social-relational. The main difference between these dimensions is the absence of face-to-face contact in dimension 4, as also usually in dimension 3. Deep personal transformation requires frequent face-to-face relationships with sisters and brothers in the local church (dimension 2, in combination with dimension 1). But global Christian community can also be transforming as it expands our vision of what the church is worldwide. Giving us a bigger vision of the kingdom of God, it helps undercut nationalism and false patriotism, materialism, and ethnocentricity. We get a wider picture of who God is and of what he is doing and intends to do. This consciousness of the world church helps free us from captivity to our own culture. It helps us see the ways in which God truly is forming "a great multitude . . . from every nation, from all tribes and peoples and languages" (Rev 7:9).

Many biblical passages speak of this broader dimension of community. The Bible refers to the church not just as a local community, but as the body of Christ in the world.[5] When Jesus says he will build his church, he is referring to the church world-wide, for his disciples are to be his witnesses "to the ends of the earth" (Acts 1:8). The writings of Paul and of Peter and the Book of Revelation picture the church as a worldwide community.

Ecumenical and other cooperative movements have focused especially on this dimension. Denominations that have a global presence also give Christians some sense of connection to the global church. At a very practical level, John and Sylvia Ronsvalle of The Empty Tomb, inc., in Champaign-Urbana, Illinois, provide resources for yoking congregations in various countries, thus working to expand this sense of the interdependence of the global Christian family.[6]

This fourth expression of Christian community, then, is *koinonia* in the sense of partnership and interdependence within the Christian church worldwide. But two more dimensions of Christian community also deserve our attention and enrich our experience of community.

5. Community with All the People of God in All Times and Places, in Heaven and on Earth, by the Spirit and in the Trinity

In the Apostles' Creed, Christians affirm "the communion of saints." What kind of Christian community is this? Do Christians today experience some sense of community with the whole people of God, beyond the limitations of space and time, including the "noble company of saints and martyrs" who have gone before us? Is there really a "communion of saints" in this sense?

There does seem to be a reality here that many Christians experience and witness to. Since this dimension of community transcends space-time limitations, it is much less "tangible" in our daily experience. Yet it does seem to be real, and it has significant implications for church life and mission.

Several biblical passages speak of, or at least hint at, this dimension. Hebrews 11:1—12:2 is particularly relevant. We read, "Therefore, since we are surrounded by so great a cloud of witnesses, let us also lay aside every weight and the sin that clings so closely, and let us run with perseverance the race that is set before us, looking to Jesus the pioneer and perfecter of our faith, who for the sake of the joy that was set before him endured the cross, disregarding its shame, and has taken his seat at the right hand of the throne of God" (Heb 12:1–2).

In church history, this dimension of Christian community seems to come to consciousness especially in worship and in the experience of the great saints of church history.[7] For many Christians this dimension becomes real especially during times of prayer and meditation.

---

5. For example, Rom 7:4; 12:5; 1 Cor 10:16–17; 12:12–28; Eph 1:23; 3:6; 4:4, 12–16, 5:30; Col 1:18.

6. See the Yoking Map at the empty tomb website, http://www.emptytomb.org/index.html. See also Ronsvalle, *State of Church Giving*.

7. See the discussion in Snyder, *Models*, 56–66, where this sense of Christian community is seen as a characteristic of the kingdom of God understood and experienced as "mystical communion."

In Julia Foote's vision of God, cited earlier, we saw that "many others" were present, though "she could not tell whether they were angels or people."[8] Here is a picture of mystical communion.

Christian hymns are full of images picturing this kind of community. For example:

> There is a scene where spirits blend,
> Where friend holds fellowship with friend;
> Though sundered far, by faith they meet,
> Around one common mercy seat.[9]

Of course, here we face spiritual mysteries beyond our present comprehension—mysteries not yet fully revealed. Are Christian believers of past epochs really with us today, surrounding us? Do we in fact have a kind of community with those Christians who have now gone to heaven? We can't be dogmatic here. Nevertheless, down through history the church has affirmed the reality of the "communion of saints"—though with varying meanings.

Biblically speaking, we can affirm at least this much: Christians who have preceded us in death, who have already crossed the line between this earthly life and the life to come, still live. The Bible affirms this in many places, including in the Book of Revelation. We can reflect here also on the experience of Jesus and his disciples on the mount of transfiguration.

Obviously what most makes this dimension different from all others is that it involves spiritual experience that is not limited by space and time. Here is a spiritual dimension *now* that already has the character of the life we will enjoy when salvation has fully come; when creation is fully healed. This dimension reminds us of the mystery of the broadest, most vast reaches of spiritual life and the widest dimensions of the reality of the church.

However, this dimension also has practical implications for our lives in Christ and the healing of creation. First, because our lives are surrounded and witnessed by those faithful who have gone before us, we gain a deep sense of responsibility to treasure and protect the legacy of faith and service that we have received from our spiritual ancestors, even if we are sometimes critical of it. And second, by the same token, we have a sense of responsibility to be faithful to God's call on our lives for the sake of those who will come after us, those whose lives we will bear witness to after our (first!) earthly lives have come to an end. In both these ways, we gain a long-term perspective of the lasting significance of our lives and actions, the lasting implications of the real choices we make in our lives today.

6. *Solidarity with the Entire Human Family on Earth and with All Creation*

How far does Christian community really reach, biblically speaking? If it includes "the communion of saints," does it reach also "to the ends of the earth," literally and

---

8. Heath, *Mystic Way*, 87.

9. Hugh Stowell, *From Every Stormy Wind That Blows* (1828), stanza 2.

physically? Certainly the Bible teaches the interdependence and connectedness of the whole human family and the entire created order. Christians trust in and worship God "the Father, from whom every family in heaven and on earth takes its name" (Eph 3:14–15). Humans exist in a relationship of mutual interdependence based in creation, common grace, Christ's incarnation and atonement, and the work of the Holy Spirit—a relationship based most fundamentally in the truth and love of the Holy Trinity.

Since we are speaking here of relationship with the whole human family—including non-Christians and many enemies of the Christian faith—obviously the concept of "Christian community" does not seem to fit here. But we can properly speak of *solidarity* with all peoples and the whole created order. Recognized or not, all humans share a common interest in the well-being of the planet, the physical environment. Together with our Jewish friends we remember the covenant recorded in Genesis 9 that God made with "the earth," "the covenant that I make between me and you and every living creature that is with you, for all future generations" (Gen 9:12). As part of those "future generations" we today seek to be faithful to the covenant.

But is this really *community*? And is it truly *Christian*? In an important sense, this solidarity with all peoples and the whole creation cannot be called *Christian* community. Still, it is not unrelated to Christian community and should be understood in connection with it. Solidarity with all creation is not Christian community because it does not directly participate in the five dimensions we've just discussed. Obviously, most of humanity is not reconciled to God through Jesus Christ and does not experience the *koinonia* in the Holy Spirit that comes through faith in Jesus.

But that is not the whole story. In another sense, solidarity with the whole human family and all creation *can* be seen as a dimension of Christian community. Through communion with Jesus Christ in the Spirit and with the body of Christ, we enter into a relationship of mutual interdependence and responsibility with the creation that God has made. The source and power of this is the love of God. Think of the many biblical passages that show the intimate interrelationship between humankind and the created order, beginning with the creation account in Genesis 1 and 2. We remember the responsibility God gave Israel to care for the land (for example, in Leviticus 25–26), and the interdependence between God's people and the land that is reiterated in the early chapters of Deuteronomy.

In the both the Old and the New Testaments we are reminded that God is the God of all nations; the Father "from whom every family in heaven and on earth takes its name" (Eph 3:15). The Apostle Paul could affirm that in a broad sense, though not in a specifically Christian sense, in God we all "live and move and have our being" (Acts 17:28).

Given biblical teaching on the unity of the human race because of our common creation and because of God's gracious concern for and involvement with all peoples, we can legitimately extend the concept of Christian community to this broadest dimension. This is true in three senses: first, in terms of our mutual interdependence; second, in terms of mission; and third, in terms of eschatology.

First is the undeniable fact of *mutual interdependence.* Although solidarity with all humanity and the physical creation is not Christian community, it is a Christian concern because we understand by divine revelation the interconnectedness of all creation. The Christian community is in actual fact dependent upon the whole earth for its own life, as noted in previous chapters. Because of God's love shed abroad in our hearts by the Holy Spirit, Christians share a concern for all peoples and for the well-being of the physical environment upon which all peoples, including ourselves, depend for physical life.

Second, solidarity with all peoples and lands is a dimension of Christian community because *Christians have been given a mission for the whole earth.* Christians are concerned to reach people everywhere for Christ. The Christian mission is for the whole world, both in the sense of all earth's peoples and in the sense of the well-being of the planet.

The third sense in which solidarity with all peoples and the earth is a dimension of Christian community is *the perspective of eschatology.* Christians firmly believe that, viewed eschatologically, "the kingdom of the world has become the kingdom of our Lord and of his Messiah, and he will reign forever and ever" (Rev 11:15). Both the Old and New Testaments prophesy a renewed earth community, "new heavens and a new earth, where righteousness is at home" (2 Pet 3:13; cf. Isa 65:17; 66:22; Rev 21:1). Here is universal *shalom* with all peoples and the whole earth: "they shall all sit under their own vines and under their own fig trees, and no one shall make them afraid" (Mic 4:4; cf. 2 Kgs 18:31; Isa 36:16). Eschatologically speaking, Christian community is restored earth community, refined and purified by God's judgment and renewal.

Christians in mission seek to live in this future now. Faithful followers of Jesus say a decisive "No!" to the alienations, divisions, and exploitations of the present order of things and a decisive "Yes!" to all the promises of God. As much as possible they even now live within the Yes and deny the No. Thus living in two worlds they realize that solidarity with the whole earth is not *yet* Christian community, but that *it will be.* And if God's future is really more certain and real than our present, Christians can even now, in audacious hope and faith, claim earth-human solidarity as Christian community. "The whole wide world for Jesus!"

This dimension provides a practical theological basis for Christian cultural engagement and a Christian environmental ethic. Christians should view creation care as faithful *human* stewardship and as *Christian* mission. As Christians we can and should cooperate with other people and organizations that struggle for healthy human culture and for the welfare of the physical environment. Christians cooperate from their own special viewpoint and insights, of course. They recognize the sovereignty of God, the salvation that has come into the world through Jesus Christ, and the final goal of God's plan: new creation, the reconciliation of all things through Jesus Christ (Eph 1:10)—in other words, the kingdom of God in its fullness.

This sixth dimension of community provides the basis for human (not explicitly Christian) community with all people of good will and sincere hearts everywhere, regardless of religion, culture, worldview, ethnicity, or social status. Here is a solid biblical basis for international cooperation to meet human and environmental need. Though this is not yet Christian community, Christian community (life together in Christ) does provide the common ground upon which Christians can play a redemptive role in the larger human community.

So it is indeed possible to view solidarity with all creation as part of Christian community in this more extended sense. This is a legitimate concern of Christians, of the church. For Christians understand through biblical revelation and the gospel the true nature of the relationship between God, the whole human family, and the physical-social-spiritual environment. Through Jesus Christ we know the secret, the "mystery" of the plan of God (Rom 16:25; Eph 1:9; 3:3–9; 6:19; Col 2:2–3; 4:3) for his whole creation.

So this sixth dimension is a proper and compelling missional focus for the church. Jesus' disciples understand that we bear responsibility for the welfare of all creation and the whole human family. This is our calling and our joy. It is part of our stewardship as humans and as Christians, our eco-evangelism and our vision of creation healed.

PRACTICING CHRISTIAN COMMUNITY TODAY

These dimensions of Christian community are immensely practical for the life, renewal, and mission of the church, and for nurturing the vision of creation healed. Here are some key implications:

1. *The experience of Christian community is deeper and richer the more of these dimensions it embodies.* We grow in our understanding, appreciation, and experience of real Christian community to the extent that we participate in all these dimensions. We experience Christian community most profoundly when we participate in it most broadly. For this reason, growth in experiencing these various dimensions is part of a Christian community's spiritual growth.

2. *These dimensions are not strictly sequential.* Though community with God (dimension 1) and with others in the body of Christ (dimension 2) are foundational, different people, and perhaps people in different cultures, may feel drawn towards or more easily experience different dimensions—either initially or on an ongoing basis.

This can help our evangelism. People may first start to understand the gospel at one or another of these dimensions. Different people may be attracted to Christ in different ways. Often people come to faith by "belonging" (which may be experienced in dimension 2) before "believing" (necessary for the experience of dimension 1).

Here's an example: Kathy, who knows nothing of the good news or of Jesus, has a passion for the environment. Getting to know Christians with the same concern, she begins to understand deeper reasons for creation care. She learns that God himself, and the church, share this concern. This discovery can eventually draw her to Jesus Christ, then on to experiencing the other dimensions of Christian community. These are some of the dimensions of eco-evangelism.

Other people, however, may find the port of entry into Christian community at a different place, perhaps in one of the other kinds of Christian community. It may be that different persons, depending on their temperament or gifts or culture, may initially be attracted to one of these six dimensions in particular. Participating in this dimension may then lead to the others.

3. *Ongoing growth is possible in all dimensions as we walk with God in Christian community, open to the Spirit.* Growth in the Spirit, in sanctification, in being "in Christ," is enriched as we see how the Christian life involves all these dimensions. The Spirit guides us into widening experiences of Christian community, and so we continue to "grow in the grace and knowledge of our Lord and Savior Jesus Christ" (1 Pet 3:18).

4. Relatedly, *these different dimensions of community help a church discern its particular gifts, callings, and ministries.* Every Christian should experience all these dimensions, but some persons will probably sense God's call to focus especially on one or two. For instance, God may call some to minister primarily in evangelism or discipleship within the first and second dimensions of community, but he may call others to work primarily in other dimensions—say, helping to bring unity and cooperation in all the church worldwide (dimension 4) or working to relieve hunger worldwide or to be an advocate for creation care (dimension 6).

What does God want each of us to do as we fulfill our callings within the priesthood of all believers? Specific gifts and callings within the church are diverse (1 Cor 12:4–7; Eph 4:7). But considering these varying dimensions of Christian community can be an important factor in helping a church discern the ministry and calling of each believer. It expands the range of true ministry options. Recognizing the diversities of gifts and interests, vital congregations open many doors and opportunities for ministry and service.

5. *Each of these expressions of Christian community may be thought of in terms of covenant.* Covenant means a relationship involving commitment and faith in God and his promises. We recall the covenants God made with all creation (Genesis 9), with his people Israel, and especially the new covenant in the blood of Jesus Christ. This reality of the covenant-making God is thus the basis for all six dimensions of Christian community.

Because God is the Lord who initiates covenant, all these dimensions are real and important to the economy of salvation. All can lead to genuine experiences of Christian community because they are all essentially relational in character. All these dimensions of community are based in God himself—the God who is both transcendent and immanent, ultimate and intimate; the Holy Trinity who has self-revealed through the incarnation, life, death, resurrection, and continuing reign of Jesus Christ in the power of the Holy Spirit.

6. *An exclusive or exaggerated emphasis on any one of these dimensions leads to a distorted gospel and to unbalanced mission.* A biblically comprehensive gospel and truly wholistic mission require a vision for and genuine experience of all these dimensions in combination. Here, then, can be an important test of biblical fidelity regarding mission today. These six dimensions in combination nourish the church as God's agent for the healing of creation.

All these dimensions are thus immensely practical. They have power to enrich a church's community life, each Christian's own spiritual walk, and the practice of mission. We all need to experience all these dimensions for our own good, for the church's health and vitality, and for the mission of creation healed.

Every Christian disciple, however, should pay special attention to the first dimension—communion with God—not only in his or her own spiritual life but also in terms of all the other dimensions. This is true for the most basic of reasons: the greatest human need, throughout the earth and in all cultures and societies, is the reconciliation, the "friendship" (John 15:13–15) that God wants to bring to persons everywhere—to all people, the whole human race, and the entire creation.

Embodying these six dimensions can renew the church. Church renewal is grounded most basically in the experience of God through Jesus Christ by the Spirit, and in our community with one another in the body of Christ as the Spirit makes the church a reconciled and reconciling community. But recognizing the other dimensions also helps transform the church.[10]

When a church recognizes that it is global and universal, not just local, this gives it a broader sense of itself and its mission. It enriches worship, for Christians now sense they are part of the "great multitude" that God is forming from all earth's peoples worldwide. A church can focus too much on itself, shrinking God to the dimensions of its own concerns and culture. These broader dimensions help the church catch God's vision for creation healed.

Recognition of the great "cloud of witnesses," including the church which is now beyond the space-time limits of earth, renews the church because it gives a sense of the spirit world and the millions of forerunners who have lived the faith before us but are still with us. This is the point of Hebrews 11 and 12:1–3.

Finally, recognizing our solidarity with the whole earth and the global human family gives us an expanded sense of our present mission of reconciliation and healing. It keeps the life of the church "grounded," "earthed" in the actual world in which we all live interdependently. This helps the church understand the eco-evangelistic role God has given humanity to "care for the garden" (Gen 2:15).

God promises to renew the face of the earth, to "restore everything" (Acts 3:21 TNIV) through Jesus Christ. This is the largest sense of renewal. But he promises also to send "times of refreshing" to his people if they will turn fully to Jesus and be fully open to the Holy Spirit (Acts 3:19).

Recognizing, and living into, the six dimensions of Christian community is a key to the church's participation in God's plan to heal all creation. These six dimensions, and some of the ways they affect the life and vitality of the church, can be pictured as follows:

---

10. As suggested in Snyder, *Signs of the Spirit*, there are five key aspects to church renewal: Personal, corporate (or communitary), conceptual (or theological), structural, and missiological. All of these aspects relate to the six dimensions of community elaborated here. Truly vital churches experience these six dimensions personally, corporately, conceptually, structurally, and missionally. Snyder, *Signs*, 285–94.

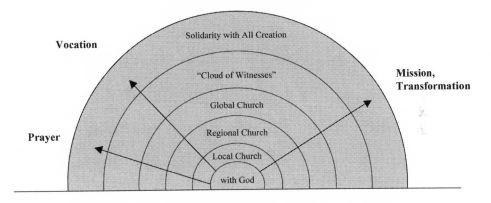

Six Dimensions of Christian Community

Conclusion

Living New Creation Now

THE BEAUTIFUL THING ABOUT the vision of salvation presented in these pages is that it fully affirms the church's historic understanding of Jesus Christ as Savior and Lord. "Christ died for our sins according to the Scriptures." He "was buried, and . . . rose again on the third day according to the Scriptures" (1 Cor 15:3–4 KJV). We still sing praise to Jesus Christ and seek to serve him faithfully, but now we see Jesus' great saving work in the larger, grander picture of all creation healed.

Ponder these brief parables: The king of a great land was about to take a long journey. He called his top three officials together. "I am putting you in charge while I am gone," he said. "I am giving each of you $50,000 to manage. You are to invest these funds carefully so that when I return my wealth will have grown substantially. Use whatever honest methods you wish."

The king was gone for five years. When he returned, he called his officials together and asked for their reports.

The first official said, "You Highness, I invested the $50,000 in real estate, and the value of the property has now risen to nearly half a million dollars."

"Well done," said the king. "Continue to manage this property."

The second official reported, "Your Highness, I invested the money in some carefully chosen venture capital funds, and the current value is nearing one million dollars. Ongoing prospects look very promising."

Well done," said the king. "Continue to manage these accounts."

The third official reported, "Your Highness, I put the $50,000 into a bank savings account, but its value has increased hardly at all, due to inflation. However, I want you to know that I love you very much, and I think about you and read books about you every day."

The king said, "This is unacceptable. I want my money to be invested, to be productive, to *do something*. What do you have to say for yourself?"

The official replied, "O, Wonderful King. How great you are! I praise you, and I even sings songs about you! I meditate about you at night! O King, now I just want to stand by your throne, praising you forever and ever!"

And the king said, "Miserable servant! You have completely misunderstood my orders. You have fatally misread my commission and my character, and the nature of my kingdom. Your praise is fine, but there is more to serving me than that. I have other goals than just being praised. I have big projects to unfold. Now, you have a job to do! Get to it! Do the work of my kingdom."

And so the official went out and did the work of the kingdom, finally understanding that that was his true service and praise. And through his faithfulness and creativity, the kingdom was made beautiful.

* * * *

Another great king was about to leave on a long journey. He appointed one of his assistants to be administrator while he was absent. "I am putting you in charge of everything," he said. "Manage my kingdom well."

When the king returned several years later, he summoned the administrator and asked for his report.

"Sir," he said, "I have managed your kingdom well. Our wealth has increased. Our population has grown and is prospering. The kingdom's economy is strong. We have started several new enterprises."

The king was pleased. But later he went for a tour of his kingdom. He discovered that some rivers were now polluted from poor farming practices. Crop yields were down because of over-intensive farming. Trees that should have been left standing had been cut down. Hillsides were beginning to erode. And the king discovered many conflicts among his people—even violence and murder.

So the king called in his administrator a second time. "How do you explain all these problems?" he asked.

The administrator replied, "Sir, I see these as minor difficulties—part of the cost of increasing wealth and developing our operations."

The king replied, "This is shortsighted. The whole kingdom must prosper in every way. Healthy relationships and healthy land are more important than increasing our wealth."

The king replaced his administrator with another who fully understood the king's wishes. He sent his former administrator to labor alongside his most faithful workers, relearning the work of the kingdom. And the kingdom was blessed.

LIVING IN THE NEW CREATION

At the end of one of his last parables—the landowner who rented out his vineyard (Matt 21:33–44)—Jesus warned, "The kingdom of God will be taken away from you and given to a people who will produce its fruit" at harvest time (Matt 21:43 TNIV).

But, Jesus said, those who faithfully follow him would be "blessed." What did he mean by "blessed"? He meant more than just happy. The Beatitudes are much more than "the Be-happy Attitudes," as some call them. We hear Jesus saying:

- Blessed are the poor in spirit, for theirs is the kingdom of heaven.
- Blessed are the meek, for they will inherit the earth.
- Blessed are the *shalom* makers; they will be called God's children (Matt 5:3, 5, 9).

Clearly Jesus didn't mean happy, or even safe. These statements all have rich Old Testament kingdom-of-God resonance. Jesus was talking about God's reign and about discipleship, which is risky and hard. Rooted in the Hebrew Scriptures, Jesus was—we now understand—speaking of the healing of heaven and earth, not transit from one to the other. "May your kingdom come. May your will be done on earth as in heaven."

What Jesus meant by "blessed," then, is this: Rejoice! You get in on God's project! You know the secrets, the mystery, of the kingdom. You have the blessed privilege of participating with God in the healing of creation, the marriage of heaven and earth. You can live now in anticipation of the great celebration: "Blessed are those who are invited to the marriage supper of the Lamb" (Rev 19:9). The wedding supper of the Lamb is the great celebration of redemption consummated; the final marriage of heaven and earth.

The Sermon on the Mount is misunderstood if not interpreted in light of the kingdom of God and the call to discipleship in Christian community, the body of Christ.

CONSIDER THE EARTH

Consider now a lesson from the earth. The naturalist and oceanographer Carl Safina reminds us: "All life is related by lineage, by flows of energy, and by cycles of water, carbon, nitrogen, and such; . . . resources are finite, and creatures fragile." But humans have not yet comprehended "how we can push the planet's systems into dysfunction."[1]

We need to pay attention to the earth, God's good creation. As Safina puts it, "In accounting terms, we're running a deficit, eating into our principal, liquidating our natural capital assets. Something's getting ready to break." Safina tallies the balance sheet:

> Population growth adds about seventy million people to the world each year, twice as many as live in California. Meanwhile, since 1970 populations of fishes, amphibians, mammals, reptiles, and birds have declined about 30 percent worldwide. Species are going extinct about one thousand times faster than the geologically "recent" average; the last extinction wave this severe snuffed the dinosaurs. We're pumping freshwater faster than rain falls, catching fish faster than they spawn. Roughly 40 percent of tropical coral reefs are rapidly deteriorating; none are considered safe. Forests are shrinking by about an acre per second. . . . Synthetic fertilizers have doubled the global nitrogen flow to living systems,

1. Safina, *View from Lazy Point*, 16.

washing down rivers and, since the 1970s, creating hundreds of oxygen-starved sea-floor "dead zones." . . . The Convention on Biological Diversity . . . says, "Biodiversity is in decline at all levels and geographical scales."[2]

But the Christian vision is one of healing, restoration, reversing the effects of the fall. The gospel envisions spiritually and physically healthy people on a healthy and abundant land.

Healing the land requires the health of the soil. Healthy soil is a vast tangle of winding roots, insects, microbes, myriad tiny creatures. A healthy field is not neat rows of corn or soybeans, sterilized of weeds and insects. A healthy field is a vast mix of living things all sustaining each other, even giving their lives to maintain the larger ecology. This is called *symbiosis*—living with, living together. Any ecologist will tell you that.

Nature abhors monoculture. It thrives on diversity. Monoculture is what caused the great Irish potato famine of 1845–49, resulting in a million deaths and the massive Irish migration to America. In 1845 one third of the Irish population was subsisting on potatoes (brought originally from South America), and when fungus wiped out the crop two years running, disaster ensued.[3]

This is true also in human society: health requires diversity, symbiosis. Genocide is the human cultural parallel to monoculture. Both are deadly—ultimately lethal to all life, even that of short-term victors. So it is for all life, including the church's life.

Plants send roots downward, spreading outward. The size of the root system is more or less equivalent to the growth aboveground. Normally we see only what is aboveground. But health above requires health below, and vice versa. Healthy human societies are similar. They depend on roots—history, stories, genealogies, ancestors, traditions, myths. Here also health above depends on health below, and vice versa. This is why we need the full biblical story of salvation—the complete glorious saga of creation healed.

In Scripture we perceive the symbiosis, the full heaven-and-earth ecology. We see it through the work and risen life of Jesus, by the Spirit. We see and ponder and actually *live* the *connections* between things—because of who God the Trinity is. As Jesus prayed: "I in them and you in me" (John 17:13).

BLESSED DISCIPLESHIP—CREATION HEALED

Here we have, then, our *blessed* call to discipleship. We get to participate in creation healed—now and on into the everlasting, when at last God restores all things (Acts 3:21). By grace, we get in on God's project.

Beautiful, blessed discipleship means nurturing our relationship with Jesus Christ by the Spirit. It also means—like Jesus—nurturing our relationships with Jesus' body,

2. Ibid., 13.

3. Killeen, *Short History of Ireland*, 50-51; Weatherford, *Indian Givers*, 66-71. Weatherford observes, "Had the Irish followed the Indian technique of planting many different types of potatoes rather than just a few, the effect of the blight probably would have been considerably lessened" (70).

the church, and with the land God loves and plans to restore. True, blessed discipleship is thus three dimensional: God, people, land. Actually, it is multidimensional, because God is Trinity, the church is diverse, and creation is vastly complex. We are called to dwell in God, to dwell in the church, and to dwell in the good earth God has made and sustains. Jesus said, "Those who abide in me and I in them bear much fruit, because apart from me you can do nothing" (John 15:5). This multidimensional discipleship can be pictured as follows (Figure 1):

Figure 1. Dwelling in God, Growing in Grace, Healing Creation

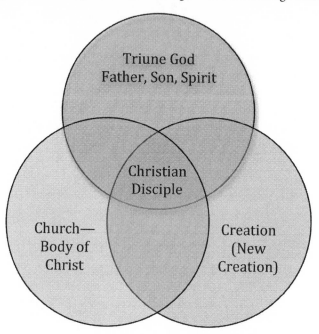

Deep Communion / Profound Indwelling

Growth in grace means continually deepening our relationship with God the Trinity, our brothers and sisters in the body of Christ (the church in all dimensions), and "Nature," God's good creation—all in anticipation of the new creation in fullness.

Jesus reported to the Father: "The glory that you have given me I have given them, so that they may be one, as we are one, I in them and you in me, that they may become completely one, so that the world may know that you have sent me and have loved them even as you have loved me" (John 17:22–23; see John 14–16).

Jesus' special friend the Apostle John wrote, "truly our fellowship is with the Father and with his Son Jesus Christ" (1 John 1:3).

Jesus said, "I am not asking you to take them out of the world, but I ask you to protect them from the evil one" (John 17:15).

PRACTICAL EARTHED DISCIPLESHIP

We can draw out the meaning of this blessed creation-healing discipleship in several dimensions:

1. Through the Spirit we have received, and must constantly develop and live into, a deep communion with the Triune God, with one another in the church, and with the created order. These are profound interrelationships, each according to the nature of the reality related to. Relationship with our Holy Lord has supreme priority, and defines the others. Living into these relationships is sanctification, holiness.

2. These three relationships strengthen and enrich each other. Growth in one area deepens growth in the other two. As we grow in our relationship with God, we deepen our relationship with one another. As we grow in our *koinonia* with one another, we deepen our relationship with creation. Deeper communion with creation deepens our relationship with God.

This works in both directions if we are Christ-centered. A nurturing relationship with creation enriches our relationship with God, and with Christ's body. All this is true *provided* our theology and practices encourage this mutually reinforcing growth (Figure 2). Each relationship is mutually nourishing and in God's intent leads to flourishing. For example, through stewardship and care we nourish the created order; we in turn are nourished in spirit and body by the beautiful earth.

Figure 2. Wholistic Growth in Grace and Discipleship

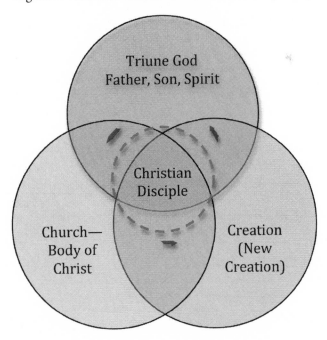

Deep Communion / Profound Indwelling

3. All this is the work of the Holy Spirit, and the perfect exemplar is Jesus Christ. He had and has a deep relationship with the Father and the Spirit in the Trinity—the source and basis of all. He developed deep community (*koinonia*) with his closest disciples and continues to do so. He lived in harmony, *shalom,* with the whole creation, while judging all that was evil. He "sustains all things by his powerful word" (Heb 1:3) and will finally bring all to sinless perfection.

4. Discipleship then is finding practical answers to the question: How can I (we together) nurture, deepen, and enrich my (our) relationship with God, with one another in the body of Christ, and with all creation? What am I doing now; what needs to be done? How can I (we) nurture an upward *spiral of health* in which we grow progressively in mutually reinforcing ways in all these dimensions?

5. All this is key to *shalom.* It is part of the great picture of salvation as creation healed. Relationship with Jesus Christ by the Spirit is the basis of the church as a reconciled, healing community, and the basis and resource for the church's mission of participating in God's work of healing all creation—everything from the prodigal son or daughter to the damaged earth.

CHRIST RETURNS!

I conclude with personal testimony. One day, about the time of my seventieth birthday, a new thought hit me with surprising force: It is *absurd* to think that Jesus died and rose again to save our souls—not our bodies and the whole creation. Why should Jesus rise *physically* to save us only *spiritually*? Do we really believe in resurrection—resurrection in space, time, and history? If so, how can we not believe in creation healed in space, time, and history? Would Jesus' incarnation really have been necessary if God wanted to save only our souls? Was a physical resurrection required? Have we forgotten the biblical promise of Jesus' return to restore all things?

I was startled with these thoughts. About this time I came across the old hymn, "It May Be at Morn." I immediately remembered it from my childhood, but I hadn't heard it for years. I found the hymn in my daily devotions as I was working through the 1910 *Free Methodist Hymnal.*[4] There it was, No. 100. The words were written by H. L. Turner in 1878, when premillennialism was rising. James McGranahan wrote the music about 1906, and the song was first published by Ira Sankey, Moody's song leader, in his *Gospel Songs No. 3.*

The song has a ringing chorus:

O Lord Jesus, how long, how long ere we shout the glad song?
Christ returneth! Hallelujah! Hallelujah, Amen, Hallelujah! Amen.

The first two stanzas begin, "It may be at morn," "It may be at mid-day." What struck me, however, was the last stanza:

---

4. General Conference of the Free Methodist Church of North America, *Free Methodist Hymnal.*

> Oh joy! Oh, delight! should we go without dying,
> No sickness, no sadness, no dread and no crying,
> Caught up through the clouds with our Lord into glory,
> When Jesus receives "his own."

Well, in good conscience, I can no longer sing those words. To be biblical, they need to say something like this:

> Oh joy! Oh, delight! to see him without dying,
> No sickness, no sadness, no dread and no crying,
> To dwell on the earth in the light of his glory,
> When Jesus reclaims "his own."

This is my hope. This is *our* hope as biblical Christians. What awaits us is a future better than heaven—because of Jesus' resurrection. "In accordance with [God's] promise, we wait for new heavens and a new earth, where righteousness is at home" (2 Pet 3:13). Our goal is not to reach heaven, but to have full fellowship with God and one another now and in the final new creation. Creation healed! This is salvation, true healing salve. It is good news.

Our response, then, is to hear again Jesus' words:

"Go into all the world and proclaim the good news to the whole creation" (Mark 16:15).

"Go make disciples of all nations" (Matt 28:19).

"As the Father has sent me, so I send you" (John 20:21).

"I am with you always" (Matt 28:20).

Bibliography

Abraham, William J., et al., editors. *Canonical Theism: A Proposal for Theology and the Church*. Grand Rapids: Eerdmans, 2008.

Alcorn, Randy. *Heaven*. Carol Stream, IL: Tyndale House, 2004.

Anderson, Ray S. *An Emergent Theology for Emerging Churches*. Downers Grove, IL: InterVarsity, 2007.

Andrews, William, editor. *Sisters in the Spirit: Three Black Women's Autobiographies of the Nineteenth Century*. Bloomington, IN: Indiana University Press, 1986.

Arias, Mortimer. *Announcing the Reign of God: Evangelization and the Subversive Memory of Jesus*. Philadelphia: Fortress, 1984.

Ball, Jim. *Global Warming and the Risen Lord: Christian Discipleship and Climate Change*. Washington, DC: Evangelical Environmental Network, 2010.

Balmer, Randall. *The Making of Evangelicalism: From Revivalism to Politics and Beyond*. Waco, TX: Baylor University Press, 2010.

Barnhart, Clarence L., and Robert K. Barnhart, editors. 2 vols. *The World Book Dictionary*. Chicago: Field Enterprises, 1976.

Barth, Karl. "The Christian Community and the Civil Community." In Barth, *Against the Stream: Shorter Post-War Writings 1946–52*. New York: Philosophical Library, 1954.

Baumol, William J., et al. *Good Capitalism, Bad Capitalism, and the Economics of Growth and Prosperity*. New Haven: Yale University Press, 2007.

Bellah, Robert N., et al. *Habits of the Heart: Individualism and Commitment in American Life*. Berkeley, CA: University of California Press, 1985.

Berkouwer, G. C. *The Church*. Translated by James E. Davison. Grand Rapids: Eerdmans, 1976.

Berry, Wendell. *The Gift of Good Land*. New York: North Point, 1981.

Bevans, Stephen B., and Roger P. Schroeder. *Constants in Context: A Theology of Mission for Today*. Maryknoll, NY: Orbis, 2004.

"Biofools." *The Economist* (April 11, 2009) 81.

Bloesch, Donald G. *Essentials of Evangelical Theology*. Peabody, MA: Hendrickson, 2006.

Blumenthal, Les. "Group Sounds Alarm on Ocean Acidity Rise." *The Sacramento Bee* (April 23, 2010). Online: http://www.sacbee.com/2010/04/23/2700093/group-sounds-alarm-on-ocean-acidity.html.

Boff, Leonardo. *Trinity and Society*. Translated by Paul Burns. Maryknoll, NY: Orbis, 1988.

Bonhoeffer, Dietrich. *Dietrich Bonhoeffer's Meditations on Psalms*. Edited and translated by Edwin Robertson. Grand Rapids: Zondervan, 2002.

Bosch, David J. *Transforming Mission: Paradigm Shifts in Theology of Mission*. Maryknoll, NY: Orbis, 1991.

Brown, Edward R. *Our Father's World: Mobilizing the Church to Care for Creation*. 2nd ed. Downers Grove, IL: InterVarsity, 2008.

Browning, Christopher R. *Ordinary Men: Reserve Police Battalion 101 and the Final Solution in Poland*. New York: HarperCollins, 1998.

Callen, Barry L. *Radical Christianity: The Believers Church Tradition in Christianity's History and Future*. Nappanee, IN: Evangel, 1999.

Calvin, John. *Commentary on 2 Peter*. Online: http://www.biblestudyguide.org/comment/calvin/ comm_vol45/htm/vii.iv.iii.htm.

Cantor, Norman F. *Inventing the Middle Ages*. New York: Morrow, 1991.

Carpenter, Joel A., and Wilbert R. Shenk. *Earthen Vessels: American Evangelicals and Foreign Missions, 1880–1980*. Grand Rapids: Eerdmans, 1990.

Chaturvedi, B. K. *Tales from the Mahabharat*. Delhi, India: Diamond, 2008.

Chenu, Marie-Dominique. *Nature, Man and Society in the Twelfth Century*. Translated by Jerome Taylor and Lester K Little. Chicago: University of Chicago Press, 1968.

Colson, Charles, with Ann Morse. "Reclaiming Occupied Territory." *Christianity Today* (August 2004) 64.

Crouch, Andy. *Culture Making: Recovering Our Creative Calling*. Downers Grove, IL: InterVarsity, 2008.

Daly, Herman E., and Joshua Farley. *Ecological Economics: Principles and Applications*. Washington, DC: Island, 2004.

Davis, Leo Donald, S.J. *The First Seven Ecumenical Councils (325–787): Their History and Theology*. Collegeville, MN: Liturgical, 1983.

De Lubac, Henri, S.J. *Medieval Exegesis. Vol. 2: The Four Senses of Scripture*. Translated by E. M. Macierowski. Grand Rapids: Eerdmans, 2000.

DeWitt, Calvin. "Ecology and Ethics: Relation of Religious Belief to Ecological Practice in the Biblical Tradition." *Biodiversity and Conservation* 4 (1995) 838–48.

Dolan, Jay P. *Catholic Revivalism: The American Experience 1830–1900*. Notre Dame, IN: University of Notre Dame Press, 1978.

Driver, John. *Images of the Church in Mission*. Scottdale, PA: Herald, 1997.

Dulles, Avery. *Models of the Church*. Rev. ed. Garden City, NY: Doubleday, 1987.

Durant, Will, and Ariel Durant. *The Age of Reason Begins*. The Story of Civilization, Part VII. New York: Simon and Schuster, 1961.

Durnbaugh, Donald F. "Free Church Tradition in America." In *Dictionary of Christianity in America*, edited by Donald G. Reid, 450–52. Downers Grove, IL: InterVarsity, 1990.

———. *The Believers' Church: The History and Character of Radical Protestantism*. New York: Macmillan, 1986.

Edwards, David L. *Christianity: The First Two Thousand Years*. Maryknoll, NY: Orbis, 1997.

The Empty Tomb. "Yoking Map for Churches." Online: http://www.emptytomb.org/index.html.

Esser, Cajetan, O.F.M. *Origins of the Franciscan Order*. Translated by Aedan Daly and Irina Lynch. Chicago: Franciscan Herald, 1970.

Faupel, D. William. *The Everlasting Gospel: The Significance of Eschatology in the Development of Pentecostal Thought*. Journal of Pentecostal Theology Supplement Series 10. Sheffield, UK: Sheffield Academic, 1996.

Ferguson, Niall. *The Ascent of Money: A Financial History of the World*. New York: Penguin, 2008.

Field, David. "Confessing Christ in the Context of Ecological Degradation" (No date). Online: http://web.uct.ac.za/depts/ricsa/projects/piblicli/environ/field_ec.htm.

Finke, Roger, and Rodney Stark. *The Churching of America 1776–2005: Winners and Losers in Our Religious Economy*. New Brunswick, NJ: Rutgers University Press, 2005.

Foster, Richard J., editor. *The Renovaré Spiritual Formation Bible*. New York: HarperSanFrancisco, 2005.

Foster, Richard J., and Gayle D. Beebe. *Longing for God: Seven Paths to Christian Devotion*. Downers Grove, IL: InterVarsity, 2009.

Friedman, Thomas. "Mother Nature's Dow." *New York Times* (March 29, 2009). Online: http://www.nytimes.com/2009/03/29/opinion/29friedman.html.

Frost, Michael. *Exiles: Living Missionally in a Post-Christian Culture*. Peabody, MA: Hendrickson, 2006.

———, and Alan Hirsch. *ReJesus: A Wild Messiah for a Missional Church*. Peabody, MA: Hendrickson, 2009.

General Conference of the Free Methodist Church of North America. *Free Methodism Hymnal*. Chicago: Free Methodist Publishing House, 1910.

Gimpel, Jean. *The Cathedral Builders*. Translated by Teresa Waugh. New York: Harper & Row, 1984.

"Global Warming: Why Business Is Taking It So Seriously." *Business Week* (August 16, 2004) 60–69.

Grant, Robert M. *The Letter and the Spirit*. London: SPCK, 1957.

———, with David Tracy. *A Short History of the Interpretation of the Bible*. 2nd ed. Philadelphia: Fortress, 1984.

Green, Joel B. *Salvation.* Understanding Biblical Themes. St. Louis, MO: Chalice, 2003.

Guder, Darrell L., editor. *Missional Church: A Vision for the Sending of the Church in North America.* Grand Rapids: Eerdmans, 1998.

Gunton, Colin E. *Christ and Creation.* Grand Rapids: Eerdmans, 1992.

———. *The Promise of Trinitarian Theology.* 2nd ed. Edinburgh: T. & T. Clark, 1997.

Hampshire, Stuart. *The Age of Reason: The 17th Century Philosophers.* New York: New American Library, 1956.

Hardt, Philip F. "'A Prudential Means of Grace': The Class Meeting in Early New York City Methodism." PhD diss., Fordham University, 1998.

Hatch, Nathan O. *The Democratization of American Christianity.* New Haven, CT: Yale University Press, 1989.

Heath, Elaine A. *The Mystic Way of Evangelism: A Contemplative Vision for Christian Outreach.* Grand Rapids: Baker, 2008.

Hempton, David. *Methodism: Empire of the Spirit.* New Haven, CT: Yale University Press, 2005.

Hertsgaard, Mark. *Hot: Living through the Next Fifty Years on Earth.* New York: Houghton Mifflin, 2011.

Hirsch, Alan. *The Forgotten Ways: Reactivating the Missional Church.* Grand Rapids: Brazos, 2006.

Holloway, Mark. *Heavens on Earth: Utopian Communities in America 1680–1880.* Rev. ed. New York: Dover, 1966.

Holmes, Richard. *The Age of Wonder: How the Romantic Generation Discovered the Beauty and Terror of Science.* New York: Pantheon, 2008.

Hughes, Richard T., editor. *The American Quest for the Primitive Church.* Urbana: University of Illinois Press, 1988.

Huntington, Samuel P. "The Clash of Civilizations?" *Foreign Affairs* 72.2 (Summer, 1993) 22–49.

Hynson, Leon O. "Original Sin as Privation: An Inquiry into a Theology of Sin and Sanctification." *Wesleyan Theological Journal* 22.2 (Fall 1987) 65–83.

Jones, E. Stanley. *Christ's Alternative to Communism.* New York: Abingdon, 1935.

Jones, James. *Jesus and the Earth.* London: SPCK, 2003.

Kärkkäinen, Veli-Matti. *The Trinity: Global Perspectives.* Louisville, KY: Westminster John Knox, 2007.

Killeen, Richard. *A Short History of Ireland.* Dublin: Gill & Macmillan, 1994.

Kinlaw, Dennis F. *Let's Start with Jesus: A New Way of Doing Theology.* Grand Rapids: Zondervan, 2005.

Kloberdanz, Kristin. "Global Warming: The Culprit?" *Time* 166.14 (October 3, 2005) 43.

The Land Institute. Online: www.landinstitute.org.

Latourette, Kenneth Scott. *A History of Christianity.* New York: Harper & Brothers, 1953.

Lee, Young-Hoon. "Christian Spirituality and the Diakonic Mission of the Yoido Full Gospel Church." Address, Edinburgh 2010 Missionary Conference, June 4, 2010.

Leffel, Gregory P. *Faith Seeking Action: Mission, Social Movements, and the Church in Motion.* Lanham, MD: Scarecrow, 2007.

Littell, Franklin Hamlin. *The Free Church.* Boston: Starr King, 1957.

Loth, Calder, and Julius Trousdale Sadler, Jr. *The Only Proper Style: Gothic Architecture in America.* Boston: New York Graphic Society, 1975.

Lotz, Anne Graham. *Heaven: My Father's House.* Nashville: Thomas Nelson, 2001.

Macchia, Frank D. "Justification through New Creation: The Holy Spirit and the Doctrine by which the Church Stands or Falls." *Theology Today* 58 (2001) 202–17.

Maddox, Randy L. "John Wesley's Precedent for Theological Engagement with the Natural Sciences." *Wesleyan Theological Journal* 44 (2009) 23-54.

Marsden, George M. *Fundamentalism and American Culture: The Shaping of Twentieth Century Evangelicalism: 1870–1925.* New York: Oxford University Press, 1980.

McCoy, Charles Sherwood. "The Covenant Theology of Johannes Cocceius." PhD diss., Yale University, 1956.

McGrath, Alister E. *A Brief History of Heaven.* Oxford: Blackwell, 2003.

———. *The Re-enchantment of Nature: Science, Religion and the Human Sense of Wonder.* London: Hodder & Stoughton, 2002.

McKibben, Bill. *Eaarth: Making a Life on a Tough New Planet.* New York: Times, 2010.

Medin, Amber. "My Eco-Conversion." *Priority!* (Fall 2008) 40–41.

Merritt, Jonathan. "Keeping an Eye on the Sparrow." *Creation Care* 39 (Spring 2010) 32.

Meyendorff, John. *Byzantine Theology: Historical Trends and Doctrinal Themes*. New York: Fordham University Press, 1979.

Middleton, J. Richard. "A New Heaven and a New Earth: The Case for a Holistic Reading of the Biblical Story of Redemption." *Journal for Christian Theological Research* 11 (2006) 73–97.

Milgram, Stanley. *Obedience to Authority: An Experimental View*. New York: Harper, 1974.

Miller, Lisa. *Heaven: Our Enduring Fascination with the Afterlife*. New York: HarperCollins, 2010.

Minear, Paul. *Images of the Church in the New Testament*. Philadelphia: Westminster, 1960.

MIT Joint Program on the Science and Policy of Global Change. "Greenhouse Gamble: Comparison of Projections: 2009 update vs. 2002." Online: http://globalchange.mit.edu/resources/gamble/comparison.html.

Monastersky, R. "Global Warming: Politics Muddle Policy." *Science News* 137.25 (June 23, 1990) 391.

Neill, Stephen. *A History of Christian Missions*. Rev. ed. New York: Penguin, 1986.

Niebuhr, H. Richard. *The Social Sources of Denominationalism*. Cleveland, OH: World, 1957.

Noll, Mark A. *America's God: From Jonathan Edwards to Abraham Lincoln*. New York: Oxford University Press, 2002.

———. *The Rise of Evangelicalism: The Age of Edwards, Whitefield, and the Wesleys*. Downers Grove, IL: InterVarsity, 2004.

Nürnberger, Klaus. *Prosperity, Poverty and Pollution: Managing the Approaching Crisis*. Pietermaritzburg, South Africa: Cluster, 1999.

Oden, Thomas C. *John Wesley's Scriptural Christianity*. Grand Rapids: Zondervan, 1994.

Olin, Stephen. *The Works of Stephen Olin, D.D., LL.D., Late President of the Wesleyan University*. 2 vols. New York: Harper & Brothers, 1852.

Pelikan, Jaroslav. *The Christian Tradition: A History of the Development of Doctrine. Vol. 1. The Emergence of the Catholic Tradition (100–600)*. Chicago: University of Chicago Press, 1971.

Peterson, Eugene H. *Christ Plays in Ten Thousand Places: A Conversation in Spiritual Theology*. Grand Rapids: Eerdmans, 2005.

Phillips, Kevin. *Wealth and Democracy: A Political History of the American Rich*. New York: Broadway, 2002.

Piper, John. *Future Grace*. Sisters, OR: Multnomah, 1995.

———. *Let the Nations Be Glad! The Supremacy of God in Missions*. Grand Rapids: Baker, 1993.

———. *The Future of Justification: A Response to N. T. Wright*. Wheaton, IL: Crossway, 2007.

Pollan, Michael. *The Omnivore's Dilemma: A Natural History of Four Meals*. New York: Penguin, 2006.

Prestige, G. L. *God in Patristic Thought*. London: SPCK, 1952.

Prusak, Bernard P. *The Church Unfinished: Ecclesiology through the Centuries*. New York: Paulist, 2004.

Putnam, Robert. *Bowling Alone: The Collapse and Revival of American Community*. New York: Simon and Schuster, 2000.

"Quotation Marks," *Christianity Today* 53.5 (May 2009) 15.

Ramabai, Pandita. *A Testimony of Our Inexhaustible Treasure*. In *Pandita Ramabai through Her Own Words: Selected Works*, compiled and edited by Meera Kosambi, 295–324. New Delhi: Oxford University Press, 2000.

Reumann, John. *Stewardship and the Economy of God*. Grand Rapids: Eerdmans, 1992.

Richey, Russell E., editor. *Denominationalism*. Nashville: Abingdon, 1977.

Richter, Sandra. "A Biblical Theology of Creation Care." *The Asbury Journal* 62.1 (Spring 2007) 67–76.

Rifkin, Jeremy. *The Age of Access: The New Culture of Hypercapitalism Where All of Life is a Paid-For Experience*. New York: Tarcher/Putnam, 2000.

Robert, Dana L. *Occupy until I Come: A. T. Pierson and the Evangelization of the World*. Grand Rapids: Eerdmans, 2003.

Roberts, Benjamin T. "Free Churches." *The Earnest Christian* 1.1 (January 1860) 7.

Ronsvalle, John, and Sylvia Ronsvalle. *The State of Church Giving through 2006: Global Triage, MDG 4, and Unreached People Groups*. Champaign, IL: Empty Tomb, 2008.

Rosell, Garth M. "Charles Grandison Finney and the Rise of the Benevolence Empire." PhD diss., University of Minnesota, 1971.

Russell, Jeffrey Burton. *Paradise Mislaid: How We Lost Heaven—and How We Can Regain It*. New York: Oxford University Press, 2006.

Sabin, Scott C. *Tending to Eden: Environmental Stewardship for God's People.* Valley Forge, PA: Judson, 2010.

———. "Whole Earth Evangelism." *Christianity Today* 54.7 (July 2010) 26–29.

Safina, Carl. *The View from Lazy Point: A Natural Year in an Unnatural World.* New York: Holt, 2011.

Sandeen, E. R. *The Roots of Fundamentalism: British and American Millenarianism, 1800–1930.* Chicago: University of Chicago Press, 1970.

Schaeffer, Francis A. *Pollution and the Death of Man: The Christian View of Ecology.* Wheaton, IL: Tyndale House, 1970.

"Scientists: Pace of Climate Change Exceeds Estimates." *Washington Post* (February 15, 2009) A03.

Simpson, D. P. *Cassell's New Latin Dictionary.* New York: Funk and Wagnalls, 1968.

Sleeth, J. Matthew, MD. *Serve God, Save the Planet: A Christian Call to Action.* White River Junction, VT: Green, 2006.

Sleeth, Nancy. *Go Green, Save Green: A Simple Guide to Saving Time, Money, and God's Green Earth.* Carol Stream, IL: Tyndale House, 2009.

Smalley, Beryl. *The Study of the Bible in the Middle Ages.* 2nd ed. Notre Dame, IN: University of Notre Dame Press, 1964.

Snyder, Howard A. "The Church as Holy and Charismatic." *Wesleyan Theological Journal* 15.2 (Fall 1980) 7–32.

———. *Coherence in Christ: The Larger Meaning of Ecology.* New York: General Board of Global Ministries, United Methodist Church, 2000.

———. *The Community of the King.* Rev. ed. Downers Grove, IL: InterVarsity, 2004.

———. *EarthCurrents: The Struggle for the World's Soul.* Nashville: Abingdon, 1995.

———. *Kingdom, Church, and World: Biblical Themes for Today.* Eugene, OR: Wipf & Stock, 2002.

———. *Liberating the Church: The Ecology of Church and Kingdom.* Downers Grove, IL: InterVarsity, 1983.

———. "The Marks of Evangelical Ecclesiology." In *Evangelical Ecclesiology: Reality or Illusion?* Edited by John Stackhouse, 77–103. Grand Rapids: Baker, 2003.

———. *Models of the Kingdom.* Nashville: Abingdon, 1991.

———. *Populist Saints: B. T. and Ellen Roberts and the First Free Methodists.* Grand Rapids: Eerdmans, 2006.

———. *The Problem of Wineskins: Church Structure in a Technological Age.* Downers Grove, IL: InterVarsity, 1975.

———. *Radical Renewal: The Problem of Wineskins Today.* Houston, TX: Touch, 1996.

———. *The Radical Wesley and Patterns for Church Renewal.* Downers Grove, IL: InterVarsity, 1980.

———. *Signs of the Spirit: How God Reshapes the Church.* Grand Rapids: Zondervan, 1989.

———. *Yes in Christ: Wesleyan Reflections on Gospel, Mission, and Culture.* Tyndale Studies in Wesleyan History and Theology 2. Toronto: Clements Academic, 2011.

———, with Daniel V. Runyon. *Decoding the Church: Mapping the DNA of Christ's Body.* Grand Rapids: Baker, 2002.

Stackhouse, John G., Jr., editor. *Evangelical Ecclesiology: Reality or Illusion?* Grand Rapids: Baker, 2003.

———. *Canadian Evangelicalism in the Twentieth Century: An Introduction to Its Character.* Vancouver, BC: Regent College, 1999.

Stafford, Tim. *Shaking the System: What I Learned from the Great American Reform Movements.* Downers Grove, IL: InterVarsity, 2007.

Stark, Rodney. *The Rise of Christianity: A Sociologist Reconsiders History.* Princeton, NJ: Princeton University Press, 1996.

———. *The Victory of Reason: How Christianity Led to Freedom, Capitalism, and Western Success.* New York: Random House, 2005.

Stearns, Richard. *The Hole in Our Gospel.* Nashville, TN: Thomas Nelson, 2009.

Steele, Daniel. *Antinomianism Revived; or, The Theology of the So-Called Plymouth Brethren Examined and Refuted.* Boston: McDonald, Gill, & Co., 1887.

Stephens, James, et al. *Victorian and Later English Poets.* New York: American, 1949.

"Suddenly, a wider world below the waterline" and "Seabed mining: The Unplumbed Riches of the Deep." *The Economist* (May 16, 2009) 29–31.

Synan, Vinson. *The Holiness-Pentecostal Tradition: Charismatic Movements in the Twentieth Century.* Grand Rapids: Eerdmans, 1997.

Tennent, Timothy. *Christianity at the Religious Roundtable: Evangelicalism in Conversation with Hinduism, Buddhism, and Islam.* Grand Rapids: Baker, 2002.

Tickle, Phyllis. *The Great Emergence: How Christianity is Changing and Why.* Grand Rapids: Baker, 2008.

Tillard, J.-M.-R. *Flesh of the Church, Flesh of Christ: At the Source of the Ecclesiology of Communion.* Collegeville, MN: Liturgical, 2001.

Torrance, Thomas F. *The Trinitarian Faith: The Evangelical Theology of the Ancient Catholic Church.* London: T. & T. Clark, 2004.

Tucker, Ruth. *From Jerusalem to Irian Jaya: A Biographical History of Christian Missions.* 2nd ed. Grand Rapids: Zondervan, 2004.

Uberoi, Meera. *The Mahabharata.* New Delhi, India: Penguin, 2005.

United Nations Environmental Programme 2005. Online: http://www.unep.org/Documents.multilingual/Default.asp?DocumentID=67&ArticleID=5125&l=en.

Van Bierma, David. "The New Calvinism." *Time* (March 23, 2009) 50.

Van Dyke, Fred, et al. *Redeeming Creation: The Biblical Basis for Environmental Stewardship.* Downers Grove, IL: InterVarsity, 1996.

Van Gelder, Craig. *The Essence of the Church: A Community Created by the Spirit.* Grand Rapids: Baker, 2000.

Volf, Miroslav. *After Our Likeness: The Church as the Image of the Trinity.* Grand Rapids: Eerdmans, 1998.

Walsh, Brian, and Sylvia C. Keesmaat. *Colossians Remixed: Subverting the Empire.* Downers Grove, IL: InterVarsity, 2004.

Ward, W. R. *The Protestant Evangelical Awakening.* Cambridge: Cambridge University Press, 2002.

Weatherford, Jack. *Indian Givers: How the Indians of the Americas Transformed the World.* New York: Fawcett Columbine, 1988.

Webber, Robert E. *Ancient-Future Worship: Proclaiming and Enacting God's Narrative.* Grand Rapids: Baker, 2008.

————. *Who Gets to Narrate the World? Contending for the Christian Story in an Age of Rivals.* Downers Grove, IL: InterVarsity, 2008.

Weiner, Jonathan. *The Next Hundred Years: Shaping the Fate of Our Living Earth.* New York: Bantam, 1990.

Wesley, John. *The Bicentennial Edition of the Works of John Wesley.* Edited by Frank Baker, Richard Heitzenrater, et al. Nashville: Abingdon, 1984.

————. *Explanatory Notes Upon the New Testament.* [1754]. London: Epworth, 1958.

————. *Explanatory Notes Upon the Old Testament.* 3 vols. [1765]. Reprint. Salem, OH: Schmul, 1975.

————. *Primitive Remedies.* Reprint of Wesley, *Primitive Physick.* Santa Barbara, CA: Woodbridge, 1975.

Westin, Gunnar. *The Free Church through the Ages.* Translated by Virgil A. Olson. Nashville: Broadman, 1958.

Wheeler, Sara. *The Magnetic North: Notes from the Arctic Circle.* New York: Farrar, Straus and Giroux, 2011.

Wolffe, John. *The Expansion of Evangelicalism.* Downers Grove, IL: InterVarsity, 2007.

Wright, Christopher J. H. *The Mission of God.* Downers Grove, IL: InterVarsity, 2006.

Wright, N. T. *Surprised by Hope: Rethinking Heaven, the Resurrection, and the Mission of the Church.* New York: HarperOne, 2008.

Yates, Timothy. *Christian Mission in the Twentieth Century.* Cambridge: Cambridge University Press, 1994.

Young, William P. *The Shack.* Los Angeles: Windblown Media, 2007.

Zahniser, A. H. Mathias. *The Mission and Death of Jesus in Islam and Christianity.* Maryknoll, New York: Orbis, 2008.

General Index

Abel, 72
abolitionism, 155–56; and creation care, 155–56
abortion, 143
Abraham (Abram), patriarch, 72, 79, 127, 160; call of, 69, 119
Acts, book of, 5–6, 210; church in, 189, 210
Adam, biblical, 66, 69, 71–73, 85, 92, 107, 163; as steward, 163
advertising, 153
Afghanistan, 52
Africa, 29, 90, 201
Africa, church in, 12, 13, 15, 37
African American worship, 171
African Americans, 75, 207–8
African Methodist Episcopal Zion Church, 207
age to come, 157; powers of, 162
agriculture, 78, 87, 90, 140, 153–54; and creation care, 153; organic, 155; perennial, 155; sustainable, 153, 202
air, 51, 121, 152, 163; circulation of, 89; pollution of, 51, 71, 164
Albom, Mitch, 40
Alcorn, Randy, 40
alienation, fourfold, 3, 66–78, 82–83, 94, 99, 101, 107, 139, 146–50; healing of, 146–51, 198–205, 215
"all things," 19, 24, 35, 54, 94, 97, 99, 103–4, 152; restoration of, 94, 97, 99–101, 107, 123, 127–28, 130, 138–39, 154–55, 183–84, 206, 215, 218, 226
allegory, allegorization, 21–24
Alopen, 12
America, as "promised land," 31

American Association for the Advancement of Science, 87
amillennialism, 57, 158–59
amphibians, decline in, 222
Anabaptists, 21, 26, 29–30, 174–75; discipleship in, 175; persecution of, 174; view of church, 174–75
Ananias and Sapphira, 72
angels, 69, 159, 208, 213
Anglican Church. See Church of England.
animals, 26, 61, 66, 77, 90–91, 93, 97, 100, 102, 117, 118, 122, 140, 159, 163; care of, 122, 204; decline in, 222; suffering of, 120, 154; transformation of, 154
annihilation, 26, 98, 154
anthropology, 38, 134, 141, 148; of church and mission, 149
anti-Semitism, 12, 22
Antioch, 9; church in, 191, 210
apocalypticism, 24. See also eschatology; dispensationalism.
apologetics, 7–8, 46
apostles, 7, 162, 190, 192–93, 197, 209–10
Apostles' Creed, 189, 212
apostolic poverty, 26
apostolic succession, 193, 197
apostolicity, 162, 188–97, 203; and the poor, 189–90, 196–97
Aquinas, Thomas. See Thomas Aquinas.
architecture, 140; and creation care, 201; church, 170–75, 201
Arctic area, 88
Aristarchus, 210
Aristotle, 16
ark, 90–91, 118–19

hope: and eschatology, 55, 57–58, 60–61, 131–33, 157–58, 161, 215; as mark of church, 186–87; escapist, 66; for creation healed, 31, 54, 56, 60, 101, 104, 109, 178–79, 183–84, 187, 201–2; for the poor, 197 "hope for better times," 30; Jesus Christ as, 73, 100, 130; living, 147; "of glory," 73; radical, 131, 138

Hosea, prophet, xv

hospitals, 35

house churches, 7, 15, 38, 174

humanism, secular, 37

humanity, 213–14; dependence upon earth, 51, 119, 121–23, 125, 142, 215; unity of, 214

humility, eschatological, 154

Huntington, Samuel, 72

Huq, Saleemul, 156

Hurricane Katrina, 86

hurricanes, 152

hymns, hymnody, 31–33, 35, 47, 55, 170–71, 175, 179, 180, 202, 226–27; and communion of saints, 213; and creation care, 202; Trinitarian, 33, 180

ice age, 86

identity, Christian, 38, 52; ethnic, 143; national, 38

ideology, 42, 46, 49–51, 52, 56, 102, 123, 133, 135, 144; moral effects of, 102

idolatry, 44, 52, 83, 160; national, 52, 123

Ignatius Loyola, 29

image of God, 13–14, 55, 79–80, 101, 103, 146, 156; and responsibility, 79; reflected in the created order, 13, 55

immigration, 49, 223

immortality, 54, 95

India, 29, 37, 70, 73, 77

Indians, American. *See* Native Americans.

indigenous peoples, 34

individualism, 33–34, 41, 46, 51, 60, 73, 97, 149, 170, 175–77

inductive Bible study, x

indulgences, 12

Industrial Revolution, 31, 34, 42, 49, 177

industrialization, 48–50, 77, 122

Inferno, 17

information age, 50

inheritance, 61, 149, 156, 187, 222; earth as, 222

insects, 93, 223

institutions, church, 15, 17, 35, 38, 130, 194–95, 204

integrity, 148

intercession, 132

interdependence, 51, 54, 139; ecological, 139, 154; in the Trinity, 151; of humans with the environment, 54, 119–21, 239

International Council for Science, 87

Internet, 37, 38, 88, 211

interstate commerce, 51

invisible hand, 50

Ireland, 12, 223

Irenaeus of Lyons, 6, 8

Irish potato famine, impact of, 223

irrigation, 155

Isaac, patriarch, 72, 160

Isaiah, prophet, xiv, 100, 109

Islam, 12, 15, 18, 20, 26; growth of, 26, 37

Israel, biblical, 57, 214; election of, 124–26; mission of, 126

Jacob, patriarch, 69, 72, 160

Jacob's ladder, 69

James, Apostle, 75

Jefferson, Thomas, 30

Jeremiah, prophet, 67

Jerusalem, 161; church in, 191; council, 210; fall of, 20

Jesuits. *See* Society of Jesus.

Jesus Christ, and the poor, 196–97; Apostle, 192–93; as *crucis*, 160–61; as firstborn, 55; as head, 94, 98, 99, 127, 130, 137, 147, 149, 164, 187, 203–5; as servant, 151, 180; ascension, 48, 61; atonement, xiii, xiv, 53, 74, 94, 96, 101–4, 130, 170, 214, 220; authority of, 137; blood of, 53, 67, 74, 98, 118, 120, 127, 139, 147, 163, 206–7, 217; character, 143, 196; death, 6, 60–61, 70, 103, 123, 130, 137, 183, 217, 220, 226; earthly life, 6, 21, 60, 65–66, 70, 73–74, 78, 97, 98, 101, 123, 130, 132–33, 193, 197, 203, 217; example, 21, 98, 182, 189–90, 226; full humanity of, 23; Great Physician, 96, 130; healer, xiv, 65–66, 92, 97, 104, 164, 203; High Priest, 175; incarnation, xiii, 6, 25, 45, 48, 53, 61, 98, 103, 105, 109, 123, 151, 181, 204, 214, 217, 226; liberator, 203; light of world, 136; Lord, 142, 162, 183, 203, 220; Messiah, 57, 130–31, 215; miracles of, 101; mission of, 136–38; offices, 97–98, 175; parables of, 45, 100; pioneer, 212; Prophet, 192–93; resurrection, ix, xiii, 6, 25, 32, 45, 60–61, 78, 92, 94, 98, 100–101, 102, 103, 107, 123, 138, 146,

Nicea, Council of, 5–7
Nicene Creed, 6–7, 46, 188–90
Niceno-Constantinopolitan Creed, 6–7, 188
Nineveh, 122
nitrogen cycle, 87, 222–23
nitrous oxide, 87, 222
Noah, patriarch, 79, 90–91, 118–20
North Pole, 89–90; mineral resources of, 89–90
notes (*notae*) of the church. *See* marks of the church.
numbers, in Scripture, 157; symbolism of, 158–59
Nürnberger, Klaus, 90
nutrition, 202. *See also* food.
nutritional supplements, 153; as food, 153

obedience, 148, 160, 208
obesity, 153, 202
oceans, 88–90, 93, 156; acidification, 89; circulating currents in, 88–90, 112; dead zones, 223; ecological connection with land and air, 88; minerals in, 89–90; threats to, 88–90, 91, 223
Oden, Thomas, 161–62
oikonomia, 6, 56–57, 91, 94, 99, 108, 139, 147, 150, 156, 163, 186, 204; and dispensationalism, 56–57, 162; and eschatology, 156; and stewardship, 162–64; as administration, 162; openness of, 162
oikonomos, 163
oikos, 6, 91, 108, 139, 162, 163
Old Testament, relation to New, 127–28
Olin, Stephen, 189–90, 196
one-another passages in NT, 9, 185, 187
openness, eschatological, 159–62
oppression, 73, 143, 181, 204, 208
optimism, 34, 58, 156, 187; of grace, 34
order, 55, 111, 199–200
ordination, 16
organism, 75; church as, 133, 181, 200
organizations, Christian, 182; roles in, 182
Origen, church father, 9, 22; allegorical method of, 22
original sin. *See* sin, original.
orphans, 181
orthodoxy, 31, 40, 55, 191
Otto of Freising, Bishop, 17–18
oxygen, depletion of, 223

pain, 92, 154; end of, 154
Palmer, Phoebe, 176

pantheism, 44
parables, 45, 100, 220–21
Paradise Lost, 17
paradise, 24
parasitism, 104
partnership among churches, 212
passions, human, 47
Patrick, Saint, 12
patriotism, 38, 44, 46, 211; uncritical, 52
patristic tradition, 24
Paul, Apostle, 5, 21–23, 44, 54, 69, 82, 84–85, 92, 94, 99–100, 103, 111, 117, 127, 137, 147, 149, 161, 162, 179, 185–86, 190–91, 193, 209, 212, 214
Pauline writings, medieval preference for, 21–23
peace, xiv, 66, 69, 73, 74, 83, 84, 95, 99, 109, 139, 159, 183, 206; as health, 69; inner, 74. *See also* shalom.
Peaceable Kingdom, the, 109, 154
pearly gates, 34
Pelikan, Jaroslav, 188
Pentecost, 4, 72, 105, 112
Pentecostals, Pentecostalism, 36, 57, 60, 61, 135, 169, 171–72, 192; and eschatology, 57
people of God, 128, 212–13; as kingdom of priests, 126, 203; holy nation, 126
Peretti, Frank, 59
perfection, 47, 108–9, 146, 212, 226
perichoresis, 180
persecution, 14, 174
perseverance, 212
pessimism, 34, 58, 156; eschatological, 58, 156–57
Peter Waldo, 25
Peter, Apostle, 4, 61, 94, 100, 101, 154, 162, 186, 209, 212
Peterson, Eugene, 96
philanthropy, 35
Philip, evangelist, 141
Philippi, church in, 191
philosophy, 7–8, 20, 34, 42, 122, 133, 143–44; Greek, 7–10, 46–50; medieval, 20
Pierson, A. T., 57
Pietist Movement, 30, 33–34, 36
piety, 77, 130, 132, 183; and mission, 183; popular, 130; private, 183. *See also* spirituality.
pilgrimage, ix–x
Piper, John, 53–54, 117
plan of God. *See* economy (*oikonomia*) of God; salvation.
Plant With Purpose, 82, 164

communion with, 225; community in, 206; diversity in unity, 151, 182; doctrine of, x, 7, 23–24, 33, 46, 53, 131, 150–51, 180–82, 205; ecology of, 151, 178; implications for ecclesiology, 178–84; mystery, 104, 178, 204; overflow of love, 180–81; Reality, 179; renewed interest in, 131; self-revelation of, 217; suffering, 181; vision of, 208; worship, 180. *See also missio Dei.*

truth, 42–44, 98, 101, 107, 143–44, 148, 149; absolute, 135; and love, 149; in nature, 42–44

Turner, H. L., 226

two ways, the, 159–62; and land, 160–61; choice of, 160–62

typology in biblical interpretation, 22, 24

United Nations (UN), 86

United States, dispensationalism in, 55–56; patriotism in, 52; reasons for prosperity, 49

universe, physical, openness of, 161. *See also* creation.

universities, 18; rise of, 21

urbanization, 20, 48, 49

Van Dyke, Fred, 91, 106

Van Gelder, Craig, 189

vegetarianism, 102

vestments, 15, 18

violence, 72, 76, 105, 143, 207

visible church. *See* church, visibility of.

visions, 208, 213

vocation, 129, 184, 207–8

voluntarism, 175, 176

Waldensians, 25, 26, 29, 174; persecution of, 174

walking, 202

Walsh, Brian, 85

war, 80, 102, 201; ecological effects, 201

warfare, culture of, 143

waste, 201

water, 51, 112, 121, 163, 201, 208; depletion of, 222; pollution of, 51, 77, 90; stewardship of, 163; supply of, 152, 201

Watts, Isaac, 32

Wealth of Nations, 49

wealth, 48, 143; accumulation of, 49; as sign of God's favor, 49; in relation to environment, 51; in the church, 197; power of, 49; pursuit of, 49–50; stewardship of, 163. *See also* riches.

weather, 122; patterns of, 86, 90. *See also* climate.

Webber, Robert, 6, 131

well-being, 69, 91, 101, 121, 214; of earth, 214–16; responsibility for, 216

Wesley, Charles, 32

Wesley, John, 14, 58, 60, 77, 85, 95–96, 102, 120, 152, 154, 176, 181, 189; and the poor, 181, 189, 196–97, 211; interest in medicine, 95–96

Wesleyan theology, 53, 57, 175

Wesleyan University, 189

wheat, 155

whole gospel, 147, 155

widows, 73, 75, 181

will of God, 31, 84, 96, 104, 136–37, 147, 161; done on earth, 31, 35, 130–31, 137, 158, 161–63, 187, 204, 222

Willow Creek Community Church, 172–73; worship model, 172–73

wisdom literature, biblical, 154, 160

wisdom, 107, 122, 160, 187; in creation, 202; of God, 66, 101, 150–52, 181, 202

witness, Christian, 46, 60, 123, 133, 193, 200, 212; ecology of, 198–205

women, roles of, 20, 70, 73, 163, 207–8; "feminine estates," 20; in relation to men, 72; in the church, 207–8; oppression of, 72, 73. *See also* gender.

Word of God, 96, 97, 98, 159, 188; made flesh, 179

work, 199

World Vision U.S., 41

World War II, 101–2, 123, 153

world, 127, 167; as home, 183–84; escape from, 47, 130; love of, 96, 187; meaning of, 93; nature of, xiii. *See also* earth.

worldstory, Christian, 134, 136, 138–44, 198

worldview(s), 29, 39, 143, 146, 215; biblical, 103, 121–23, 130, 134–36, 138–41, 144, 184; Christian, ix–x, 8–9, 13–14, 26, 31, 34, 39–61, 135–36, 140, 198; Copernican, 17; dualistic, x, 9, 13–14, 18–19, 26, 41, 45, 53, 138; ecological, 138–41; Greek (Hellenistic), x, 9; hierarchical, 47; medieval, 14, 20, 47; Neo-Platonic, 138; Ptolemaic, 17; shift in, 138

worship, ix, 26, 44–45, 54, 106, 117, 125, 132, 151–52, 175–76, 179–80. 198, 200, 211, 214, 218; and communion of saints, 212–13; and earth, 180; ecology of, 180;

worship: evangelical patterns of, 169–78; missions and, 117, 180; music in, 180; of nature, 44–45; Pentecostal-charismatic pattern, 171–73; reciprocity in, 180; revivalist pattern, 170–72; rock concert pattern, 172–73; traditional-liturgical pattern, 169–71; Trinitarian, 180
wounded healers, 149, 203

Wright, Christopher, 127
Wright, N. T., ix, 48, 100, 104–5, 107, 109, 183–84

Yoido Full Gospel Church, 93–94
youth, 25

Zwingli, Huldrych, 29

Scripture Index

Made in the USA
Columbia, SC
20 December 2023

28962084R00167